TEACHING ENGLISH

Teaching English

TRICIA EVANS

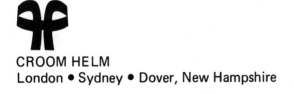

CROOM HELM
London • Sydney • Dover, New Hampshire

©1982 Tricia Evans
Croom Helm Ltd, Provident House, Burrell Row,
Beckenham, Kent BR3 1AT

Croom Helm Australia Pty Ltd, Suite 4, 6th Floor,
64-76 Kippax Street, Surry Hills, NSW 2010, Australia

Croom Helm, 51 Washington Street,
Dover, New Hampshire 03820, USA
Reprinted 1985

British Library Cataloguing in Publication Data

Evans, Tricia
    Teaching English
    1. English language – Study and teaching
    I. Title
    420'.7'1   PE1065

ISBN 0-7099-0901-2
ISBN 0-7099-0902-0 Pbk

Printed and bound in Great Britain by
Biddles Ltd, Guildford and King's Lynn

CONTENTS

To Ann Crosley

TEACHING ENGLISH

INTRODUCTION

It has become a commonplace to introduce books concerned with the
teaching of English with a reference to the 'significant, even radical
changes' in the teaching of the subject and to outline the 'conflicting
ideologies' which confront the English teacher. Such books then
proceed to chronicle the changes and document the ideologies
eloquently while leaving the practitioner stranded in a limbo where
aims are undisputed but achievement is left in doubt. At times the
generalizations are both bewildering and demoralizing:

> As we begin the 1980s, things are very different. The Great Debate
> gave a renewed respectability to those who feared the new 'political'
> English and its pedagogy. A new Government, falling rolls and
> teacher surplus have combined to cause a loss of nerve. The English
> teachers, who five years ago felt so clear about their direction in
> the classroom, the school and even in society, have lost their way.
> They may be hanging on grimly to their hard-won freedom to deter-
> mine their curriculum and classroom practice, but their hold is
> fragile, not least because it is no longer informed by a political
> perspective. (Andrew Bethell, *Divide and Rule: Radical English Loses
> its Nerve*)

Scant solace apparently for those who are still finding their way
through the platitudes which hedge almost every aspect of English
teaching.

We must discriminate between what educational writers would like
to see happening in an ideal world, the middle ground of the school
chalk-face where a striving after excellence is conceived of in terms of
what is possible in the context, and a cynical acceptance of the lowest
common denominator of educational achievement where successes are
seen as freaks or as the preserve of a particular type of pupil. This book
is concerned with the limbo, the middle ground, and thus with the
means to the end.

In fact less has changed in the teaching of English in the last decade
than some educationalists who have been saved from the classroom
would care to accept and, while they are in the vanguard of innovation
and preach the new gospels, the crunch really comes when theory meets

the practice of a school, a timetable and an English department. The
dilemma begins when the student or teacher, accustomed to the inadvis-
ability of splitting English into its component parts is told, 'Spelling
practice on Mondays, comprehension on Wednesdays and class readers
on Fridays'. Observation suggests that while text books come and go,
and sometimes only the latter, much in terms of method, rightly and
wrongly, remains unchanged. There are few reasons why the
teaching of English should have changed so radically. With the
exception of certain Mode III CSE syllabuses the essential formula
for English exams at A and O Level and CSE Mode I remains
almost unchanged and the influence of these exams percolates
inexorably down to the junior forms. The details may change but the
ubiquitous essay and written comprehension test survive triumphantly
despite sieges from 'N and F'[1] and 'Waddell'.[2] One has only to explore
the stock cupboards of English departments to realize that there has
not, despite the advent of MACOS[3] and the Humanities Curriculum
Project,[4] been a revolution in resources for English teaching. Ridout's
earlier books, though fortunately seldom used, are still there and their
replacements for the most part implicitly reinforce the idea of teaching
English in tidy segments to a homogeneous level of ability, nor have
teachers been given the time, training or financial backing to produce
adequate resources of their own. And what of the teachers who have
most influence over the way English develops in the department, the
compilers of aims, the buyers of books, the setters of standards, in
short the heads of department? What opportunities have they had to
expand their initial training, to innovate with the impetus of in-service
training courses and to finance such innovations? Precious little in a
decade of inflation and public spending cuts. But the prospect is not as
bleak as this might seem to suggest. If nothing else a tightening of
educational belts should result in a commensurate tightening of
objectives and more rigorous analysis of how best to achieve these,
given the inevitable restraints.

To suggest that English is about the exploration of the visions of life
offered by literature, about new experiences and encouraging pupils
to reveal their linguistic potential, though incontestable, will only take
the teacher of English so far, certainly not as far as the end of the first
lesson with a large mixed-ability class. An analysis of theory, while
crucial in any book about English teaching, will be kept to a minimum
here since there already exist many books which collectively have
dealt comprehensively with the theoretical side. This is a book which
must briefly state and then assume certain aims, just as secondary

schools everywhere must. What is at stake here are our *objectives* and how we are to fulfil them, given the resources at our disposal. To that end this book will be unrepentantly practical and will describe approaches and stimuli which have been shown to have worked in a number of environments and in a number of contexts.

Teaching for twenty-five hours a week or more is quite a different proposition from the selfconscious lessons of teaching practice, staged for the supervisor's visit and quite different from the sporadic sorties of education lecturers into the classroom. In some schools it is not melodramatic to talk of 'survival'; in all schools it is sheer common sense to determine personal priorities. Both demand strategies, not the cynical lowest common-denominator approach referred to earlier but a realistic appraisal of the context and content, objectives and obstacles. This presumes forward planning, not just the stereotyped lesson-plans of teaching practice but a more fundamental interest in, and thus knowledge of, the pupils, which is a pre-requisite of the good relationships so vitally important in the teaching of English.

A great deal has been written about the child's need for safety and security, very little about the teacher's need to feel at home with the content and demands of his own subject. Paper qualifications will go some way towards instilling this confidence but in an increasingly graduate profession the test is not the teacher's ability to write a good honours-degree essay on 'The importance of imagery in the work of John Donne' or 'Aristotle's contribution to the vocabulary of literary criticism', nor his or her ability to induce pupils to mirror these erudite feats. Far more important than an intimate knowledge of English literature as taught at university is a knowledge of the potential of the English language in general, of the class as a collection of individuals in particular, and an understanding and therefore a choice of possible routes to preconceived objectives. This book deals predominantly with the latter.

An examination of the teaching of English must concern itself with the nature of relationships, social interaction and organization within the classroom. Exploration, the trying-out of opinions, the give-and-take of discussion presume trust, since seldom will these opinions be the final word on the subject; inspired, half-formed, at times half-baked, they will be stifled at birth if the environment is hostile. As trust is the corollary of security so security is the necessary antecedent of enjoyment, not the flabby complacent safety of knowing that there are no risks ('We've done it before, Sir. It's easy') but taking risks where fundamental concerns are never in doubt, where whatever the outcome there will be something constructive and interesting to be learned even from picking up the pieces. Any guide to the teaching of English must explore the means of establishing and maintaining good relationships and while 'control' has in some quarters been seen as a dirty word, it is, if interpreted carefully, no more than a synonym for 'security'. We cannot afford to dodge the issue; an understanding of the subject, even an understanding of a repertoire of strategies will be of little use if the teacher has not grasped his and his class's emotional and social needs.

Notes

1. The Schools Council N and F proposals for the reform of sixth form curricula and examinations, 1977.
2. The report on proposals for a common system of examination at 16+. Chairman Sir James Waddell (DES, HMSO, 1978).
3. Man: A Course of Study. An American humanities curriculum project much influenced by the ideas of Jerome Bruner.
4. Set up in 1967, financed by the Schools Council and Nuffield Foundation, director Lawrence Stenhouse.

1 AIMS AND OBJECTIVES

But why are we doing this, Sir? (Secondary school pupil)

In Search of the 'Real' English

Before we can decide our aims we must define our subject. If the
Newsom Report is to be believed the common interpretation of English
in schools is a counterfeit:

> in practice many of the weaker pupils never seem to reach the point
> at which real English begins. Some teachers . . . give them a watered
> down version of what they remember from their own grammar
> school experiences. Much use is made of text books providing end-
> less exercises in comprehension, composition and the like. There are
> rough books and best books, the former filling up more quickly
> than the latter with laborious writing. Commas are inserted, spelling
> corrected . . . Poetry is 'done': drama may occur on Friday after-
> noon and towards Christmas . . .[1]

This was written in 1963. Ironically at the time most teachers of
English would have confidently defined 'real' English as literature,
composition and grammar. Such confidence was in part born of an
academic monopoly. The CSE was not examined until 1965; the
grammar schools, through O Level language and literature, controlled
examination success. The secondary modern schools attempted the
GCE exams but, as the Newsom Committee observed, for the 80 per
cent in these schools English was a dilution of the rigorous and exam-
orientated diet of the grammar schools, and this diet was apparently
immutable; formal composition, grammatical analysis, précis and a
cultural tour through the literary classics.

Today the English teacher's definition of his subject would probably
be less confident and precise but more comprehensive, less restricted
by notions of a classical grammar school syllabus. He might stress the
importance of developing pupils' skills in using language for a variety of
purposes in a number of ways. He might well extend the definition of
'literature' to include all that is worthy of careful perusal, and see
English as an exploration of the pupil's experiences and of the wider

11

social issues which impinge upon them. This would probably involve
recognition of the crucial importance of the mass media and their
contribution to the pupil's perception of life. The emphasis would be
less on formal exercises and more on developing powers of discrimination through discussion and a wide range of reading. He might well
quote a contemporary of the Newsom Report:

> English, well taught, should train a 16-year-old secondary school
> pupil to use the language confidently, appropriately and accurately,
> according to the circumstances in which it is used. He should be able
> to speak his own mind, to write what he has thought and to have a
> care for the correctness of written and spoken English. He should be
> able to understand what he reads and hears, to master the ideas and
> restate them in his own way. He should have some understanding of
> the different uses of language, of the language which relates,
> describes, evokes, persuades and is the instrument of the creative
> imagination.[2]

Of course there is no guarantee that this summary is any closer to the
'real' English than the mediocre interpretation that the Newsom Report
attacked. Few today would argue with this summary in essence; it is
an eminently reasonable if inevitably vague interpretation. Few would
contest that the four modes which it indicates (reading, writing, talking
and listening) are essential in any definition of English. It is the relative
emphasis placed upon each and particularly the relationship between
literature and language which has caused most argument in the last
fifteen years. This is not the place to chronicle a dispute which has
been competently explored elsewhere;[3] suffice it to say that literature
has been seen at one extreme as just one of many language activities,
'one of many Englishes', and at the other as our cultural heritage, a
'vital civilising factor in the battle for personal integrity and discrimination'. Somewhere between the two lies an acceptable compromise:
'our attention will be focused not on the work of literature as a thing-
in-itself . . . but rather upon its capacity for interaction with the
individual pupil, its relevance to his present emotional and intellectual
needs . . .'[4]

Fortunately or unfortunately, depending on one's point of view, this
debate, given great impetus by the Dartmouth Seminar[5] of 1966, has
barely impinged upon the day-to-day concerns of most teachers of
English. There have been other, more vital, and pressing issues; after
the DES Circular 10/65 comprehensive schools came to be seen less

as an aberrant minority and more as a future reality for the majority of secondary school pupils. Debates about standards, school and classroom organization, the O Level, CSE and 'ROSLA' (the raising of the school leaving age, Summer 1973) pupils proliferated. It is then little wonder if in the years following Dartmouth English teachers 'got on with the job' without concerning themselves too much with the finer checks and balances:

> In the field of English, much of the writing, lecturing and dis-
> cussion since 1965 has addressed the minority of enthusiasts, the
> kind of teachers who are attracted to a voluntary association such as
> the National Association for the Teaching of English.[6]

'Getting on with the job', living from week to week, may seem an unfortunate necessity at a time of great pressure. It becomes dangerous escapism if prolonged. By the mid-70s comprehensive schools catered for nearly two-thirds of secondary pupils and in several notable cases were both settled and gaining a reputation as centres of excellence, an excellence that no longer depended upon the narrow interpretation of exam results. A broadening of subject options, a more enlightened approach to pupil grouping and curriculum development were bearing fruit. There was time to surface and a more pressing incentive for taking stock. 'Post comprehensive' anxiety about reading standards initially prompted the inception of the Bullock Committee in 1972.[7] Their report, *A Language for Life*, published in 1975, ranged further than an inquiry into standards of literacy; it examined language in education and 'ranged from the growth of language and reading ability in young children, to the teaching of English in the secondary school.' The report provided the closest thing to an official view of the aims and achievements of English teaching and its part in a policy for language across the curriculum since the Newbolt Report of 1921.[8] While the views of those involved in the language-literature debate seemed confusing and irrelevant to many, the Bullock Report found a wider and more receptive audience. Cynics would suggest that this was in part because its description of English was vague enough to find an almost universal acceptance. The report outlined three main, but not mutually exclusive approaches:

> Some teachers see English as an instrument of personal growth,
> going so far as to declare that 'English is about growing up' . . .
> Others feel that the emphasis should be placed on direct instruction

in the skills of reading or writing . . . There are those who would prefer English to be an instrument of social change.

For the Bullock committee there was no doubt that English was about language as a whole: ' . . . language competence grows incrementally, through an interaction of writing, talk, reading, and experience, the body of resulting work forming an organic whole.' This was an attempt to free English from its cellular division into spelling, grammar, comprehension, poetry, composition, debate and so on. Today many would like to see English as an integrated whole, particularly where the move from reading to writing, from writing to discussion, is prompted by the needs and interests of the individual pupil rather than the demands of the teacher or the exam syllabus. This is the ideal; it is extremely difficult to decide to what extent such an ideal is realised in individual classrooms. We are forced to make the distinction between what English should be and what it is and this will inevitably involve generalisation, since it is abundantly clear that any interpretation of English is very dependent upon the context of the individual school and upon the gloss put upon it by each English teacher.

It is easier to gain a clearer picture of what English *should be* by eliminating what it is not. English is not about:

arid exercises in classifying parts of speech;
'free for all' discussion where pupils are free to listen to the teacher who does all the talking;
reading 'set books' interminably round the class before summarising them;
detonating pupils' imagination in the self-indulgent way of those most uncritical supporters of 'creative writing' where spontaneity is all and quality of communication hardly assessed;
sacrificing the quality of expression to the god of accuracy;
cutting 'the classics' down to examination proportions where both literature and students suffer;
thinking and writing 'in best' where the tentative and exploratory are discouraged.

By inversion English concerns itself with language of many sorts in a number of contexts and a number of ways which are all meaningful to the pupil. It exploits the pupil's own opinions and experiences through constructive discussion; it broadens these opinions and experiences through a wide range of literature. It encourages the pupil's initiative to stimulate written work and uses spelling, punctuation and grammar rules in the pupils' interests, waiving them where quality and quantity rather than undistinguished accuracy are the priorities. It is about planning and pruning and experimenting with ideas and approaches.

Who Needs Aims?

Engish has a unique place in the curriculum. It is both a subject in its own right, taking literature as its special preserve and, as language, it is a service medium for learning elsewhere; the 'core' subject *par excellence*. It is not for nothing that when standards of spelling, handwriting or articulation slip in other subjects that the English department is blamed.

English does not lay claim to a body of knowledge which can be circumscribed and quantified. In no sense is it a linear subject, emphatically not where the teaching of the 'basic skills' of reading, spelling and punctuation are concerned. The English teacher is thus in a more precarious and vulnerable position when it comes to deciding aims, objectives and the content of a lesson. He cannot resort to a reference to higher authority in quite the way that the History or Science teacher can, in order to validate opinions, nor can he adopt the approach, 'This may seem tedious but you must grasp this in order to understand what is to follow'. The English teacher, more than most, will lean heavily upon 'aims'.

The most fundamental aims of the English teacher will correspond to the expressive, emotional and vocational aims of the school as a whole:

> to develop a wide range of communication skills;
> to encourage tolerance of the views of others;
> to encourage independent and critical thinking which will guide pupils' own behaviour and responses;
> to encourage maturity in personal relationships;
> to foster interests and talents and allow all pupils experience of success;
> to develop sensitivity to detail and mood;
> to prepare pupils for work in a complex industrial society;
> to help pupils to use their leisure time constructively.

These aims can be taken as read, so generalized that we will have little difficulty in agreeing their worth, but for English teachers they are only the beginning: 'An objective consideration . . . shows how remarkably free they are to design their own lesson patterns, select their own teaching material and even pursue their own aims.'[8] Such autonomy is both rewarding and disconcerting, disconcerting because the greater the freedom the greater the responsibility. The English department must supplement the school's aims with its own and use these long-term strategies to discipline this freedom. The English department aims to:

make English enjoyable as a subject and effective as a means of communication;

develop the basic means of communication: talking, writing, reading (and by inference listening);

widen experience through exploration of a wide range of language experiences;

encourage fluent expression; both oral and written;

encourage appreciation and experience of the linguistic demands of different contexts, e.g. narrative, poetry, description, instruction, etc;

encourage accuracy in the interests of effective communication;

develop the pupil's ability to read with pleasure, understanding and discrimination, distinguishing between the valuable and the second-rate, the genuine and the sham;

encourage delight in the depth and variety of English literature, not neglecting the best and the greatest available;

extend vocabulary and encourage delight in words, their meanings, uses and power;

encourage an informed and tolerant attitude to the views of others;

dispel self-consciousness and develop the pupil's confidence to express views openly and coherently;

allow pupils some control over the course of the lesson in order to develop personal initiative and individual creativity;

make English meaningful and relevant through its links with life outside school and the exam syllabus;

provide a flexibility in lesson planning which takes account of the demands and constraints of mixed ability teaching, the examination syllabus, resources, the immediate environment and the interests and needs of the pupils;

help pupils achieve success in examinations;

help pupils use language effectively in order to achieve goals in employment, personal relationships etc.

This is typical of the lists produced by most English departments. A comparison of this with the earlier, equally typical extract from the school's aims, suggests that the English department assumes a major responsibility for the expressive and imaginative needs of the pupil. Recent research confirms that if English were to disappear so too would most pupils' expressive writing.

It is usually possible to agree about aims; it is the ordering of those aims which causes disagreement. Those who see literature rather than language in general as the essence of English will make the eighth aim pre-eminent. Those who are moving towards a more child-centred approach will stress number twelve. Others will see this as an invitation to anarchy. Some will feel squeamish about the inclusion of number ten; after all, we all know exams exist but do we have to acknowledge our dependence on them publicly? Unfortunately we do, distasteful though it may seem, because there can be no doubt of the destructive backwash effect of exams. To ignore this reality is to sacrifice our pupils to our own privileged ideology and to avoid the worst effects of this academic strait jacket. There will be those who insist they forget exams until the last possible moment but who will reveal the truth through barely disguised exam dummy runs, which will distort the syllabus of even first and second year pupils. There is no easy answer; there is no 'correct' list of aims and even where we agree with the list devised by the Head of English or thrashed out at departmental meetings we will be free to abandon them privately, for there is another side to freedom. The freedom of non-accountability and non-inspection means that we will be able to agree to one theory and do another. It is only too easy to fall into the trap of abandoning good intentions in order to 'keep control'. Perhaps aims, unless they are obviously extreme or scrupulously ordered are ultimately meaningless because they are inevitably generalized. If aims are long-term, and ultimately unrealisable strategies, then objectives are the short-term tactics for getting things done, and it will be localised objectives for a lesson which will be far more indicative of the intentions of the teacher and the probable content and course of the lesson.

The Importance of Objectives

Objectives will indicate what we are trying to achieve in terms of a particular context, skill, method, group or individual. They will provide a basis for evaluation since they will be realisable. A consideration of objectives will force us to plan and determine priorities; is it more important that a pupil should spell each word correctly or write imaginatively and at length, and is there a way of bridging these two? It will force us to consider the organisational implications; if we wish to make fifth-form pupils aware of the metaphorical complexity of Shakespeare's language and wish to encourage student initiative we may arrange group discussion with the minimum of teacher intervention.

Our objectives may extend to the whole class, 'to appreciate the rhythm and musical quality of narrative verse through reading a wide variety of poems', but under this umbrella there will be room for individualised objectives: 'to encourage Sukinder to think twice before saying the first thing that comes to mind'; 'to reassure Susan that if she doesn't understand she can always ask again'. This is the ideal; these personal objectives will never reach the file of even the most conscientious student-teacher or able professional's lesson-plan. They will only be crystallised by unexpected success or failure or the staff-room discussion. The successful teacher will recognise his pupil's individuality through the objectives he has for each of them.

Often force of circumstance will modify objectives: 'I set out to demonstrate how a mundane plot can be transformed through careful characterisation, descriptive detail and minor twists, but a query about homework showed that my instructions had been ambiguous. We talked through several interpretations of the homework task and then only had time to consider what we meant by "plot".' 'I had hoped that the pupils would proffer a lot of the ideas but it ended up with me doing a lot of the talking.' 'I wanted the class to experiment with the different ways of reading selected sections of dialogue but they were very late coming back from a swimming lesson, too late to make all the rearrangement worthwhile. They did silent reading instead: this settled them down and meant we could make a clean start next lesson.' Future objectives will be revealed by the progress made, or lack of it, in a lesson: 'I wanted to capitalize upon their obvious enthusiasm for translating Act III Scene II of Henry IV part I into a twentieth century setting, and I wanted to extend their initial discussion using a variety of approaches, written, oral and dramatic,' 'In the previous lesson Dawn and Lesley interpreted the suggestions on the board as prescriptions. I wanted to find a way of cutting their imagination loose.' Often careful assessment of classwork or homework will reveal future objectives: 'I've just confused them by giving them those rules for the difference between "they're, their, there". They seem to be avoiding them like the plague now, or making mistakes when before there was no problem.'

With almost all our lessons there should be no need for any pupil to ask why he is doing a particular activity (nevertheless we should be prepared to answer pupils who do ask). We should outline the course of the lesson in the opening moments, simultaneously making it clear what we hope the class as a whole will achieve and 'what is in it' for the pupils. While we may be clear about our own objectives, if we do not carry our pupils with us, reconcile our objectives with their own, then the lesson is doomed to failure; 'When I thought back to our last lesson and how successful it was I thought we'd continue on similar lines, but this time we'd make it a bit more difficult for ourselves . . . that way the results really should be something to show off about. . .' Having declared the overall intention, the teacher will visit individuals in the course of the lesson to interpret the general objectives on a more personal level: 'Lee, how about checking over that last piece of work and if you and I are happy with it you could concentrate today on . . . '; 'I want to see that piece of work written out clearly so that I can read it and understand it . . . Do you understand what I'm saying?' The last quotation demonstrates that a localised objective will amount to an order on occasions. Lazy pupils do exist; they are not always a fiction devised by the teacher to escape the suspicion of ineffectual teaching, and lazy pupils, like lazy adults, need the jolt of a clearly framed objective.

No extensive research has explored those objectives most commonly adopted by teachers of English, although Malcolm Yorke's inquiry into objectives for the teaching of literature[10] demonstrates a surprising consensus; 'With only very minor variations these junior, middle, secondary, preparatory, comprehensive, and public school teachers share much the same priorities in much the same order of importance when they teach literature.' His teacher-sample stressed the emotional pleasure to be gained from reading and hoped to encourage long-term reading habits. Of less importance apparently was the pupil's ability to give an account in his own words of what he had read. Teachers strongly rejected objectives which suggested that pupils should 'list, quote, recite or know anything by heart', and dismissed objectives concerning the pupil's ability to define abstract concepts and give an account of grammatical rules. A knowledge of literary history was considered unimportant.

It would be tempting to conclude with a 'check list' of objectives. We could perhaps derive some comfort from ticking them off week by week, but we would soon find ourselves with a list as seductively linear as the Contents page of one of the many apparently fool-proof English course books. We would soon lose sight of the distinction between teaching and learning, between aim and achievement: 'Yes, I taught them inverted commas on Tuesday . . . '; 'I've done Falstaff with them.' We might dodge the fact that to state whole class objectives and to ignore individual differences is to play the lecturer. No list could do justice to the flux of objectives which form and re-form before, during and after each lesson and which change for one pupil within a single lesson.

Every English teacher must decide why he teaches as he does; because it's the easiest way out? Because it seems to bring results? Because that's how I was taught, at school, university, department of education? Because that's the way the Head of English does it? If these provide the basis for what and how we teach, then we have to back-track rapidly. Is it in the pupil's interests that I teach as I do? How do they see English, judging from my lessons? What will they think I am aiming at? Is this a true picture? If not, what do I put in its place? To what extent can I overcome the constraints placed upon me? This is a circular debate. We do not immortalise our aims on paper, file them and rest secure; 'If anyone asks, that's what we're doing'. The environment, organisation patterns, constraints will change; ideally we should not wait for an HMI survey or DES report to jerk us into a guilty appraisal; it is not only the student teacher who should be able to state the why and the how.

Notes

1. The Newsom Report, *Half our Future* (Ministry of Education, HMSO, 1963), p. 152.
2. 'The Certificate of Secondary Education', *Examinations Bulletin* no. 1, Secondary School Examintions Council (HMSO, 1963), p. 34.
3. David Allen, *English Teaching Since 1965* (Heinemann, 1980).
4. Thompson (ed.) *Directions in the Teaching of English* (Cambridge, 1969), p. 25
5. John Dixon, *Growth through English*, (NATE, Huddersfield, 1967); a report of the Anglo-American Dartmouth Seminar of 1966.
6. *English in the 80s*, Schools Council Working Paper 62 (Evans/Methuen, 1979), p. 13.
7. The Bullock Report, *A Language for Life* (DES, HMSO, 1975).
8. The Newbolt Report, *The Teaching of English in England* (HMSO, 1921).
9. See 6.
10. Malcolm Yorke, 'Teaching Literature: an Inquiry into Objectives', reported in *Use of English*, vol. 29, no. 3, summer 1978.

2 THE ENGLISH ENVIRONMENT

Children are liable to work better if taught in an atmosphere
of confidence that they can and will succeed in the tasks they
are set. (Michael Rutter *et al., Fifteen Thousand Hours*)

The children all have certain definite and precise expectations
of how teachers should behave. First among these is that the
teacher should keep order. (Roy Nash, *Classrooms Observed*)

The young and affable English teacher called the Third Form to order,
for the third time; 'Come on, just shut-up and turn round the lot of
you . . . Let's get some work done, ten minutes've gone already'. Gary
and Paul struggled in belatedly, calling to their friends in the back row
as they did so. Mr Jones looked heavenward as he continued to lob
text books over the heads of the front row. 'Not this again,' whined
Julie, and she started to rummage through her make-up bag in protest.
Mr Jones helped two students hunt for several missing pages which had
spiralled elegantly to the floor, before moving towards the blackboard. His repeated calls for silence were lost behind his back and
among the chatter and scrape of chairs. Sandra, the trustie from the
front row, was sent next door to 'ask Mrs. Higgins if she's got a
board rubber'. In the mean time Mr Jones used a combination of
saliva and his handkerchief to remove mistakes. He turned round,
consoled to find that everyone was sitting down.
    'Turn round and open your books.'
    'Sir, what does it say on the board? . . . Looks like my Mum's
shopping list . . . What's the date, Sir? . . . I haven't got my homework
back, Sir, and you said you'd have it for today . . . What's the point of
. . . ?'
    'Just listen — last week we got to page forty-three . . . I think. Can
you find it?'
    'No Sir, it was further on than that'
    'Right, if you're so clever, Nigel, come out and show me . . . No, not
you as well.'
    'I've got it Sir, it's page forty-five where she says . . . '
    'O.K., thank you Louise . . . Right you can sit down now, Nigel. . .
and David . . . Mind those bags . . . I said SIT DOWN.'
    'Sir, why can't we do what the other lot are doing with Mr. Woods?

They're doing plays and things.'

'Well, we're doing a play.'

'But it's not the same Sir, this is boring.'

'Yes, it's boring Sir, can't we do . . .

'BE QUIET – if that's the way you feel . . . since I can't trust you even with this we'll do something less interesting. Mandy, collect in the books – we'll do a summary instead. No, the *text*books, Mandy . . . Trevor, give out the worksheets. Aren't they there? Well, you'll have to wait while I get them from the staff room . . . '

There is good reason for beginning this chapter with an eye-witness account of the beginning of an 'English lesson'. Those of us who have witnessed or participated in such a lesson will have learned the hard way that any lesson is not simply the sum total of aims, objectives, lesson-plans and resources. These provide the framework but the all-important flesh and substance is provided by the individuals in the class-room. Teaching is about building relationships which allow learning to take place and the teacher 'cannot avoid his responsibility for maintaining in the group an atmosphere in which learning may go on.'[1] The teacher who disregards this will never succeed. Or to put it more starkly, as many successful teachers would; if you can't control what happens in the classroom then you might as well tear up your aims and objectives and meticulous lesson-plan.

The English teacher will rightly emphasise the importance of self expression, the pupils' freedom to express opinions, and talk fostered by trust, respect and their associate control. But what is this all-important control, or 'good discipline'? How does it manifest itself and why do some teachers have it, others obviously not? Young teachers and women teachers have been known to complain, not unnaturally, 'It's all right for him. His pupils know he may clout them or cane them but how am I expected to cope when I can't and won't and when that's the only punishment they seem to understand?' For the vast majority of teachers control is not and cannot be dependent on threats of corporal punishment, nor even on the minor sanctions at our disposal, which can only be used sparingly if they are to carry any weight. Our concern should be less with cure, less with punishment, than with preventing problems concerning relationships arising in the first place. Too many lessons fail not because of the teacher's lack of academic expertise, nor even because of a failure to plan the lesson content, but because of a failure to foresee organisational hazards and a failure to react positively to these when they cannot be foreseen.

All this means a concern for the environment of learning, an environment which should be understood in physical and emotional terms. It consists of the fabric: walls, windows, floor and ceiling, the props, blackboard and furniture, and the personnel, teacher and pupils, brought together because the law of the land decrees that pupils should receive full-time education until the age of sixteen.

The Physical Environment

We will have to accept the fabric, unless the classroom is obviously far too small or far-flung, along with pock-marked walls and well-used desks. We should not accept the blackboard which is fixed so that some of the class cannot see it, wobbly or broken chairs and inadequate heating. These should immediately be reported to the relevant authority. The physical environment signals our attitude to the subject and our concern or lack of it for our pupils. Where the classroom is our own base there is no excuse for not making the room inviting and reflecting the subject as attractively as possible. Obviously the room will also double as a tutor room and space will be needed for pastoral notices, but the remainder could well be divided between the different classes taught, showing a regularly renewed selection of recent work with a sprinkling of educational posters for longer term reference. Few teachers alone and unaided will maintain a regular turnover. We will need to use volunteers to mount and fix work during lesson time, or better still in break and lunch time (as with all volunteers their work should be recognized and rewarded appropriately). The display should set standards for quality and presentation, bright coloured backing should be used, titles should be distinctive and clear and the whole display should engage pupils' attention, through carefully planted pictures, questions, and of course through the inclusion of work by all pupils over a term or half-term period. Where the English department communally uses a suite of rooms responsibility for display becomes a departmental one and departmental meetings should consider the state of these rooms.

Mounting a display is relatively easy but our concern cannot end there, since the physical environment is threatened by every lesson in the room. We should never passively inherit a classroom from another teacher, without comment, tacitly accepting a littered floor, spread-eagled furniture and poor ventilation. We cannot race to each lesson before our pupils in order to tidy and rearrange. Where the majority of the class can queue up quietly in the corridor without obstructing it, a small band of pupils can put the classroom to rights. Alternatively pupils can be told to take responsibility for tidying their own section of the classroom before sitting down. There is no question of soldiering on in depressing surroundings and clearing up at the end of the lesson, although of course a routine check will still precede dismissal. We then owe it to an inevitably disgruntled class to discover who is to blame for the disorder, and deal tactfully with the situation, usually with the help of the head of department. No lesson should begin until the teacher has checked the position of desks and chairs, that bags are removed from gangways, that there is sufficient ventilation, and the board is clean. The look of the room is obviously affected by those within it and pupils should look as tidy as the layout. This may mean the removal of coats, the tying of ties and shoelaces. All this is a clear indicator; 'If he cares this much about little things like straight desks and knotted ties how much more will he care about good behaviour and good work?'

Where large and younger classes are concerned it is well worth perfecting movement routines for all time, at the beginning of the year. At the start of the lesson should pupils wait in the corridor quietly or sit down and wait for the teacher? Much will depend on local factors, who arrives first, double lessons already in progress in the next classroom, narrow corridors and the likely state of the classroom at the beginning of the lesson. No regrouping of furniture in the course of the lesson should be undertaken lightly. Young and larger classes should never move simultaneously, but consecutively, small group by small group as quietly and rapidly as possible, under the teacher's watchful eye. A 'Freeze!' signal can restore instant silence, as in drama, when the choreography goes awry.

The Emotional Climate

Inexperienced teachers, observing the lessons of successful 'old hands', can easily jump to the wrong conclusions. They may well find themselves part of an apparently informal lesson where the lesson plan is nowhere to be seen. The teacher appears relaxed, sometimes sits on the front of his desk, jokes with certain pupils, even gives a couple a light-hearted flip with his fingers in passing and is as likely to respond to the occasional slight misdemeanour with a quip as a curt reprimand. The lesson appears to proceed effortlessly; pupils seem to know what to do next, indeed the teacher does not seem to be doing much more in the middle of the lesson than chatting in a relaxed manner to pupils as he moves around the classroom. The inexperienced observer may not realise that this is the culmination of a great deal of hard and some-times subtle work. The teacher has earned the respect and best endeavours of the class over months rather than weeks. The constant bickering, which destroys so many lessons and relationships, never materialised because this teacher make it clear early on that he would insist on a few sensible prohibitions. He refused to talk against even one pupil muttering in the room and would stop a pupil in mid-sentence if he was interrupted by another. He would send pupils out, even the 'sophisticated' fifth year if they arrived unkempt and still talking. He penalised the conditioned reflexes of those who packed up at the first sniff of the end of the lesson. In short, he stuck to his guns because he had good reason to do so. In the early days he smiled and joked a little less but always praised more than he punished. He did not mistake friendship for respect and was well aware of the element of fear which is a necessary part of the latter. He was 'Sir' and he expected the courtesy that he in turn accorded the class. Although the lesson-plan was not apparent it was there nevertheless, and though he had taught the material before the lesson was tailor-made for the group. He was quite clear how it should unfold but was always prepared for the relevant query which might seek explanation and revision or prompt interesting and relevant illustration.

If we are to produce an emotional climate where learning and good relationships can flourish and feed off each other, if we are to avoid Mr Jones's chaos, we will have to work hard to manage the key moments, key factors in classroom control and organisation; the beginning and end of each lesson, the distribution and collection of materials, pacing the lesson, the prevention and cure of discipline problems, and noise levels. Mr Jones's experiences indicate that the first of these, the beginning of each lesson, is crucial in deciding who will control whom.

The Beginning of the Lesson

The teacher must set an example; we should never arrive late for the obvious reasons that it wastes precious time and invalidates censure of pupil late-comers. When an emergency makes our late arrival unavoid-able we should apologise to the class just as we would expect our pupils to apologise to us. Where pupils are coming from different parts of the school we will need some idea of how long these journeys should justifiably take and have a teaching strategy prepared for those who will arrive earlier, perhaps checking homework, silent reading or answering a question on the board. As many materials as possible should be given out before the lesson proper starts. These should engage the attention of pupils as they sit down and avoid unnecessary interruptions in the course of the lesson. As the class gathers the teacher has an opportunity to check the placing and appearance of desks and individuals. Now is the time to weed out any gum-chewers or coat-wearers; it is not the time to confront pupils about weightier problems, which can wait until a later and calmer moment. The beginning of the lesson should not be postponed until the class is complete; pupils should not conclude that it is in their interests to dawdle from class to class. Our tolerance level should be defined and the official beginning of the lesson signalled forcefully and deliberately; 'Right, it is now five minutes past the bell. Let's get started. Let me have a good look at you.' A good look should finally alert and identify those who are still day-dreaming or rummaging in their bags. It should also produce a moment of absolute silence as the teacher scans the class, and a much-needed opportunity for teacher and class to gather their wits and prepare for what is to come. Some teachers register the class before proceeding to instructions or recapitulation, partly because this demands silence; others feel that it holds up the start and invites rest-lessness, and thus postpone registration until the class are working quietly. No instructions should be given until all the class are listening, and we should not get into the habit of repeating instructions many times over for those who cannot be bothered to listen the first time. The pattern must be, 'I shall say this once and once only, so listen carefully.'

Distribution and Collection

Though some, often senior, members of staff wing books around classrooms, calling out pupils' names as they do so, this is an unnecessarily careless and often noisy method. If we have impressed upon pupils that books must be treasured and protected, throwing them at desks and pupils seems a blatant contradiction of our concern. There are two obvious methods of distribution, both with their own advantages and disadvantages; materials may be passed from the front to the back, which removes any excuse for pupils to leave their places but does involve most pupils in turning round. The second method is slower; one or two pupils, depending on the size of the class, distribute materials. Unless we need an excuse to contact a large number of individuals it is usually best to stand back and supervise this exercise.

Collection is a special case. All materials must be counted and seen to be counted. Losses or mutilation must be followed up. The collection of homework deserves a special routine. Pupils should be reminded near the beginning of the lesson that it will be collected in, and immediately asked, 'Is there anyone who, for whatever reason, has not got their homework ready to be handed in?' These pupils should be noted in the mark-book and seen in the course of the lesson. In the closing minutes, those due to present missing work at the end of the lunch-hour, detention or subsequent lesson should be reminded of the fact; it is best to insist that this is recorded at the back of the exercise book. As a final rather cynical check, and as a marking convenience exercise books can be collected in open at the homework.

Pacing the Lesson

There are two common and fundamental errors where timing is concerned; both are only too familiar to every student or inexperienced teacher. The first involves sticking too closely and inflexibly to a lesson-plan's time allocations in the face of misunderstandings, queries or unforeseen phenomena. The second is its obverse, the abandoning of the lesson-plan prematurely. Amazed at our good fortune in engrossing the whole class, we might prolong the activity to a point where appetites are jaded, attention wanders and tempers fray. As a general rule no task should continue indiluted or unmodified in some way for more than fifteen minutes. This is particularly important where the less able of any age are concerned. Their attention and concentration span is likely to be shorter than that of more self-restrained and academically orientated abler students. Strategic modification does not have to be contrived and dramatic. Where pupils are busily writing it might mean a shift to reading their work so far, whether silently or aloud, thus allowing time for thought and evaluation. A double period needs to be paced particularly carefully. It might be seen as two quite different lessons with a 'break' in the middle. The break might amount to a trip to the library for older pupils, or allow younger pupils the chance to read silently or discuss a task with a neighbour. Pupils will feel more secure and committed if they are allowed to share the lesson plan: 'I thought we'd hear a few examples from your last homework, move on to the next chapter and then give you the chance to read on your own.' 'We shall be playing host to a guest in the second part of the lesson . . . and I thought we'd spend the first part of the lesson deciding which questions we'd like him to answer.'

Discipline Problems: Prevention and Cure

Knowledge of the subject and knowledge of our pupils are great allies here but neither is quite as straightforward as it may seem. In an increasingly all-graduate profession knowledge of the subject in one sense is assumed, but a first class honours degree does not guarantee success in the classroom. Indeed it may actually impede it if the teacher is blind to the distinction between academic facts and the ability to put the subject across, or fails to take account of and build upon pupils' existing knowledge. Teaching English is essentially not about knowing the probable order of Shakespeare's plays but about finding the right local route to making a study of Shakespeare pleasurable and meaningful. Too many lessons fail, too many discipline problems arise, because the material or approach is quite unsuitable, demoralisingly difficult or offensively easy. Once pupils begin to think, or worse mutter, 'Who does she think she is . . . ?', 'Who does he think we are . . . ?' learning and relationships are at risk.

Knowledge of our pupils at its simplest means learning names as quickly as possible. Pupils whose names are muddled or forgotten after the first couple of weeks will feel insulted, and communication, particularly praise or reproach, is far more effective where identification is immediate; 'Peter, open the window please', rather than a vague and generalised question-imperative, 'Will someone near the back open the window please?' Those of us with poor memories will need a memory aid, whether a formal seating plan (which must take account of friendships), a less formal insistence that pupils always sit in the same place until half-term at least, or cryptic and concealed jottings in the mark book which distinguish between similar-looking pupils with similar names.

In addition, we shall gain all the information we can from pupils' records, the form tutor and parents, balancing this with the realisation that pupils will react differently to different teachers, will mature and develop and will need the chance to turn over a new leaf with a new relationship. The opinions of other teachers and details of the pupil's family background should never be quoted, never allowed to destroy a unique relationship between teacher and pupil. We should never indulge in the cheap comment; 'I suppose this is all we can expect from you, Gregory — you're going to end up just like your older brother'. 'I'm not the only one who feels this way about you, Susan — Mr. Edwards says your work is very untidy and Mrs. Roberts says she's given up with you entirely.' Such retorts not only help to destroy the relationship between teacher and pupil, they also drive a wedge between the pupil and his family and the school as a whole, and between the pupil and other members of staff, who are unaware that their confidential comments are being irresponsibly exploited outside the staff room.

Scrupulous classroom organisation is at the heart of any scheme for preventing discipline problems. This means obvious tactics, dividing and conquering the 'villains' who congregate conspiratorially in the back rows, and doing this at an early stage while the relationship is still relatively intact. It also means guaranteeing breathing, and learning, space between desks so that pupils are not simply pressurised into talking to colleagues because of their proximity. Examination desks are placed at strategic intervals for good reason. We may scorn the elevated desk and chalk and talk teaching methods that placed the teacher firmly at the centre front, but from here he could, and pupils knew he could, see recalcitrant heads, legs, laps and eyes. There is much we can learn from this all-seeing presence who nipped all plots with one shrewd glance from his compound eyes. We will not resign our classroom perambulations but we will be more careful in positioning ourselves so that we can talk comfortably to the individual and simultaneously see the rest of the class. Rather than burying ourselves in the pupil's desk we will lift the work to eye level thus keeping all the communication lines open. Without reducing the class to a state of twitching paranoia we will talk from whichever vantage point seems appropriate, occasionally taking a centre back position. We will only leave the classroom in an emergency and will keep trips to the stock cupboard to a minimum (it is not unknown for teachers to be locked into their own stock cupboards by their triumphant pupils).

It is far more sensible that the teacher should move to the pupil, rather than the other way round, particularly where the class is a large one. 'Come out when you've finished and show me your work' and 'Come out and get the next sheet when you've finished the first one' both invite chaos, or at best the unknown, since several pupils may well need help or the next stimulus simultaneously, forming a queue or worse still an undignified scrum. The queue puts a great deal of pressure on the teacher to deal with pupils' work or problems quickly. It is easy to find our *bonhomie* slipping away, particularly if, as so often, the queue who are now bored with waiting start to chat among themselves, and simultaneously block the view of the rest of the class. 'Put up your hand if you really need help or have finished and I will come to see you' is much the better alternative, even where the next work-sheet is required, since it at least guarantees that the teacher will check the pupil's work before handing out the next piece of paper.

The observant teacher will have far fewer discipline problems. He will notice the growing irritation between two former friends, that Ann is self-conscious about her shorn hair and needs sympathetic and tactful handling. The teacher who finds the time to say to the pupil returning after a two day absence, 'Are you feeling better now? Your form teacher told me that your gums were playing up again' is unlikely to have truancy problems. Such careful attention to 'detail' is a sure sign that the teacher *cares* about each pupil, and all pupils are shrewd enough to recognize, and reward this. Such observation is usually built upon a methodical foundation, an insistence on taking the register *and* following up absences, if only so that, when confronted by the Deputy Head inquiring, 'Was Ernie Doors in your lesson last Tuesday afternoon? It's important we know since he may have been involved in a theft at that time' we do not splutter weakly, 'I'm afraid I don't know.' Observation requires a special 'Memo' section in the mark book to record that 'R and T are not to sit together next lesson'; 'Make time to hear about D's trip to parliament; 'Return B.K.'s book with thanks'.

When all's said and done we all have discipline problems, however slight and sporadic, and if we insist that we don't it is usually more a matter of luck than charisma; the luck of not landing 4X for a double period on Friday afternoon in room 27, the luck of Gavin's removal to another school. When discipline problems occur we should not ignore them nor over-react but respond decisively and fairly, using school sanctions in a discriminating way. Venial offences should not be punished by a formal school detention; a serious offence should be referred to the appropriate pastoral authority, whether year head or senior teacher, immediately. As there is a hierarchy of offences so there is a hierarchy of reprimands; the 'tut', the aggrieved look, the stern stare, the sudden rap on the desk, verbal reproach of many kinds and the movement and exclusion of pupils. We should never lose our tempers. We should avoid standing pupils in the corridor where they may distract other classes, deface the walls, rifle the cloakrooms or disappear homewards (although convulsive giggles or a flood of tears will probably only be calmed by a cooling-off period outside). We do not disappear to seek outside help on the rare occasions when it may be necessary. Instead a trusted pupil can carry a sealed message to a senior member of staff who is known to be available on such occasions.

It is perfectly possible to fit the reprimand and the reward to the individual and the circumstances, without being unjust and without showing favouritism. For those embarrassed by public praise, unmoved or angered by public reproach, a quiet private word will be more effective. For most pupils a stern look from the 'with-it' teacher[2] will be quite sufficient, although there are occasions and pupils which require public admonition, which impresses on other pupils the extent of the teacher's tolerance. A public rebuke should never make a martyr out of the culprit nor sink to sarcasm; it should be succinct and rational, not 'I've had enough of this sort of behaviour from you, it's just not good enough,' but 'I asked you to sit down so that I can see who is working with whom.' If we justify our demands we are placed in a stronger position when coping with breaches of the rules. There are very good reasons for asking pupils not to swing on their chairs, interrupt the teacher or each other, call out without putting their hands up and move from their desks without the teacher's permission. When invited, pupils are able and willing to explain these rules in a mature and cogent way. Of course rule enforcement can be taken to foolish and naive lengths. It is important that we distinguish between those occasions when to ignore a misdemeanour publicly would be to risk our credibility and invite cries of 'But that's not fair — when Carol did it you told her to stay behind', and those occasions when misdemeanours which are only apparent to the teacher should be quietly ignored. We should not slate a distraught pupil for chewing gum nor fracture a period of diligent calm to swoop on an infringement of the uniform rules. Most obviously we should not reward the attention-seeker with the very spotlight he seeks. Having once reprimanded a pupil it is important to find, sometimes manufacture, an opportunity for reinstatement if a grudge is not to be fuelled. This may mean steering a pupil towards a task where he is an expert and can earn praise, or finding him special responsibility, inviting a younger pupil to clean the board or take a message, or appointing an older student as chair-person of a discussion group. Reinstatement must be managed subtly; older pupils in particular will see through the all too blatant ingratiating smile and hand on the shoulder, and if they are to retain their own peer-group credibility will have no alternative but to reject both peace offerings.

When it is all over, when we have got over our suppressed anger and sense of failure, and the painful incident is balanced by the many unexpectedly successful moments in the school day, then we analyse and evaluate: 'Was it really her fault or did I hound her into a corner where she had no alternative but to act as she did?'; 'Could *I* have avoided these detentions without endangering my credibility?'; 'Why do I get these problems in this lesson and not in the parallel lesson on Thursday?' Sometimes the unravelling of the thread back from the incident will reveal an apparently trivial trigger to events; 'It was a hot day, the blinds were stuck and I kept forgetting to tell the caretaker. Pupils near the windows had to shade their eyes and their work. They were hot and sticky and the boys were annoyed because I wouldn't let them take their ties off. Eventually they had to be moved, which squashed all the pupils into half the classroom. I was hot too, and annoyed that a carefully prepared lesson was being sabotaged by the class's restlessness and reluctance to sit where I told them. I started to nag, which made a few of the normally docile girls start whining. I can't stand whining pupils and when Michael moved from his place without permission, knocking over his chair as he did so, I just exploded at him.' The 'moral' is usually as clear as in this example.

Noise Levels

Acceptable noise levels must be decided by the nature of the activity, the proximity of other classes, the teacher's ability to reimpose silence, and of course the nature of the noise. Thus the freedom of an isolated mobile classroom is no excuse for noisy work, if such work is not positively furthered by vigorous and constructive discussion, and if the teacher feels unhappy at the apparent impossibility of reimposing silence when this becomes necessary. As with all classroom rules we should justify our demands: 'Since most writers can only plan their work in silence we'll make that the rule for the first ten minutes . . . '; 'Remember that in your groups only one person should be speaking at any one time, so I will expect to hear only five voices in the whole classroom.' Once having declared the rules we stick to them, without nagging, choosing our moments carefully for the warning 'ssshh', sudden movement or reproachful look. It is important to make the point emphatically but quietly, since we should not contribute to the noise level. Too often the noisiest individual in the classroom is the teacher who almost panics pupils into a counter-reaction by the constant and progressively ineffectual 'Be quiet!' As the teacher feels increasingly vulnerable his voice becomes more strident, the pupils smell the heady whiff of desperation and the vicious circle takes shape. We too need to make every word count and to think before stirring up ripples unnecessarily. Comments, instructions and reprimands[3] should be delivered firmly, but as quietly as is commensurate with effective communication. Teachers who shout at pupils, particularly those who, like Mr Jones, shout 'BE QUIET' make a rod for their own backs. The ridiculousness of dramatically adding to the noise in a vain attempt to quell it should be apparent, and we will soon lose our voices to little effect if we persist. If we attempt to achieve silence by shouting then the relationship has already reached the stage where silence is little more than a truculent and precarious truce. There are more sensible ways of cutting through classroom chatter, an insistent 'ssshh', or hand-clap or rap on the desk. Paradoxically, the quiet but telling comment delivered to the front rows may stop or at least curtail the noise, as pupils pause long enough to hear what has been said. At moments of extreme frustration a resigned folding of the arms and a stolid silence will achieve more than a desperate shout.

The end of the lesson should balance the calm of the beginning; it should draw the threads together and have its own orderly routine. Pupils need to be warned of the time remaining to them at least five minutes before the end of the lesson, and a generous time allowance will be required for the collection of materials and last minute queries. This is the safety-net of time which allows pupils and teacher to wind down in an unfrenzied way before proceeding to the next lesson. This is the time to compliment individuals, read out interesting excerpts, invite relevant anecdotes, place the immediate task in the context of past and future work, ask for opinions, remind the forgetful, reassure the insecure and laugh with the class clown. Finally, exit from the class-room should be orderly and silent.

Successful teachers are not born; they work hard at learning from their occasional but inevitable mistakes. They all have in common a genuine regard for their subject and their pupils, which is manifested not through a facile familiarity but through a firm insistance that all pupils are capable of progress and all have a great deal to contribute. They are just, and ensure that they are seen to be just, but temper praise and blame to the individual. Their own pedagogic and organisational skills produce ample opportunities for praising pupils. They have an eye for detail and yet a grasp of the fundamental priorities. They have a shrewd grasp of what is required of them, by the school, pupils, parents and the community. They know the part, look the part and act the part.

Notes

1. The Bullock Report, *A Language for Life* (DES, HMSO, 1975).
2. J.S. Kounin, *Discipline and Group Management in Classrooms* (Holt, Rinehart and Winston, 1970) for the importance of 'withitness' in the classroom.
3. K.D. O'Leary *et al.*, 'The Effects of Loud and Soft Reprimands on the Behaviour of Disruptive Students', *Exceptional Children*, vol. 37. no. 2, (October, 1970) pp. 145-55.

3 TALKING FOR EFFECT

What's the point of telling him? He knows it all already.
(Secondary school pupil)

Why is classroom discussion so important? This is not an arbitrarily
speculative question. It is one which must be tackled if only to reassure
the disconcerted parent who reports, 'Kevin said you didn't do any
work last lesson, you just talked'. Work for many pupils, parents and
teachers is equated with writing, and writing with facts, since after all,
it is argued, isn't teaching about the conveying of information, information which can be conned and reproduced? Isn't talk an unnecessary
extravagance at best and at worst a harbinger of chaos? Teaching does
currently concern itself with the conveying of information, with the
transactional function of language[1] but *learning* is concerned with so
much more and pupils need to talk in order to learn. We need go no
further than our own experiences to find proof of the importance of
talk. We communicate for at least ninety per cent of the time through
the spoken word and this is true even for those in the word-intensive
business of journalism and pedagogy. If we collect a typical week's
written output much of it will be routine; form filling, cheque writing,
comments on the work of others. Seldom will it be creative and it will
scarcely scratch the character and complexity of the writer, for this we
suggest through what we say. We bring to what we say all the paralinguistic means of amplifying and elaborating upon our words. Spoken
communication is taken for granted and yet we don't need the hypotheses of professional linguists and cognitive psychologists to convince
us that some communicate more effectively, persuasively and
articulately than others. The ability to communicate intelligibly in a
number of contexts to a number of ends is a skill which is capable of
improvement. Language must be practised in the way that a doctor
practises medicine, as James Britton suggests.[2]

But the fact that we all communicate predominantly via the spoken
word is hardly conclusive justification for stressing its importance in the
classroom. The second argument in its favour is both more crucial and
more difficult to document, since it is concerned with the much
charted but ultimately unmappable straits between teaching and
learning. This is not the place to delineate learning theories; it is
enough to describe the enormous contribution talk can and should

make if the pupil is to connect new data with past experience and internalise 'complicated patterns for structuring new knowledge, so that he may approach new situations with greater understanding and more comprehensive strategies,[3] or as the Bullock Report put it, 'Language has a unique role in developing human learning; the higher processes of thinking are normally achieved by the interaction of a child's language behaviour with his other mental and perceptual powers.' Talk provides the context, the framework for a new fact, idea or experience; the very differences between spoken and written language make talk a liberator, a means of experimenting with hypotheses, juggling with ideas and bouncing opinions off other people. Talk of the right kind makes a fact personal; it bridges the gap between the knowledge 'out there' and the experience within. Pupils can only grasp what is placed before them by a metaphorical leap which relates the new, via talk and thought, to an old and familiar pattern. While thought and talk are not synonymous, the latter allows us to delve into, manipulate and improvise our thoughts. If talk lays claim to and personalises information it also crystallises and confirms ideas. We talk through a problem with another for just this purpose, to see our ideas reflected and corroborated through the eyes of the 'other' and at its simplest the very act of making the infinite (our thoughts) something finite which can be reflected upon (our words) is a therapy in itself. And we don't always need an audience: young children in particular, but adults less frequently, indulge in a running commentary, a soliloquy intended to break a problem into manageable sections which can be ticked off; put metaphorically, the control tower helping the passenger to bring in the pilotless plane, the policeman with loud hailer extricating the potential suicide. The ability to divide any topic into rational and manageable sections is part of the process of learning anything. Talking through ideas is thus a way of thinking through ideas, a means of eliminating the redundant, preserving the relevant and testing this relevance against the reactions of others: 'So-called knowledge is not knowledge if the thinking powers are not applied to it, and . . . the only way to get a child to think about it . . . is to get him to talk about it.'[4]

But why the need to adopt this defensive pose? Do teachers of English need convincing of the importance of talk? 'Chalk and talk' still rules the classroom but all the available evidence suggests that while more exploratory and expressive talking and writing is likely to be found in English lessons talk is teacher-dominated in two senses; three quarters of the talk is commonly teacher-talk and where the pupils are encouraged to contribute too often their responses must conform to implicit but nevertheless rigid teacher-imposed templates. These are soon learned, but the templates are by their nature limited and, more importantly, inhibiting, in that those pupils who cannot grasp the teacher's frame of reference are left to flounder. They cannot contribute since their contributions do not 'fit' into a sequence which has been devised to take the lesson forward according to a teacher-imposed logic. And we are not just describing the less able since the most able 'divergent' thinker may well feel inhibitied and penalised too. 'Learning becomes heavily dependent upon the child's ability to take over by an act of imagination whatever linguistic constraints operate upon the teacher,'[5] as this excerpt from an English lesson where third year (13-14 year-olds) are discussing a prose extract exemplifies:

> *Teacher*: Right. Let's look back at the third paragraph . . . found it? Do you think (have you found it? . . . No, not that one) that he conveys the atmosphere well? Yes, it is getting a little draughty. I think we'll have that window closed now . . . Look for the adjectives . . . you know what an adjective is?
>
> *Pupil* 1: Nice . . . nasty.
>
> *Teacher*: Definition! You tell us, Tony.
>
> *Pupil* 2: Er . . . a describing word?
>
> *Teacher*: Yes, a describing word. Now let's get on . . . let's find an adjective . . . umm . . . *decrepit* will do nicely. What does this suggest? Can you think of another word instead of *decrepit*?
>
> *Pupil* 3: Old?
>
> *Teacher*: Any more than that? . . . Well, it means *dilapidated, falling down* . . . 'his face a decrepit facade.'
>
> *Pupil* 4: My gran took me to a fortune-teller on the pier once, Miss. I didn't want to go but my gran said, 'Let's for a laugh. See what she says' and . . .
>
> *Teacher*: Is this going to get us anywhere, Terry? We haven't got time for stories and I've already heard enough from you for one day . . . '

This demonstrates, however briefly, why it is not enough to accept the importance of talk in a lesson without defining both what commonly happens and differentiating between this and discussion in its true sense. The extract shows clearly how a teacher can monopolise the discussion, allowing pupils to enter it only on her terms, thus pupils' responses, though not rejected, have to be modified before they can be accepted and Terry's 'story', though it may ultimately be both highly relevant and entertaining, is not given a chance. There are several other inhibitors, and although a transcription is necessarily limited this does convey the linguistic and listening demands which are imposed on the pupils. The teacher's first speech jumps from a whole class imperative to a question with threatening overtones directed at an individual, back to the whole group, to another thinly veiled imperative directed vaguely at no more than two individuals sitting near the window in question, back to the whole group. The speech veers from the vague and colloquial to the precise and formal, 'Look for the adjectives'. The teacher is obviously aware of the importance of explaining the terminology of her subject, as with 'You know what an adjective is?', but seems to deter pupils with the substitution of another example of terminology for the one she was attempting to explain. Through lack of class response she is forced to turn to her 'safety net', a pupil who can be relied upon to give the right answers when all others fail, but even Tony ('Mekon' to the class) seems unsure, or perhaps afraid of becoming even more alienated from his peers by the teacher's embarrassing patronage. The teacher has no idea whether the rest of the class have grasped the concept 'adjective'. If they have not what follows will probably be meaningless since there is insufficient analogous explanation to make it clear. The teacher becomes increasingly side-tracked from her original stated objective: 'to encourage enjoyment and understanding of an interesting prose extract'. To the pupils it must appear that the key to enjoyment and understanding of the passage is dependent upon the definition of an 'adjective' and the original question 'Do you think that he conveys the atmosphere well?' is frightening in its breadth and diction. A question such as 'What does this suggest?', while it will mean something quite positive and paraphrasable to the teacher, may mean very little to the majority of the class. Only the brighter pupils who have grasped and remembered the significance of these pseudo-questions may be able to follow the teacher's logic. Pupil 3's response is left in cold storage while the teacher prods for an improvement, but the class and pupil 3 are in some doubt about what the teacher has in mind and to whom her next question is directed, to pupil 3 or the whole class? Her stance and head movements are somewhat ambiguous. The teacher, reluctant to resort to Tony again, provides the right answer but leaves it in a vacuum, since *dilapidated* merely substitutes another difficult word for the original and *falling down* is little better than pupil 3's suggestion and bears little relation to the context 'his face a decrepit facade', where an understanding of the phrase is dependent upon an understanding of the metaphorical *facade*. By this point a note of dreary irony is apparent in the teacher's voice and it may well be that this neglect of a full explanation is due to a weary resignation. It is perhaps not surprising then that Terry's jaunty introduction to his story is treated in a deprecatory manner, which is a pity since she could have exploited the opportunity to reinstate Terry who has been ticked off for a venial offence earlier in the lesson. Her response relegates 'stories' in the English hierarchy to a Platonic position of deception and irrelevance, certainly inferior to adjectives. The pupils are having to learn how to interpret the teacher's comments; the learning takes place on her terms and there is very little evidence that she is making the imaginative leap which is so necessary if the assimilation and accommodation of the new information is to take place, if the dialogue is to have meaning on both sides and if the class is to be seen as less a monolithic mass and more a collection of individuals who may have little more in common than their title, 3P.

But it is too seductively simple to criticise from the safety of an armchair. All teachers will admit in their more honest moments to lessons which have grated disconcertingly, to classes they have left feeling a sense of failure. The interest and understanding were there to be plumbed but the combination was missing. More dangerous and destructive are the exclamations, familiar in all staff rooms, where the blame is placed fairly and squarely on the pupils; 'I couldn't get a thing out of 2S this morning, what on earth's got into them?' Here the teacher has securely dissociated himself from any responsibility for the learning process, and has neglected the relationship between his own conceptual framework and those of his pupils. Teachers must take responsibility for the learning experiences of their pupils and particularly for the talking environment which is determined by the assumptions of the teacher. We cannot, though, dodge the quite natural reservations of teachers who fear the consequences of breaking the mould for lessons where 'discussion' means question and answer, where the only problem-solving is that of grasping what will please the teacher, where answering becomes a conceptual cloze test and as the teacher's questions become longer the pupils' responses become shorter. This is after all the prevalent interpretation of discussion, but more insidiously it is the easiest too, seen as a means of controlling the pupils' attention, conserving the teacher's energies and demonstrating the teacher's sequencing of knowledge. At its best it allows for positive feedback about pupils' perceptions of this knowledge, but there are implications for control here; 'uninhibited' is synonymous for some with indiscipline and it might be objected that discussion where all responses are not filtered through the teacher as specialist and expert is a recipe for chaos; 'The predominant teaching technology is still that of exposition interspersed with bursts of question-and-answer. But if pupil participation is therefore indispensable, it also presents formidable managerial problems because of the number of potential participants. Once the teacher stops lecturing, how are turns taken? How is the rule of one speaker at a time maintained?'[6] Group discussion can appear unnessarily time-consuming when exams loom threateningly; that is, until one relates a teaching method which recognises a pupil's need to structure his learning to one which implies a passive acceptance of the teacher's monopoly of knowledge. The first produces positive results, the second, pupils who are later castigated for their inability to 'think for themselves'. Any shift in teaching method is a potential risk and so with talk, if we are not clear of our objectives and their context and if we are not careful to adopt organisational strategies for meeting these goals.

What can talk 'do'? Joos[7] and others have attempted to classify styles of language; frozen, formal, consultative, casual and intimate. We can discern dialects, registers and idiolects. We can, with Andrew Wilkinson,[8] divide it into the conative, affective and cognitive or adopt Halliday's models:[9] the instrumental, regulatory, interactional, personal, heuristic, imaginative and representational; or, to put it more simply, language can be used to satisfy needs, to control the behaviour of others, to interact with others, to establish identity and express feelings, to learn about and explore, to pretend and to pass on information. We know from experience that language can be used to persuade, inquire, reiterate, analyse, instruct, describe, justify, anticipate, conclude, infer, interrogate and eulogize, and just as pupils need to meet and explore the various literary genres so they must have the opportunity to experience a wide range of language uses. Perhaps the most sensible classification of language functions for the teacher of English is to be found in Joan Tough's *Listening to Children Talking*[10] which, for example, subdivides 'self-maintaining' language thus:

1. Referring to physical and psychological needs and wants.
2. Projecting the self and self-interests.
3. Justifying behaviour or claims.
4. Criticising others.
5. Threatening others.

While we would not encourage pupils to criticise or threaten, we all indulge in antisocial language, and an awareness of the difference between constructive and destructive criticism and how words can threaten is obviously necessary. Though intended as part of a project dealing with early childhood, Joan Tough's comments make it clear that the classification is relevant to any age group; 'the classification not only offers a basis for the appraisal of children's language, but also provides a set of objectives that can be kept in mind as we talk with children. It provides a guide to the kind of strategies of language that all children need experience of using.'

The English teacher has traditionally been seen as the guardian of the individual's feelings and imagination, English as an expressive safety-valve which counteracts the more rigorous language of the science lab or games lesson. This is an unfortunate burden since of course expressive language and imaginative freedom should not be seen as the sole preserve of the English teacher, but a precious responsibility too, for it is not for nothing that personal revelations are more likely in the English lesson than elsewhere. It is not unusual for the danger signals of domestic problems to appear in the English discussion or homework rather than through the usual pastoral channels; 'Special value is given to the anecdotes children offer as a contribution to whatever is being considered. These can be thought of as small segments of lived experience, and become the touchstone for much of the work.'[11] But our pupils will offer nothing if we do not invite their gifts and gifts are what they are, for silence is the easy way out. No pupil, and particularly no prickly adolescent, is going to offer his soul for inspection if he feels he may be turned aside by an indifferent or ironical comment. There is too much to lose and here it is less the teacher's favour and far more peer group approval that counts. In many classes there are too many good reasons for not courting approval for teachers to tread lightly over pupils' ideas on love, the family, racialism and the other 'themes' which find their way into CSE classes. And there are other reasons why we must tread delicately; English teachers have been rightly criticised for squashing incoming first-years' anecdotal contributions, but for some pupils the damage has already been done. Before we first meet them they may already have experienced destructive criticism, have already innured themselves to the relative safety of being labelled 'inarticulate', 'dull', 'introverted' or 'unresponsive'. It will take more than an encouraging smile to convince such pupils that they have a meaningful contribution to make, and more importantly that any contribution will be judged sympathetically and not against a predetermined and inflexible rule. Only a relationship based upon trust and respect, both of which may be slow in coming, will catalyse their involvement.

Trust suggests safety and it is the teacher's responsibility to create an environment in which meaningful discussion can take place, but safety should not suggest a reluctance to take risks, to defend opinions and invite criticism. Part of our job is to encourage pupils to see beyond their immediate concerns to consider those of others, to practise language-use in a number of situations which, through their very novelty, will make unusual demands. No development will be possible if the teacher does not have control of what is going on in the lesson. 'Control' is an emotive and in some quarters a dirty word but it is worth remembering that what 'uncontrolled' classes have in common is a refusal on the part of the pupils to meet the teacher half way, to suspend their disbelief in silence, and trust that, based upon accumulative past experience (or more cynically sheer fear), there is a rationale, a pattern which will be unfolded and will make sense. A silent trust and interest is replaced by flippant remarks, looks heavenward, wearied comments; 'Why don't you do something, Sir?', 'I'm fed up with this. We want to learn something even if you don't' and an attempt to fill the gap with gossip, fidgeting, furtive reading of magazines or worse. Should the teacher be courageous or foolish enough at this stage to suggest, 'Now we were talking about the summer holidays. What have you got planned, Leslie?' he is likely to be met with bland indifference, at best.

It is a common mistake to assume that a lesson which has as its aim constructive discussion requires less organisation than a written task. In most cases it requires more, and communication models, though inevitably limited, suggest why:

```
┌─────────────────────── CONTEXT ───────────────────────┐
│ Communicator 'Message' Form Medium Receiver Interpretation Response │
└───────────────────────────────────────────────────────┘
```

This model is as limited as any which attempts to categorise, to squeeze multifaceted human beings into two-dimensional diagrams. It is a gross simplification since it suggests that the message is linear, but the speaker is also listening to what he is saying, crystallising and modifying his thoughts as he goes along and most probably already anticipating and allowing for his listener's interpretation and response. The latter is already preparing his reply to a message he hasn't yet received in full. He may decide to interrupt, that a question is appropriate, in which case he may be completing the circle, or a single affirmation may bring the dialogue to an end. This description merely hints at the many complex physiological and mental operations which are taking place simultaneously, but it does suggest that listening and talking are both highly complex and far from passive activities. The context may not be as stable as the diagram suggests; it may for example veer and make the completion of the 'message' impossible. More tellingly, in a classroom context, the diagram assumes that there will be something to be communicated and someone to listen and respond. English has been defined as a means of communication but before communication can take place there must be something to communicate and someone or something to communicate to and therein lies the nub. Teachers complain 'They've got nothing to say for themselves so I end up doing all the talking' or 'How can we have any sort of discussion when they don't listen to any one but themselves?' Organisation for meaningful discussion is not as simple as hitting upon a good subject and asking the right sort of questions, even when these are enlightened and open. We must be clear about our objectives which may vary from pupil to pupil and from one context to another and we must devise organisational strategies in line with these; 'The teacher's role is partly as the provider of an array of imaginatively organized talking situations: carefully planned class discussion, small group discussion with or without a teacher present, larger groups reporting the fruits of their discussion back to the class, the teacher talking to individuals – all these deserve a place in the programme.'[12]

Our communications model will take us so far but it cannot stress the importance of a context in which talk is consequential, and not seen as a time-filler (a sure sign that the teacher is being led up the garden path), but with a goal which may be explicit at the beginning of the discussion or become so as the discussion unfolds. Nor can the model emphasise the importance of having an interested and discerning audience. An indifferent, uncritical audience will not encourage constructive statements and one scathing remark from the teacher may cut discussion dead. But an audience does not suggest its attitude to its speaker solely through a verbal response; everything about that audience, its stance, its gestures, its dress will convey something about its attitude to the speaker before he even opens his mouth and this is true for pupils and teacher. We must consider the paralinguistic, visual and proxemic means of communication, in other words tone and voice quality, appearance and positioning in organisation for discussion. We will already have suggested a great deal about the value we place on our subject, ourselves and our pupils both through first impressions and accumulatively but we cannot afford to sit back on our laurels and assume that past successes will see us through. They will certainly help in building a feeling of trust and respect but what we wear to the lesson, our own punctuality, even our gestures as we enter the classroom will set the scene for what follows. If we arrive with everything we need and make it clear that careful preparation has preceded our interest then the currency is self-evident; only the best will do if the teacher's challenge is to be met. Standards of excellence, tidiness, organization can be compared with the teacher's own. If these are slipping then we cannot complain if pupils take us at face value and follow our example.

Having considered the groundwork we must next turn to the more distinctive components and options. Let us take as our generalised aim that of encouraging uninhibited, yet controlled and constructive discussion, leading to a meaningful goal. Who are the possible participants? Thirty mixed-ability second-year pupils, eleven sixth form A Level English students, twenty fourth-form 'bottom set' pupils; there are many permutations. All will make different demands; all should affect our approach to the lesson. To leave it, as some student teachers do, at that is to miss the factors which may radically alter the atmosphere of the lesson. We obviously should know as much as possible about our pupils' general background but more immediately should relate this lesson to their previous English lessons, and with the lesson from which they have just emerged. Perhaps the last English lesson was surprisingly successful and that success should be exploited immediately through discussion; perhaps it was a failure or satisfactory in a rather routine way, a containing exercise or a lesson that was popular with the pupils but 'not really English'. Perhaps the English teacher has been absent and the class have done 'nothing much, Sir' with the deputy head who kept extricating himself for more important business. All these are possible factors which must determine our approach. Are the pupils ripe for a sudden change in emphasis, a shock to their systems? While routine is valuable, indeed inevitable, sporadic unexpected shifts in the use of materials, in teacher-role, in the arrangement of the classroom are vital if pupils are to see English more as an intellectual challenge and less like an academic treadmill, and incidentally if the teacher is to remain interested and sane.

Chapter 2 emphasised the folly of passive acceptance of the state of a classroom. This is particularly important when considering organisation for discussion. Our options are on the face of it broad; pupils may, where this is possible, sit at individual desks facing the front. This usually implies an acceptance of the norm; it suggests a rather frigid and inappropriate segregation for an activity which implies cooperation and interaction. 'The teacher . . . is the obvious focus of attention. He can direct his talk to any part of the room, while the natural flow of pupil-talk is either to him or to other pupils through him. It is a setting which makes it difficult for the teacher to avoid talking *at* pupils, or to break up the interaction into more localised encounters.'[13] Pairs of pupils may be seated side by side at desks facing the front. This has the advantage that it takes little or no time to arrange but it presumes discussion only between the pair; pupils are tied to positions which are normally associated with written tasks. Desks can be seen as symbolic barriers between speaker and listener and they may become temptingly distracting during long awkward silences. For teachers in a hurry, particularly in a lesson where group discussion is only a brief interlude between other activities and where pupils are already paired, it is convenient to turn the front pair of pupils round to face their colleagues over a central pair of desks. The barrier is still there but note-taking is made easier. Pupils may be seated in a square, rectangle or circle. Many upper school classrooms, particularly sixth-form rooms, are habitually arranged like this and teachers may prefer to arrange their specialist rooms like this for nearly all their lessons. It suggests a greater informality more in key with the give-and-take of discussion, and face-to-face contact, which is so important, is guaranteed. But unless the classroom is inherited in this state, the group is relatively small or the lesson is a long one, it is a potentially noisy and time-consuming business to form a pattern which includes desks. It is then important to realise that some pupils find writing legibly on their knees very difficult. Writing should therefore be deferred, abandoned or attempted only in rough. It is the brave or foolish teacher who arranges thirty mixed-ability lower school pupils in a circle and then expects meaningful discussion. For many this arrangement is even more inhibiting than the normal one which at least provides the emotional defences of a desk and accustomed companions. Circles, even large ones, may be ideal for drama, games and music but seldom for discussion where large numbers of younger pupils are involved. They may also accentuate discipline problems, though some would contest that they improve matters since for once the teacher can at least see every pupil clearly.

The most obvious compromise between the large group and the segregated pupil is the small group, using the junior school model of a central table or pair of desks making note-making simple and adding a necessary structure to the whole arrangement. The teacher has two basic courses for grouping pupils; pupil choice ('Get yourselves into groups or four or five') or the more structured, and thus safer, teacher choice. If the teacher genuinely doesn't care who discusses with whom then better the former, but if there's the slightest doubt then the teacher must decide. This decision should be predetermined; pupils feel insecure and sometimes annoyed as the teacher agonises over who should sit where, particularly when odd number groups mean that friends will be parted. Much better the clinical ruthlessness of reading out group allocation. This can be decided according to ability, behaviour, friendship, sex and variety of opinions, at best a combination of all five, though the final criterion may only assume importance with more mature pupils. If pupils need the security of sitting next to their best friend in order to unlock their opinions then this should be allowed; where one friend dominates another they should be divided. Where rivalry, bullying, personality clashes may threaten the discussion it is safer to keep the antagonists apart. Introverts should not normally be grouped together, nor extroverts, nor all the most able, nor all the remedial pupils but there should be interesting exceptions: why shouldn't the most able meet some real competition from equally able peers, why shouldn't pupils be given the opportunity to reconcile differences through discussion, why shouldn't boys discuss a topic which is of particular concern to them? Of paramount importance is the quality of discussion but teachers cannot always predict and ensure this through the make-up of groups. The most enthusiastic and spirited contributions sometimes come from the most unlikely quarters; we need look no further than Billy Casper in Barry Hines' 'A Kestrel for a Knave'. Pupils must be given the security in which they can do their best but they must also be increasingly challenged. The task and clientele will finally decide the number in these groups; the larger the group the easier it will be for the introverted and unmotivated to hide behind their colleagues' contributions. Conversely, a smaller group may not provide sufficient breadth and range of opinion. The teacher may, unusually, have the opportunity and energy to arrange the classroom before the pupils arrive but, allowing for registration, this is only normally possible after a mid-morning (or afternoon) break. It is far more likely that the pupils will have to be relied upon to do the moving and in any case they will be responsible for rearranging the room if need be, to meet the demands of the next class. As has already been suggested in Chapter 2, furniture moving should be formalised and disciplined.

   Discussion is special; though traditionally much neglected, seen as a non-lesson by some pupils and teachers, it requires special organisation and a realisation by the teacher of his own role options and positioning possibilities. For many the most natural position will be at the front of the class, surrounded by the paraphernalia of the profession. This is hallowed by tradition and can instil a sense of security in both teacher and pupils. In reinforcing the *status quo* it can however suggest to some that a formality and attention to detail and standards of accuracy more associated with written work are the priority here. Of course the quality of discussion and the quality of the individual's contribution will still be assessed but obviously not in exactly the same way as written work (see Chapter 8). While it may be possible to hear all that is being said from the front with small groups, this will prove impossible with larger groups where the teacher will inevitably have to circulate. The danger here, rather like that of exam invigilation, is that the perambulation will be counterproductive. A conscientious desire to see all and hear all can backfire when the teacher's threatening shadow leaves the pupils self-conscious or disgruntled. Position is most sensibly decided by the context and teacher's role, which is itself built into the organisation of the classroom. Thus to see the teacher as the centre of all discussion, as an intellectual filtration system separating the dross from the ore, may well be to see him firmly in control from the front. This is of course only one interpretation of management and control, and discussion can be managed and controlled in a number of ways in the continuum between the teacher as fountain of all wisdom and the teacher who abjures all responsibility for the course of the discussion. The teacher who would like, as far as is realistically possible, to be seen as an equal and fellow enquirer, or somewhere midway in the continuum as a point of reference, guide and umpire, will inevitably need to move around groups, particularly where the class is a large one, and react shrewdly to cries of help. Some will be false alarms, some sheer laziness; to interrupt too soon may endanger the progress of other groups. A word or two well placed (or a detour) may be all that is needed to cut through despondency, but if the aim is to encourage the *pupils* to talk, the less that is imposed, as distinct from being requested, the better. Some groups, some tasks will work better without even this carefully posed intervention; here the teacher will leave the group 'to get on with it', having provided them with all the basic information needed. Discussion here may be seen as a test of initiative, particularly where simulation is involved. This does not of course mean a bonus free period where the teacher can hide behind a pile of marking. Aims must be evaluated, the individual's contribution must be assessed; the work cannot be seen in a vacuum and some sort of follow-up is inevitable. If the teacher comes to see discussion as a soft option pupils will inevitably too, and while discipline may seem less of an issue with older, smaller or more mature groups the teacher's eye and obvious interest are great motivation.

To distinguish between role options is inevitably to simplify what happens in a well organised lesson which may fall into several dove-tailed sections each of which demand a different role from pupils and teacher. Local issues and incidents will also decide the quality of pupil-teacher, pupil-pupil interaction, as in the following description:

Context. Thirty mixed-ability twelve-year-old pupils in a mixed comprehensive school; medium sized classroom with opportunity for rearrangement of furniture; second half of Spring Term; time allowed — two forty minute lessons.

Aim. To encourage meaningful and enjoyable discussion.

Objectives. To move away from more formal whole-class lessons and individual project work, which has demanded co-operation over the sharing of resources and information, to explore the co-operation demanded by group discussion where questions are more open-ended and conclusions more personal and problematical.

Teacher as Manager. The teacher greeted the class, checked for absentees, briefly introduced the task and stimulus and related it to past lessons. He allocated the pupils to groups of six based upon friendship pairs but guaranteeing a range of ability and boy-girl mix. He gave the signal for the well-practised movement of furniture and warned the pupils to sit in silence and await further information when the move was complete. One nominee from each of the five groups collected a folder of materials and distributed it to the waiting group. The teacher elaborated the description of the task and materials and drew their attention to the questions printed on the sheet in front of them:

1. What happens in your passage?
2. Why do you think Johnny did what he did?
3. What would you have done and why?
4. Could Johnny have avoided all this trouble?
5. Tell your group about a similar problem you have faced. What did you do? Was it the best thing to do?

Pupils were asked to nominate a notetaker cum spokesperson; the teacher took down these names and allowed the pupils the remainder of the lesson for discussion. He asked the pupils for any 'final questions'.

In this introductory and organisational section the pupils looked to the teacher for all the information. There was little opportunity for appeal though the teacher did say in retrospect that he would have allowed pupils to deal with questions in an alternative order if they wished. He was particularly adamant that the groups' make-up, once decided, would be inviolable (his class had come to expect this). He had taken into account possible confrontations when deciding upon the groups. He was in two minds about the size of the groups but risked quite large ones since the plenary session would be easier to manage with a smaller number of groups. Information was made as simple as possible and presented verbally (twice), the second time to catch those distracted by the beginning of the lesson and on the sheet for those who found oral instructions difficult to follow. He was more concerned with making the discussion initially enjoyable, undemanding and relevant for all the pupils than covering a great deal of ground. He hoped in future to give pupils a variety of stimuli and to arrange for different groups to discuss and report on different issues.

Teacher as Guide and Umpire. Having checked that the ventilation was adequate, that pupils could all see each other properly and communicate comfortably, the teacher perched quietly on the edge of the teacher's desk at the front. He deliberately did not offer help in general terms, nor did he circulate since he feared that pupils would resort to 'personal calls' rather than reading the already adequate information carefully. This paid off and pupils generally appeared to be engrossed in the task. Having warned the teacher in the adjoining classroom of what was taking place, he did not put a ceiling on noise level but in fact pupils were happy to talk in turn in a rather conspiratorial way as though afraid of disclosing secrets to adjacent groups. Because of the competitive nature of some of the class there was a danger that pupils would rush the work in order to finish first and the teacher was particularly on the watch for this. There were two requests for confirmation of information that was only implied in the story. In each case the teacher responded with 'What do you (i.e. whole group) think?', which sent the pupils back to the circumstantial evidence. Two chairs collided and the teacher resisted the temptation to interfere; the two occupants sorted out their territorial claims quietly and amicably. There was one stifled inquiry, 'How much time do we have, Sir?', and three requests from note-takers for spellings despite the fact that the teacher had emphasised that spelling and writing need only be intelligible, not absolutely correct.

Teacher as Group Leader. With ten 'working' minutes of the lesson left three pupils came back from their remedial lesson; 'Mrs Banks said she had to go early, could you have us, Sir?'. There had been no warning of this. Since the teacher wanted to involve them in the follow-up to this initial lesson he arranged a small discussion group, taking the initiating role himself, still perched on the desk in order to see this group and the whole class. He described the situation in the story simply and referred them to the written sheets for reference, but knowing that some of the words would be difficult for at least one poor reader there. He explained what the class was doing and would be doing and quietly flattered the group by implying that they alone knew what was in the future. He invited their initial reaction to the story and then asked them to think about what Johnny could have done as an alternative and talk about this among themselves.

Teacher as Manager and Confidant. With six minutes to go he warned the groups that they should now be inspecting their conclusions and checking that the notes reflected group opinions. Two minutes later nominees handed in the reports and materials together in folders, labelled with group numbers. At the teacher's signal groups moved furniture back, two groups at a time, waited for the teacher's signal, put their chairs up and then stood quietly behind them. In the two minutes left before the bell went the teacher finally inspected the classroom, particularly the floor, asked about the work the class had been doing in history, looked forward to the next lesson, complimented two pupils as they left and shared a joke with a pupil about the local football team. As the class left, two pupils loitered and returned to ask advice — one about an entry for a literary competition and a remedial pupil asked, 'Sir, is it true that I'll go into 2Y next year?'

Teacher as Audience, Commentator and 'Student'. In the follow-up lesson pupils were given time to recap on their findings, during the first five minutes. They then presented them to the whole class. This entailed a grouping of furniture as before with some modification so that speakers were visible to all the audience. Report making was deliberately formalised to make the best use of the time and to allow a forum for all pupils. The note-taker cum spokesperson reported first and then other members of the group were given opportunities to elaborate or disagree with the initial statement. Each group reported in turn and on two occasions the teacher invited responses from individuals: 'I seem to remember Gary had something interesting to say here . . . '; 'Sarah, didn't you say a similar thing happened to you?' In both cases the pupils lacked confidence but seemed happy to contribute once given a platform. Cross-pollination was possible as the teacher drew a few conclusions from the mass of comment while simultaneously probing the distinction between the 'best' thing to do and the 'right' thing to do. When planning the lesson he had decided to take his lead from the pupils and only extend this debate if the pupils spontaneously showed interest in it. On at least three occasions he made it clear that he regarded the speakers as experts and without heavy-handedness and self-consciousness asked for further detail: 'Would you advise someone who didn't know to do it in that way too?'; 'That's something I hadn't thought of. What made you see it that way?' The teacher attempted to draw the three remedial pupils and one absentee into the lesson at the beginning by asking two pupils to describe what they thought they had been doing in the previous lesson; he didn't put pressure on them to contribute to the discussion though.

This is a limited, two-dimensional attempt to chronicle one teacher's shifts of role in two forty-minute lessons. It does not even scratch the surface of the individual pupil's perception of those lessons with all the concomitant rewards, pressures, distractions and perplexities, nor does it show how their roles were also determined by the context and their colleagues. It does not demonstrate how some pupils almost visibly relaxed when they were in discussion groups, not to the point of complacent inertia but so as to encourage a feeling of group identity and security. Conversely it does not suggest how teacher control was augmented by group pressure: 'Don't talk so loud . . . we can hear you!'; 'Hang on, don't go so fast.'; 'John's already said that.' For the more extrovert, the more domineering, this was irksome; although the teacher's *ex officio* authority could be tolerated, this was seen as a personal threat, a tampering with peer-group class status and more annoying since the criticisms were usually justified. Any résumé cannot convey the fun; laughter seemed nearer the surface in these small groups, often produced from momentary diversions from the main route, diversions which tested the teacher's restraint and trust. Overofficious interruption would have killed the joke and conceivably the discussion dead. Perhaps most significantly, this account does not reproduce the pauses for thought and the attentive silence of the good listener. If listening can be seen as a skill to be practised there were many children who were inevitably discovering how learning to suspend disbelief, bite back their egos, and finding out that to listen can be infinitely more difficult than finding just the right thing to say.

Hopefully this description demonstrates the importance of careful planning, making instructions unambiguous, pacing lessons carefully and perhaps most important, and certainly most ephemeral, the delicacy with which teachers must tread if over-reaction and imposition are to be avoided. The corollary of restraint is perhaps a sense of balance here; trust falsely placed will result in insecure pupils. There is no question of the teacher devolving responsibility for the whole lesson to the pupils; the teacher is in control throughout. The localised freedom of the discussion groups is on the teacher's terms, not the pupils'. In fact it is part of the freedom of discussion that pupils should be freed from the responsibility for making the main rules for themselves. Certain restraints will be inbuilt: school rules; the result of convention, routine; 'You must not leave your seats; if you need to ask something put your hand up and I will come to you.' The timing of the lesson will be the teacher's time, but most pupils work best when the time has been 'laid out' before them; 'I shall give you about fifteen minutes to discuss this and then the spokesperson in each group will report back'. The fact that more or less time is taken is ultimately neither here nor there. Pacing the lesson again calls for a certain delicacy and flexibility. One group may be moved on for strategic reasons, while another may be sent back to think again. Most importantly there will be room for the pupils' suggestions: 'We thought that if we concentrated on this . . . '; 'I think that what we should be asking is . . . '; 'Could we have longer?' Restraints may apparently be lifted ('I'm not going to say you can't talk louder than this. I think you're sensible enough to decide when you're annoying other groups yourselves') only to be devolved; here the group will have a part to play in decision-making beyond the narrower limits of the task. Obviously there will be occasions, when their sensibilities will need nudging!

We should at this stage anticipate the objection that this type of discussion lesson appears unnecessarily staged and artificial. Is there not a place for the unprepared, unrehearsed off-the-cuff lesson which develops with a will of its own? Given that we do not mean by this an ambushing of the lesson-plan by wayward pupils or inconsequential chatter, there is obviously a place for discussion which unfolds, revealing as it does so, butterfly-like, a number of surprises. This is perhaps the ideal: on occasions it is both inevitable and memorable; snow falls in May, the fire-practice has intervened, Matthew has brought in his unpredictable tame crow, Chris went to the House of Commons to collect her prize, the sixth-formers are wearing fancy dress again. Rather than ignore we exploit such phenomena; in many cases Matthew's crow and Chris's trip provide a much-prized chance for the pupils and *teacher* to learn from an expert. We must be opportunists, prepared to accept inevitable grammatical lapses, half-framed sentences, 'umms' and 'ers' patiently. The reward is our pupils' involvement, inspiration and triumph.

We might also object that organisation for discussion involving mixed-ability first years is distant from that involving less able fifth years or motivated sixth formers but the same rules apply, though here perhaps the restraints will be less overt, more implicit and assumed. The need for a sense of security, an atmosphere of trust and forbearance, the discipline of a reliable goal and the pleasure derived from a task which is seen as challenging and relevant remain the same, but 'relevance' is perhaps seen retrospectively in the sense that no teacher can predict which issues will appear relevant on one particular occasion for one motley group of individuals. It is the foolish teacher who presumes that Matthew's relationship with Joe Crow is irrelevant but that adolescent love is so pertinent that almost any approach to it will guarantee success. The teacher carefully constructs the framework in which opportunities emerge and that framework, the starting points for discusssion, may appear unsurprising, circumscribing, but it is there to be abandoned cuticle-like as the group outgrows it and takes flight. So what will stimulate discussion? Let us start with the pupils themselves, since so many teachers start with pieces of paper:

Pupils

1. interesting/provocative question/statement.
2. inability to grasp a concept/term.
3. refusal to accept teacher's/other pupil's viewpoint/explanation.
4. desire to confirm opinions through appeal to wider audience.
5. changes in pupils' appearance or situation.
6. pupil's explanation/discussion of his own work.

The Environment

1. unexpected changes in the environment.
2. recent significant events, within class/school, nationally/internationally.

3. class visits, class visitors.

'Materials' (pupils' and teacher's choice)

1. written language e.g. prose, poetry, plays, letters, diagrams, lists, etc.
2. spoken language e.g. tape, records, TV, radio, film, formal speeches, preceding conversation, improvisation.*
3. art.
4. music.

*Discussion based upon TV programmes and advertisements and radio programmes (and newspapers) will come naturally into an inquiry into the mass media, but discussion based upon these should not wait until the CSE course. Improvisation is too enormous and fundamental to squeeze into any particular category of stimulus, but it illustrates that the most constructive discussion is that of the problem-solving, transitional, 'if . . . but . . . whether' type rather than the final draft record, performance or résumé. If English lessons do not provide as many opportunities for problem-solving as the Nuffield Science courses then improvisation provides problems of many types; sharing, co-operation, allocation, selection and projection in a context where there can be no single right answer (see Chapter 9).

It might be objected that the range is over-wide; to include discussion based upon art and music is surely an intrusion into the preserves of the art and music departments. We must return to our aim: to encourage uninhibited, yet controlled and constructive discussion. We might include as an objective here: to sharpen discrimination through an exploration of the language of subjective feeling and opinion, to free the speaker from the subject specialist's reliance on categories, on typifying the object of discussion, in favour of an approach which puts emphasis on communicating to an audience what the speaker feels about the music or piece of art in a way which convinces the audience of the speaker's integrity and interest and which satisfies the speaker. Here, as throughout discussion, speaker and audience are being tested but here there is a deliberate attempt to cut loose from a facile reliance on the shorthand of a shared specialism where the interpretation of clichéd terms is taken for granted. Here the speaker must delve within himself for the often metaphorical language which will convey vividly to his audience a feeling or opinion which may be only half grasped for the speaker, but which is made clearer through its encapsulation in words.

For some English teachers sanctioned talk in class was and is synonymous with formal speech-making and debates. With the recent enthusiasm among educationalists for oracy skills it has become fashionable to deride speeches and debate, or at best to ignore them, apparently on the grounds that these are not talk so much as a painful and futile mental obstacle course. Speech-making, as with all else in teaching, will prove futile if we are not clear why we are doing it. Once having justified it as a worthwhile activity in which all pupils can play a meaningful part then it should be possible to plan for enjoyment. We can hardly expect our pupils to enter wholeheartedly into what should be a demanding and thus potentially rewarding activity unless we are clear in our own minds of its worth. Speech-making at its best is a compendium of skills; it tests the individual's ability to select, initially perhaps the subject but in every case the appropriate subject matter. It relates this to the audience's age, maturity and interests and in some cases it must find appropriate methods of persuasion for its listeners. It tests the speaker's ability to research, true even for autobiographical experiences, and to pace information so as to retain the audience's attention and interest. Speech-making demands the confidence necessary to look an audience squarely in the eye, however much the speaker must occasionally glance at his notes, and the confidence to diverge from notes where the original plan seems inappropriate. As with any other creative activity confidence is nine-tenths of the battle; it will produce an entertaining speech at short notice from a nonsensical title; 'Now you have one minute, Kevin, to tell us anything you like about paper-clips'. It goes without saying that talking, for however short a time, to a whole class or even part of the class demands quite a different form of courage to that required for group discussion. In the former, despite all the teacher's reassurance 'drying up', the glazed eyes of an indifferent audience, annoyed fidgeting from the back row, disconcerting grins from your best friend may make the whole enterprise a nightmare. Any novelty, indeed any worthwhile task, will undoubtedly be nerve-racking to the least able and most nervous. We must somehow express the task in terms which are intelligible, manageable and which help to convey the enjoyment: in other words convey our own enthusiasm and suggest what the pupils can hope to get out of it. It is too easy to present speech-making as a difficult chore; 'Now we must practise this for your CSE oral exam.' Here it may appear to the pupil to have little relationship with real life, to be as divorced from the language of breaktime as a Petrarchan sonnet. In a sense of course it is; we cannot pretend that speech-making does not require a discipline and coherency not normally associated with informal conversation. What it provides, in a way that informal discussion cannot, is an opportunity for pupils, particularly those who find writing cramping and fraught with technical traps, to take control and express themselves however briefly without interruption from others, to impress their personality and interests indelibly on the class. At this stage the realists and cynics will quite naturally object that a rambling shambles of a speech is indeed as ineradicable as indelible ink, and how are we to restore any semblance of confidence in a pupil after such a fiasco? The answer must be that while tempering our expectations realistically to the individual, but while still keeping these expectations high, we make it as easy as possible for our pupils to succeed. We make success realisable.

With this end in sight we plan carefully, and ideally our plan is long term, a strategy for success that begins unambitiously in the first year of the secondary school. Initially we must create the climate for speech-making, or more realistically, since speech-making isn't the be-all and end-all of the English syllabus, we should introduce speech-making at a point when the class is ready for it, but as the Bullock Report noted, waiting for 'readiness' may mean waiting for ever. Many will need encouraging, some will need coaxing, a few may need the rules bending if they are to join in at all. Speech-making requires a sympathetic environment where pupils will silently give the speaker the benefit of the doubt while paying him the compliment of not passively accepting every word. Pupils need to have experienced organised discussion as a pleasurable activity before moving on to more formal speech-making. They also, and this will be uppermost in their own minds, require something to speak about. With any group, but particularly with a mixed-ability first-year class who may have little feeling of group or school identity, it is not enough to leave the choice of subject up to them; it is far better to provide a select but quite open-ended choice of subjects. These do not have to be highly original since the orginality should come through the pupil's interpretation of the subject. A specimen selection might be:

My hobby;
The person in the world I would most like to meet and why;
The person in the world I would least like to meet and why
(facetious suggestions excluded);
What I would do with £100 and why;
Holidays;

A subject of your choice.

These are all old favourites; our grandparents were writing essays on just such topics sixty years ago. This does not invalidate their worth; in practice I have found this sort of list an acceptable compromise. It presents a sensible range of topics, but the very fact that it is such a sensible list encourages the divergent and more original thinkers to manipulate topics blatantly and, better still, take up the last suggestion. I have always found that whatever the class there is no duplication of subject matter; every speech has been a unique experience for both speaker and audience. Though mention of time may seem unnecessarily restricting it is important that pupils should have some guidance if they are not to flounder among a mass of possible material; 'You will need to prepare a speech to last for about a minute or more.' No ceiling should be stipulated at this stage and the 'about' allows flexibility for those who may express a great deal succinctly and for those who dry up. In practice any time limit soon becomes irrelevant as speech-making, question-answering and the handling of exhibits eat up many minutes.

Having discussed possible subjects in an informal way, pupils at this stage should be given both homework time and class time to prepare their speeches; the first initially since many will want to call on the help of their families and friends and local libraries. One of the bonuses of speech-making is that it soon turns into a collaborative activity. Pupils swop and share information, particularly where both were involved in the original experience, but they must be provided with the opportunity for doing so. Pupils will need a follow-up lesson since problems will undoubtedly have arisen and insecurities crept in: 'They didn't have the book I wanted, Miss'; 'If I forget can I read my notes, Sir?' The second question needs careful consideration. I usually resort to a rather embarrassing but apparently entertaining and effectual series of introductions to Monty Mumble, Randolph Readalot and Fenella Fidget which demonstrate how all three can respectively murder a potentially good subject. We must be prepared to be patient with those who find their eyes inexorably sucked into the safety of their notes.

One can give advice about how to plan a speech on paper, suggest headings, even abbreviations, but in the final analysis advice about planning speeches is very much like advice about planning essays; seldom heeded. We must have faith and trust in the student who appears with his earth worm, 'We've been doing them in Combined Science, Miss' and cheerfully reassures us, 'I don't need any notes, Miss,

I know all about him.' Having dismally anticipated a rather formal, and truncated, dissertation on the feeding habits of earth worms we may be pleasantly surprised to find that Eric the Earth Worm is a focal point for all the speaker's most entertaining and Mittyish fantasies. It is positively kind to encourage speakers to bring in relevant exhibits. Many a good speech has been made into an excellent one and a mediocre one saved from disaster, by an interesting and annotated display. Pupils should have access to the board, an overhead projector, even a projector and screen if necessary. All this requires that the teacher knows exactly what the pupils are to talk about in advance; it also requires a carefully stated policy concerning exhibits since pupils will take us at our word and bring in snakes, 'my brother's motorbike' and 'Dad's old books' if these seem relevant. Suggestions should be vetted carefully: a mature rabbit in a wooden hutch brought with parental permission and co-operation and hidden safely in a stock cupboard may be acceptable, a rather terrified rabbit in a cardboard box, prey to the enthusiastic fingers of thirty other pupils, will not. In any case it is sensible to give the form teacher (and colleagues who may hear some very odd noises through the wall) warning. The enterprise will be dependent upon their co-operation, since we may well need to remind pupils to bring in materials on the appropriate day.

Having seen how much effort pupils (and incidentally parents) are prepared to put into the finished speech, it is only fair to repay this effort and trust by planning the classroom and lesson carefully. With lower school pupils I have always tried to make an occasion of it by being politely formal; 'We are fortunate to have as our speaker today someone who knows a great deal about . . . ' knowing full well that this will be greeted with a friendly chortle. The artificial formality forms a novel smokescreen around the control that the teacher is inevitably exerting. We are in a theatre or a television studio where a chairman or compère seems eminently reasonable. Speeches nearly always take longer than expected, particularly if questions 'from the floor' are permitted. These provide an excellent means for bringing out the diffident speaker who has some very interesting ideas but lacks a framework in which to express them. Question-time requires careful organisation; audience and speakers will obviously need to be warned that there will be scope for questions but more obviously still, if chaos is to be avoided, pupils will have to put their hands up and wait for the teacher's go ahead. Here again a whimsical formality can be a help with younger pupils ('I think Mr Brown has a question for you') and it can also disguise some awkward moments, for example where a question could be considered embarrassing ('Are you prepared to answer Mr Phillips's question?'), allowing the speaker a graceful exit from a disconcerting predicament. If questions are unforthcoming the teacher can exert the chairman's right to pose questions of his own and can use the opportunity to highlight important parts of the speech, 'I believe you mentioned that . . . Can you tell us a little more about this . . . ?'

It is important that the teacher should keep a record of the quality of the speeches during the lesson, allowing credit for content, evidence of research, presentation, exhibits and response to questions. There is no need for a mark but it is important that speeches are seen as important in the teacher's eyes by the pupils, that their efforts or lack of them have been noted and that the teacher can refer to an area of real success when it comes to giving verbal or written reports. If a pupil is out of favour with his form tutor or other subject teachers it may boost his morale and behaviour to know that he is doing very well in one subject at least, and that his English teacher has impressed this upon the form tutor.

Depending upon the make-up of the class and the teacher's relationship with them, more or less formality may be considered appropriate. The writing of speeches can be disciplined by the teacher's inspection of the finished notes before they are used. A concluding session may reveal what has been remembered from a number of speeches, but a delight in the spoken word should not be strangled by ensuing written work. Pupils will be only too accustomed to lessons which are always 'validated' by a routine piece of written work.

It is of course conceivable that only a small group of pupils will be selected or choose to present a speech. It is possible that the speech will be presented to a subsection of the class. In practice these speeches are usually so pertinent and entertaining that all the class inevitably become part of the audience. It seems sensible to allow for this through whole class participation unless it is clear that the speaker only feels happy performing to a small group. Once it has been established, for pupils and teacher, that speech-making is a pleasurable and meaningful activity then some of the suggestions for developments will ideally come from the pupils themselves. Failing this, speech-making can be seen as the culmination of written work which aims to explore two possible approaches to an issue, arguing for and against a particular course of action, taking up a contentious and topical decision reported in the media. This is a difficult task for the younger and less able pupil, but nevertheless a necessary precursor of open-minded and unblinkered argument which is important at any age, in any context, but particularly important when considering the themes so often studied in CSE English courses and any literature worthy of analysis. The whole process can be formalised and thus explored more easily through an initial written task, which is then put to the test in a short speech delivered to an audience who are encouraged to pick up, question and confirm points. As with questioning any speaker, the enquirer and speaker are both being tested and assessed. A single speaker may speak for and against, or a pair may collaborate upon the collation of arguments and then divide in order to present the two opposing view points. The latter is more potentially fruitful not only since 'two brains are better than one' but because it makes the common ground more explicit: 'Is that an argument for or against?'; 'Can we use it in different ways for both?'; 'What if they object that . . . ?' As a pair or a team, pupils are less vulnerable, any objection from the audience becomes less of an attack since the evidence was arrived at jointly. It goes without saying that since we are expecting pupils to take on the role of Members of Parliament speaking in the Commons, or guest speakers in a television forum, they too should be allowed adequate time to prepare for and present their arguments. This may well mean lesson-time to visit the library and opportunities to consult knowledgeable members of staff and members of the community. Even with the most mature students the teacher cannot bow out; he must be there as a sorting-house for ideas, a human 'enquiries' desk, since one of the objectives here is to give pupils practice in identifying the information they need, locating sources, selection and presentation, bearing in mind the target audience; nine tenths collation, one tenth presentation. Both speaker and audience should learn from every speech.

The for and against approach can obviously develop into a full-blown debate with chairman, proposer and opposer and their seconders and with plenty of scope for questions and comments from the floor. This might be seen as the culmination of work which has demonstrated class interest and disagreement. It could initiate a study of an issue which will be explored through one or more key texts (purity in *Tess of the d'Urbervilles* and *Of Mice and Men* spring to mind). It could be seen as a lunch-time, after-school or end-of-term activity but it should not be entered into lightly; debates are only worth doing if they are done scrupulously with an attention to detail and discipline; in which case it may well be sensible to set a good example through a debate where staff take the parts of chief proposer and opposer, with pupils as seconders and a guest adult or pupil as chairman. If this seems adult-heavy then more time can be allowed for questions from the floor. Some schools of course will have debating societies, but these are often an upper-school affair, and where they are not may give the impression that debating is a rather fossilised art reserved for the most able. If pupils are to make sense of parliamentary and television debates, if they are to learn of the fragility of facts and the capriciousness of 'truth', then we must allow them opportunities to play out and practise their own ideas.

These are the basic approaches at their most elemental. There are approaches which take speech-making and debate closer still to the world of drama; adopting a new persona, voice, appearance, costume will add fresh dimensions to a speech. It may allow the speaker and audience to enter more completely into what is after all no more than a reflection of the world outside. Characters may emerge from novels, poems and plays into the classroom to argue the case for a particular course of action. They may attack their creator, debate pros and cons 'from the dead'. We can adopt and extend Browning's dramatic monologue and Milton's Satan; Chaucer's Clerk and Shakespeare's Iago may well appear more accessible and entertaining while still hopefully retaining their complexity and mystery. Finally of course we can bring in visitors who have some relevance to the work in progress and can deliver a 'professional' speech.

This chapter began rather defensively; if attack is the best form of defence then we can conclude more assertively and claim categorically that pupils learn best when they are interested, interest is increased by personal involvement and discussion provides the most obvious means of involvement. It demonstrates to pupil and teacher what is and has been learnt and more significantly what has not. If the English lesson is seen as the custodian of expressive writing, then it is fair to conclude that it has a similar association with expressive speech. Though we may regret and attempt to redress this imbalance the English teacher cannot duck a very real responsibility; not just that of setting a good example but more practically and simply of helping pupils to learn and show that they have learnt. 'Talking for effect' demands courage; in the midst of the O Level literature syllabus where 'plot', 'characterisation' and 'theme' are firmly in charge, it may seem reckless to 'waste' precious time on the tentative circumlocutions of discussion. Teachers fall prey to the preconceptions of their critics; while privately advocating real discussion they may feel pangs of guilt where a lesson has included no formal written work. It may seem to the conscientious a delegation of responsibility to allow pupils' ideas to dominate a lesson, to the insecure an invitation to insubordination to allow the pupil to teach the teacher.

It is true that the ground will be covered more slowly. What is beyond dispute is that the ground will bear fruit, the sterility of revision facts and other people's knowledge will be superseded by a more personal commitment; 'I disagreed but I know now why I disagreed because I had a chance to talk it out with others'; or, as one 'alienated' fourth year pupil remarked, 'Funny, I never thought there was much to it, English I mean, but ever since we got talking about it I kind of know what I don't know, and I think I'm beginning to learn a thing or two'.

Notes

1. J. Britton *et al*, *The Development of Writing Abilities* (11-18), Schools Council Research Studies (Macmillan, 1975).

2. J. Britton, *Language and Learning*, (Penguin, 1970).

3. M. Mallett and B. Newsome, *Talking, Writing and Learning 8-13*, Schools Council Working Paper no. 59 (Evans/Methuen, 1977).

4. *The Teaching of English in England* (HMSO, 1921).

5. D. Barnes, *Language, the Learner and the School* (Penguin, 1969).

6. Edwards and Furlong, *The Language of Teaching*, (Heinemann, 1978).

7. M. Joos, *The Five Clocks* (Bloomington, Indiana, 1962).

8. A. Wilkinson, *The Foundations of Language* (OUP, 1971).

9. See 'Relevant Models of Language' in A. Wilkinson (ed.), *The State of Language* (University of Birmingham School of Education, 1969).

10. J. Tough, *Talking and Learning*, Schools Council Communication Skills in Early Childhood Project (Ward Lock Educational, 1977).

11. See 3.

12. Ibid.

13. See 6.

4 READING IN CLASS

> You'd better come and see a proper lesson: they're reading
> their own books today. (English teacher)

Anyone familiar with the common conception of the secondary school
English lesson will scarcely be surprised by this teacher's defensive
remark, which was addressed to a student teacher. It could be para-
phrased thus; 'You will waste your time witnessing an essentially quiet
activity which causes me no supervision problems. You will not see
me tested nor will you see me performing. Since they will be reading a
range of books I shall not be leading them from the front. Instead I will
seem more like a primary school teacher interacting on a one-to-one
basis.'

Beyond this teacher's remark lie a number of significant assumptions; that 'proper' lessons are those where the teacher's organisation
and intervention are blatant and open to inspection, and where
sequencing and pupil-progress presume an almost constantly monitored
interaction between pupil and teacher, usually through question and
answer. The 'proper' lesson works towards a tangible product which can
be removed, dissected and offered as proof that something constructive
has occurred in the lesson.Thus lessons where pupils spend all or nearly
all their time reading are by these criteria improper: teacher intervention
and interruption are minimal; the end product is indefinite and unquantifiable and the teacher has apparently delegated responsibility for
choice of book and pace to the pupils. At the heart of the lesson lies
the book and the individual's relationship with that rather than with the
teacher as synthesisor and assessor. Can we justify extended silent
reading in the classroom or is it a prime example of dereliction of duty?

Towards a Reading Policy

The Schools' Council survey of Children's Reading Interests[1] came to
the conclusion that a fairly large group of proficient readers in secondary schools choose not to read books in their own time. The Effective
Use of Reading[2] project team decided that 'a large amount of classroom
reading is fragmented in nature . . . Even in English lessons only 10 per
cent of reading observed at first year secondary level would meet a

63

minimal criterion for being termed "continuous" '. The Bullock Report noted: 'At its most extreme the system of class reading at the rate of one or two books a term must put literature in a somewhat artificial light in the mind of the pupil'. It is difficult to escape the conclusion that many schools may actually be helping to put pupils off books and reading, and that many pupils currently lack opportunities to choose their own reading books and to read them at length. The library lesson and the reading lesson, far from being improper, would seem a valuable recognition of the importance of wide individualised reading within the class and a guarantee that, when exam pressures threaten, note-taking and teacher-talk do not obscure reading for understanding and for enjoyment.

'We are all of us learning to read all the time'; for many pupils I.A. Richards's confident assertion rings hollow since, if we learn to read by reading, the less chance we have to practise the less hope we have of improving. It is too easy to equate the decoding of words with effective reading, and a reading age of 9+ with proficiency, and thus fail to recognise the line of development:

> The primary skills of the early years mature into the understanding of word structure and spelling patterns. The intermediate skills, so essential in word attack in the early stages, are at work in skimming, scanning, and the extraction of meaning in the more complex reading tasks of the later stages. The comprehension skills themselves do not change; it is in the increasing complexity of the purposes to which they are put as the pupils grow older that the difference lies. In the middle years there should be three major emphases. The first is to consolidate the work of the early years, and to give particular help to those children who for one reason or another have failed to make progress. The second is to maintain and extend the idea of reading as an activity which brings great pleasure and is a personal resource of limitless value. The third is to develop the pupil's reading from the general to the more specialised.[3]

These are the aims — and the obstacles? Large classes, insufficient knowledge of the skills involved in reading, and inappropriate reading materials. These obstacles may lead even the conscientious English teacher to abandon the book and reading at length in favour of the worksheet or the course book's segments.

There is a general assumption among English teachers and teachers in general that reading and particularly the reading of 'literature' is the life-blood of English teaching, indeed is the only patch that the English department can jealously guard as its own. Language may belong to the whole curriculum; the reading of literature does not. The English teacher connot afford to join the ranks of those, the majority, who see reading as something which our pupils just do, assuming that they can make the necessary leap between reading to decode, and reading for reflection, for note-taking, for summary work, for the comprehension exercise and for pleasure. The English department needs a reading policy and any such policy will be based on a series of principles:

1. Reading is an on-going skill which can be improved.
2. Reading can be sub-divided into a number of skills which can be identified and assessed.
3. We comprehend most readily when we are interested in what we are reading.
4. Our pupils will need a wide range of reading experiences in order to prepare for adult life, a range which is not adequately covered by the set book and comprehension passage alone.
5. Our pupils will read a diverse range of materials outside school, an indication of their shifting interests and different personalities.
6. Our pupils' extra-mural reading habits may not seem ideal but, given that they read less than we would wish, we cannot afford to condemn their choice.
7. For most, 'great literature' will be a meaningless tag. If we wish to convince our pupils of the quality of the 'classics' the onus is on us as teachers to make them accessible through a critical analysis which is enjoyable and constructive rather that obsessive and destructive. Greatness cannot be presumed and should not apparently be equated with obscurity and irrelevance.
8. Too much of what is taught, 'ploughed through' in the name of literature, is a product of the back-wash from the examination set texts. If the reading experiences of pupils are being damaged by the syllabus corset then we should seek to change or replace the syllabus, or at the very least reform the stock cupboard, rather than compromise our principles.

'Literature'

Once free from the notion that 'O Lit.' will dominate the course of study for all our pupils, what and why shall we read? In answer to the latter, we may see ourselves as crusaders, evangelists, custodians of culture: 'For the sake of the human future, we must do, with intelligent resolution and with faith, all we can to maintain the full life in the present – and life is growth – of our transmitted culture.'[4] 'All the pupils, including those of very limited attainments, need the civilising experience of contact with great literature.'[5] While such exhortations may not be greeted with howls of derision they will probably be relegated to the 'public aims' file by those gingerly awaiting 5F on a Friday afternoon.

F.R.Leavis and others have made great claims for the civilising influence of great literature and while no-one would dispute that for certain individuals certain literature can inspire a moral awakening, this is the exception rather that the rule. We certainly cannot prove that 'great' literature (whatever that epithet means) makes its readers better, more civilized human beings, but we can claim that by broadening our pupils' horizons we can hope to make them more enlightened, discerning and tolerant. Literature, whether 'great' or not, can reveal alternatives, not simply in the use and interpretation of language, but in possible courses of action. Conversely it can provide support, confirmation and reassurance. The reader can confront problems at one remove and in relative safety. While refusing to make unrealistic claims for literature we can still agree that 'its significance for personal values, for the width and depth of an individual's mind, and for his growth as a thoughtful member of society is self-evident'[6] and that 'English teaching divorced from literature is often dull, flat and mechanical.'[7]

The alternatives to Leavis's and the Newsom Report's crusading zeal seem equally extreme; even the usually cautious Bullock committee claimed, 'Books compensate for the difficulties of growing up'. They obviously do not, and it is the misguided English teacher who insists on seeing literature as therapy or in an equally blinkered way selects only those materials which seem immediately relevant to the class's own situation. This can reach its laughable worst in the fourth year where literature is selected to reflect, some would say fuel, those 'well-known' traumas of the adolescent, maladjustment, juvenile delinquency, identity crises, sexual problems, drugs, abortion, and so on. Such issues are not the sole preserve of the adolescent and should not be over-emphasised at the expense of other equally 'relevant' topics and interests. Any selection of literature based solely on narrow conceptions of relevance is inevitably dangerous, since a single teacher will decide what he considers relevant for a large number of individuals who would find great problems articulating what is relevant for themselves. What is 'relevant' is what works at any one time with any one individual or group of individuals. It will work at different levels for different readers and much of the material's interest will be revealed by skilful teaching. Quaint language, unfamiliar situations, do not necessarily make Sophocles or Shakespeare irrelevant, while an unconvincing modern short story may seem emotionally light-years away from the interests of the class. There is nothing inherently dynamic in the modernity of the modern and nothing intrinsically venerable about the writings of the dead. They come together in the classroom reading, the defending champion and the upstart street fighter. A skilful teacher and the give-and-take of classroom discussion should provide the ringside judges with the criteria for awarding points.

If what is relevant is what works where shall we draw the line? Should those transactional accounts of hare-coursing, those gruelling descriptions of Hiroshima or Mayhew's London truly form part of classroom literature? Though some few purists would disagree, the answer is yes, so too should Pepys, the newspaper editorial, Genesis and the train timetable. All are examples of prose which attempts to explain, to make sense of the 'facts', in a number of ways. An understanding of the differences between fiction and non-fiction, between opinion and fact, is of vital importance if our pupils are to grasp that words can be manipulated to the writer's own ends and therefore withstand rhetoric and propaganda. The principle must be moderation and variety in all things. English is not social studies, occupational therapy, amateur psychology or ethics. The bias must be towards the literary and the imaginative, in part because pupils meet so much transactional prose in their other subjects, but more fundamentally because fiction allows us to interpret, make sense of and manipulate reality.[8]

There is no easy answer to the question 'What shall we read?'. We might decide that 'literature' means the best of any genre, whether morally edifying or not. Thus no-one would suggest that doggerel is a particularly elevated form of poetry but some doggerel is more effective, some less. The best of any genre can only be tested against the second-rate and we must allow our pupils to meet and discuss the mediocre and unsuccessful on occasions. The minefield here is obvious; pupils are extremely shrewd perceivors of the teacher's true estimate of a piece of literature, even when it is introduced without comment and then may feed the teacher with the required response as the easiest way out. We also fool ourselves if we expect our pupils to condemn our selection if it is just the sort they, and we, enjoy reading at home. Finally, we cannot realistically expect pupils to distinguish the good from the bad, to have the courage of their convictions, particularly in the fourth, fifth and sixth forms, if they have never been encouraged to speak out and disagree with the teacher in the past. From this still quite idealistic and inevitably subjective starting point, 'literature means the best that has been written of any genre', we can chart the continuum through 'literature means the best but only where the pupils are likely to find it immediately interesting' to the cynical *'anything* that works' or 'anything forthcoming from the stock cupboard'. A survey of English departments reveals that 'literature' as taught is a complex amalgam of the lot.

Few Heads of English start from scratch; there are already sets of books in the stock cupboard. Some are eminently disposable and should go. More, representing not quite the best currently available, cannot be replaced overnight. Some will remain because of the possible demands of future syllabi or for quite idiosyncratic reasons: 'Frank always uses that with his third years. He knows the West Riding like the back of his hand'. Where funds are quite inadequate a policy of merely 'topping up' currently popular but depleted sets, though sensible, may lead to a dreary cycle where staff become stale as they repeatedly teach the same text without the spur to break loose and take risks with more exciting alternatives. There is no place for the passive teacher who allows the Head of English to decide what is ordered and for whom; indeed most department heads are only too happy to receive realistic suggestions. Where this is not the case each English teacher must be prepared to argue persuasively for what he or she considers the best. There must be opportunities for departmental analysis of how and why books have failed or succeeded with particular groups, one of the most valuable and easily organised forms of in-service training.

There is a greater connection between the books used, and the teaching method employed, and the quality of the teaching and learning process than many educational commentators would care to admit. To guarantee that all English staff were provided with the books they really wanted would be a great leap forward for many departments. Staffroom conversations along the lines of 'I got *Villette* this term – heaven only knows what my fourth years will make of it,' suggest the poverty of many English stock cupboards and the desolation of trying to teach an unsuitable book to an unsympathetic class.

It is ironical that so many experts in the teaching of English sensibly preach the folly of using a book which the teacher dislikes, and yet so many teachers speak of 'making the best of' unlikely examination set texts. This is true even with CSE classes where the glorious freedom of choice of text can be practically demolished by the stock cupboard veto. It is more ironical still that we choose a book which we have enjoyed from another age and standpoint, and presume that a heterogeneous group with multifarious interests will all enjoy it too. So as we smugly secrete our virgin set of thirty copies of *Moonfleet* is there still a place for the class-reader?

Reading Matter

Kenyon Calthrop's investigation into the use of the class-reader in a variety of secondary schools[9] would suggest that there is:

> All the teachers I interviewed felt that the shared experience of reading a common book was something of great value to themselves and to their classes. They regarded it as something quite different from the pleasure to be gained from individual reading and took the view that the feeling of sharing something worthwhile, the common sense of enjoyment, and the resulting sense of community was a deeply educative process.

There is no doubt that the shared interest provided by the class-reader at its best cannot only add immeasurably to an understanding of the book, as it is approached from a number of angles, but can have a socialising effect, welding group identity and even improving discipline within a class. The class-reader can provide a sense of communal achievement which avoids the loneliness of the individual and his personal text.

Why then should the class-reader have become an old and bad joke for some English teachers and their pupils? For many teachers of exam classes, even those teaching a CSE syllabus, the class-reader can seem an inescapable straitjacket. For many, one set of readers with access to a course-book and a few anthologies is everything, as far as the stock cupboard is concerned. In a few schools readers cannot even be taken home because they will be needed by another group. For some teachers the class-reader in inextricably linked with their own memories of deadly sessions of reading around the class in turn, where the teacher would hope to catch out the day-dreamers or those who had jumped ahead, by altering the order unpredictably. The brighter, the impatient the *interested* would leap pages, frustrated by their colleagues' stumbling rendition. Some would have missed the previous lesson and thus the previous chapter; others would find the gap between one lesson and the next too great to grasp even the plot. Unless we follow the defeatist theory that if the class-reader, the 'set text', is an inevitable part of the exam years, we must acclimatise our pupils to the chore in the first three years, then there is no reason why our pupils should all read the same book simultaneously. Conversely, the fact that the experience of the class-reader has been painful for many is no argument for denying its value where it is selected and used skilfully. The fact that I have personally never favoured its use with large mixed-ability first and second year groups does not prevent my appreciating its worth when used well with smaller, or setted groups. This prompts two questions: what are the alternatives to the class-reader, and what are the alternatives to reading it around the class?

For those who feel that choosing a single book to appeal to a large number of distinct individuals is well nigh impossible, there is an alternative which almost promises the best of all possible worlds; it is based upon the English department 'library'. If the library is to be a credible improvement on the class-reader it must provide for differences in ability, interest and maturation. It must also relate a concern for the best literature available to the nature of its clientele. It will therefore include books which whet the appetite for a more challenging book dealing with the same theme or form. The range should cover first and third person narrative, the diary, autobiography, biography, science fiction, collections of short stories, poetry anthologies, and several dictionaries geared to different reading levels. Books will be chosen and catalogued according to theme and probable reading age range. No book should be recommended until it has been read by the teacher; this is particularly important, given the recent proliferation of attractively produced 'teenage' paperbacks dealing with controversial issues, such as abortion, drug-abuse and promiscuity within a fictional framework. Staff must be able to justify their recommendations to parents and governors who may, rarely, query bad language or subject matter.

Ideally, each teacher will have the space and financial backing to establish his own library in his own classroom, where the books are available at any appropriate moment. In practice this may prove impossible, particularly of course where the teacher nomadically progresses from room to room. He may have to rely on the school library instead, or on a departmental library which is centrally housed, or both. The classroom library, particularly where pupils have contributed their own suggestions or books, is infinitely preferable since the selection becomes an expression of the group's interests and books are less likely to be abused or lost, as too often happens in the school library.

The old debate about hardback for endurance or paperback for economy is hardly relevant where the English library is concerned, since much of the most interesting and successful of recent fiction will belong to well-established paperback series: Peacock, Puffin, Topliners, Knockouts, Lions, Piccolo. There will be hardback exceptions though, since the 'classics' will continue to earn their place.

Having made an initial, modest selection of perhaps four to six copies of six to eight titles for each class we shall ensure that our pupils' reading is not limited by this selection. We shall encourage our pupils to use the main school library and the local library. This last aim sounds like one of those only too familiar platitudes from the Head of Department's manifesto. Preaching the value of libraries is one thing, helping our pupils to use them is another. It is too easy to give up too soon and presume that if our pupils avoid the library there is little we can do about it. Using the library is a skill to be learnt, and even the highly motivated will need initiation into its intricacies and mysteries. Library use should be officially recognised by the timetable. In reality this usually only holds true, if at all, for lower school pupils, and then often at the expense of English teaching time. In any case access to the library whether school, departmental or class should be systematic, allowing a weekly or fortnightly opportunity for pupils to borrow and return books.

In addition to a pattern for return and withdrawal, individual reading will require purpose and safeguards if it is not to be seen as a facade, a 'soft option'. This does not necessitate a routine and lengthy written book-review which effectively destroys all fond memories of the book. Pupils can present their opinions to the class or small group orally. Pupils reading the same book can compare their views or write a brief punchy review for the department magazine or for display. We should beware of the stultifying imperative, 'Say why you liked or disliked the book.' when the more complex the book the more impossible the task. How are we to analyse literature's effect upon us, to quantify its influence, since, as with music and works of art, words can trivialise the experience or mask it in an attempt to define the indefinable? Analysis and evaluation is made more realistic if the task is broken down into more accessible segments: 'Select and describe a scene which shows the author at his descriptive best. What techniques does he use to make his description convincing and vivid?'; 'Which of the characters would make the most suitable companion for a week's coach tour in Britain? Give reasons for your answer.'

The use of the department, or class, library does not of course exclude the class-reader, just as the class-reader does not exclude other approaches to reading in class, though it may conceivably be replaced by them. A collection of short stories, used sporadically, can be more effective, particularly with a mixed ability class, than a single text. They are satisfyingly complete and can be read totally within class time. Unfortunately no one anthology will be right for a class, even those as successful and popular as Roald Dahl's, Patricia Highsmith's or Bill Naughton's collections. The teacher must be prepared to search and research if the right blend is to be found. If approached carefully, the short story can inspire pupils to take up a similar theme or the same author in their own time. Care is needed, for a short story is a specialised literary form; it is not easily imitated and it should not be seen as a replacement for the novel. The latter is more lethally true for the extract, much favoured by course-books and worksheets. Where the extract is dreary or too difficult pupils can be put off the author; this happens only too often with 'the greats', such as Dickens and Lawrence, whose works are indiscriminately plundered to provide passages based around an arbitrary theme. Where the extracts have been carefully chosen and are stimulating and interesting their abrupt endings can be frustrating for the reader who would like to know more. The extract's strength of course lies in the opportunities it provides for comparing writing styles or several approaches to a similar theme, and where the range of literature is greater there is less likelihood of boring and demoralising a significant proportion of the class.

Reading Method

Having decided what our pupils are to read, how are we to organise for reading? If the timetable does not set aside 'library periods' we will need to allocate a period once a week or fortnight for the return and withdrawal of books from the school, department or class library. This should protect the individual reading-period which, while it does not need the validation of written book-reviews or formal speeches to the class, does demand that the teacher keeps a record of what is being read and by whom. This should help to ensure that pupils are not trying to

read unsuitably easy or difficult material nor concentrating too heavily
on one particular type of literature or author. This is particularly
important of course for the less able, who may cling overlong to the
same subject or format, terrified of striking out into the unknown. The
individual reading period also demands that the teacher should take a
discerning but apparently informal interest in what is being read. We
walk the tight-rope here between over-officious interruption and apparent indifference. Pupils will not resent our sporadic perambulations
when we ask them to tell us why or how they chose the book, what
has happened so far, or which parts they have enjoyed reading most or
least. Should our intervention end there or is there a case to be made
for asking pupils to read to us in order to assess individual reading
progress? Asking pupils to read a sensibly long extract is expensive in
time and can be a fraught business, as the teacher tries desperately to
pay full attention to the reader while keeping an eye on the other
'silent' readers who are only too aware that the teacher is now effectively out of action. It is a process which, because of lack of time,
almost inevitably singles out the poor readers who are further demoralised by this embarrassing attention. More to the point it is a poor,
artificial test of reading progress where the pupil self-consciously tries
to make sense of a disembodied chunk of text under test conditions.

There are more subtle ways of encouraging and monitoring reading
progress; group play readings, sitting beside a pupil and asking him to
read a passage ostensibly for another purpose, asking pupils to read
their own work in order to praise their success in writing — and hopefully reading. Those who favour reading around the class where all the
pupils take a part in turn would claim that it does at least demonstrate
how well pupils can read. It certainly, sometimes painfully, suggests
how well pupils can read in a rather frigid and potentially nerve-racking
situation as pupils await their turn. For the less proficient it is usually
just further proof of their lack of fluency, for the more proficient a
frustrating spectacle as their colleagues haltingly destroy what they are
reading. We can extrapolate from our own experiences in such situations; what is read publicly is never properly comprehended and
remembered. It is a 'dead' extract, a conscious performance. We might
object to this attack on reading in turn that the least able obviously
need more practice in public-reading if they manage so poorly. This
'practice' will be sporadic and erratic though, and our pupils will only
rarely be called upon to read publicly outside school. Far more important is the ability to make sense of private reading, whether the tax-
form, newspaper or novel, and disastrous attempts at public reading

may destroy any interest in private reading outside school. This does not mean however that the teacher is therefore bound to do all the public reading. In many classes our more enthusiastic readers will not allow us to monopolise class reading. We shall put an unnecessary strain on our voices (already probably over-used in the classroom) and on our pupils' powers of endurance if we ruthlessly refuse to accept that pupils can read in a lively and dynamic way. It is possible to ensure the less able but enthusiastic a chance to perform publicly but safely through an interesting but modest part in a play reading, or as a contributor to small group reading. The reading group, based upon friendship patterns, or a shared text, helps to provide security and yet relative freedom. Reading within the group, whether public or private, may be seen as a prelude to discussion or as a jumping-off point for a comprehension exercise. In a small but carefully balanced mixed ability group even the least able will have the courage to read aloud when the occasion demands, and the courage of their convictions. For many comprehension will be made easier by the absence of the teacher-examiner.

'Comprehension'

When one subtracts the inordinate amount of time spent listening to the teacher talking and the time spent writing there is little time for reading, even in the English lesson. The situation is complicated by the fact that many teachers class the comprehension exercise as reading practice when too often it is merely a transcription task. A pupil who is given a time limit in which to answer a series of factual questions on a passage is likely to spend at least three quarters of that time writing, and only about a quarter skimming through the passage for contextual clues. Indeed in test conditions answering comprehension questions may be much like completing a crossword, a matter of deciding how the questioner's mind 'ticks' and deciding which are the key clue words. It may be that with a poorly framed comprehension exercise the successful pupil is the one who does not read every word. 'Comprehension' is not limited to the reproduction of a series of correct written responses to a set of questions based on the recall of facts: 'Comprehension means understanding. But there are at least two levels at which understanding may operate. At the lower level, it is sufficient that the reader satisfies himself that the matter which he reads makes some sort of sense. . .grammatically and conceptually.' But, 'To learn by reading, a student needs to penetrate beyond the verbal forms of the text to the underlying ideas. He must compare these ideas both with what he already knows and with each other, so as to pick out what is essential and what is new, and thereby alter his previous conception in line with the novel information.'[10]

Too much of what is seen as 'comprehension' in the English classroom fails to provide scope for those higher-order skills associated with reading for learning, as opposed to reading for regurgitation. When we ask questions beginning, 'Who said . . . ?', 'What happened after . . . ?', 'Where is . . . ?', where the answers are revealed by a quick skimming of the text, we are ignoring our pupils' powers of comparison, deduction and imagination. For 'comprehension' is a portmanteau term covering at least five basic skills, all of which should be tested in a meaningful comprehension exercise. These skills can be itemised and mentally ticked off as we plan the pupils' analysis of a text or extract. Does the exercise really test whether the pupil can:

1. Understand the meaning of certain *key* words, phrases and sentences.
2. Extract facts and follow instructions regarding their organisation and categorisation.
3. Extract the most important ideas and distinguish between these and mere illustration or detail.
4. Understand and extract a sequence of ideas.
5. Draw conclusions and form judgements.
6. Predict the likely consequences.
7. Understand relationships: relate cause to effect.
8. Distinguish fact from opinion, hypothesis from proof.
9. Identify problems of interpretation, particularly ambiguities.
10. Read critically and appreciatively.

These can be further summarised: word interpretation (1 above); literal comprehension, i.e. the extraction, paraphrasing and summarising of ideas (2, 3, 4); deduction (5, 6, 7); evaluation (8); critical appreciation (9, 10). To what extent does the following comprehension exercise test these skills?

Context. Twenty-seven fourth year pupils, considered 'good to average' CSE prospects, nevertheless quite a range of motivation and ability within the group. Pupils have met similar passages with similar questions before but despite the fact that 'they seem to settle to this sort of work quite happily' the results have been disappointing. The

teacher feels they need extra vocabulary and context practice. The
pupils are approaching the passage 'cold', that is it does not fit into a
theme or book they are currently studying. They are asked to write out
the answers in best and to follow the instructions (as quoted) exactly.

Teacher's Objectives: to encourage a more critical awareness of all
reading matter; to encourage careful, reflective reading of an unseen
passage; to encourage understanding of the power and significance of
words; to prepare pupils for similar exercises in the fifth year Mode I
written exam.

Passage.

War is not what it was in the good time of Falstaff, when armies
would not take the field without trains of picturesque sutlers hanging
about them — sages and thieves and humorous potboys and sinister
crones and debonair goddesses not inexorable to men — an auxiliary
host of 'character parts' who may have got in the way of the war,
but did good beyond price to people writing historical novels and
plays. And yet the semi-official, and even the demi-semi-official
campaigner is not quite extinct. He has turned army chaplain, or
works for the YMCA, or she keeps a refreshment hut or a hospital
at the base. Of such was my friend John Macleary. He came to
France and the northern bank of the Somme in 1916 as a more or
less uniformed instrument of Australian kindness, bringing gift
coffee, biscuits, and tea to serve to Australian troops in their very
few hours of ease. He also brought, on his feet and two-thirds of his
legs, a pair of top boots that stirred the imagination in man.

Leriche, our French interpreter, noticed them first. He had a
nose for antiques. After saying 'Quel type!' as the French always did
after meeting Macleary, he added, 'His boots, too! Something of
storied, of ancient. In them I find a bloom, a fragrance of — no, I
cannot tell of what age, of what dynasty.'

I could not either, fantastic in cut, fantastically unfitted for use
in this of all wars, they looked even quainter than the quaint
Burgundy fortifications where he and I sat and dangled our legs out
idly over the castle wall of Péronne. How was it? Had we not
known? Was Australia not young, after all? Or why should her boots
come trailing these clouds of an uncharted glory of ancientry? (*A
Propos des Bottes* by C.E. Montague)

Questions: spend 15-20 minutes on this exercise.
1. Explain the meaning of the following words, with the help of the passage: inexorable – auxiliary – picturesque – debonair – crones – sages.
2. What does YMCA stand for? .
3. List those who might have been expected to follow Falstaff onto the field of battle.
4. Where were the author and John Mcleary sitting?
5. Explain the meaning of the following in your own words: 'come trailing these clouds of an uncharted glory of ancientry?' 'had a nose for antiques'.
6. Why did John Macleary come to the Somme? What did he bring with him?
7. Why did the French always say 'Quel type?'?

The following was typical of the answers the teacher received and corrected in some detail:

The results obviously are disappointing, so what has gone wrong? To try to answer this we must return initially to the teacher's objectives. The emphasis here is on reading carefully and critically and the first three objectives are clearly valid *per se*, though we may dispute the need to practise exercises of this sort so far in advance of the final exam, particularly since this passage is quite untypical of the usually more enlightened and interesting CSE comprehension passage.

The teacher's choice of passage must be related to the context. Does this extract stand a good chance of interesting and stimulating this group? Is it long enough and challenging enough to repay critical appraisal? The answer to the first question must be no. No subject is necessarily dated, but the treatment of it may be, and this is the case here. These teenagers will find it difficult to imagine and make sense of any war, but particularly where the description is hedged by such idiosyncratic prose, which, to take only one example, compares a pair of top boots with Burgundian fortifications. There is nothing wrong with a fictional passage dealing with the First World War, nothing necessarily wrong with quirky prose or archaic language, but throw all three together in a disembodied chunk and we have the makings of a confusing and uninteresting comprehension extract. In answer to the second question, yes, the passage certainly is challenging, if only because it is difficult to make sense of such a short extract which is dense with unfamiliar vocabulary and geographical references. Given that this is an unwise and unlikely choice of extract, do the questions help the pupils to rise to that challenge and achieve the teacher's objectives? The pupils are given the minimum of instructions. They have fifteen to twenty minutes to answer these questions in best. Judging from the typical response the pupils had time to finish in a fashion, though the quite unnecessary time pressure might have encouraged skim reading, rather than 'careful, reflective reading'. Almost from the moment the teacher mentions 'in best' the exercise moves from being a reading one to a writing one, where spelling, layout and handwriting are apparently considered as equally important evidence of careful reading. It may well be that the pupil who reads carefully and thus does not finish in the time limit and who presents his work untidily will earn more disapproval than the pupil who strikes lucky, and fortuitously settles on the right answers.

In answer to the first of the teacher's questions we may dispute whether it is important that these pupils should know the meanings of this arbitrary collection of words, either for general use or for what follows. The first question, indeed most of the questions, amount to a time-filling, time-wasting exercise. 'Inexorable' is a difficult enough adjective at the best of times; here it is used in a particularly obscure and old-fashioned way. 'Auxiliary' and 'picturesque' are more familiar and more useful but 'debonair — crones — sages' are unlikely to repay the attention they are accorded here. One suspects that YMCA was selected because it was there, not because it has any significance within the passage or for the pupils. Questions four and six encourage cue-matching, mere copying, as the pupil fixes on the two cue words 'came' and 'sat' and copies out their neighbours in the hope that somewhere in the dross the answer will shine through. In the 'typical' pupil's case the trick has paid off to the tune of sufficient half-marks to gain a pass.

The teacher has chosen an unsuitable passage, put the pupils in an inhibiting situation and asking uninspiring and unnecessary questions, but given all this are the questions *organised* so as to encourage careful and accurate answers? The answer again must be no. No concessions are made to the ability range within the class, which at the very least would require easier questions at the beginning in order to give all pupils the confidence and stimulus to go on. Far from it, probably the most intractable question comes first, to be followed by questions which veer from the banal to the obscure. Some of the instructions are confusing in their vagueness; 'Explain the meaning of the following words, with the help of the passage' – does this also mean 'as they are used in the passage'? Ironically more perceptive pupils will probably find these instructions more tortuous than the slapdash. The first part of question five is probably impossible, given the class and the passage. The phrase is torn from the quick of the sentence, which further discourages careful contextual reading. We may question whether it is necessary, interesting and realistic to ask these pupils to put this highly metaphorical phrase into their 'own words'. The carelessness suggested by the poor ordering and phrasing of the questions is reinforced by lapses in accuracy which will hardly encourage pupils to read and write carefully. The mis-spelling 'Mcleary' is conscientiously copied by the pupil, and 'Quel type?' distorts the original and therefore invites the pupil's wrong response (though right given the question). Question three misinterprets the original and is punished by a perfectly logical response, in the circumstances. We must call a halt to this dissection but the reader should be able to detect other faults in the selection and organisation of questions (*and* in the apparently arbitrary way the work has been marked.) Suffice it to conclude that this exercise-test inadequately assesses only the first two of the five comprehension skills, and if this practice continues these pupils will never improve their performance in this and, significantly, in more meaningful comprehension exercises and certainly will never fulfil the teacher's admirable objectives.

The better alternative to the fortunately extreme example above will use an interesting and longer extract or extracts. It will recognise that the group is a heterogeneous one and will therefore start with easier questions based on word interpretation and literal comprehension, move on to questions which invite pupils to demonstrate that they have grasped the gist of the passage and can follow its sequence, to questions of the 'How do you know that. . .?' type which demand deductive reasoning. It will pose questions which ask for pupils' own opinions: 'Do you feel that he was right to. . .? What do you think Mr Harris will do next? Why? Would *you* do the same in similar circumstances? What in this passage do you feel most readers would agree with? What do you feel is a matter for discussion? Are the comparisons in the final paragraph convincing? Do they give you a clearer idea of what is being described?' There will always be a choice for those who finish the 'core' of questions, since speed, provided it is accompanied by accuracy, should not be penalised by dreary tasks. It is easy here to fall into the rut of the obvious, 'Show what happens next by continuing the story. . .' or 'Re-write the story so far from the point of view of another of the leading characters. . .' Pupils can afford to go off at a tangent, to do some associated reading, tape work or drama work suggested by a single thread from the original.

So much attention has been paid here to the written comprehension exercise because so much attention is paid to it in English lessons from first to sixth form. It is just possible that to revise our interpretation and approach to comprehension is to re-energise English and re-motivate our pupils. But, having revised and reinstated the comprehension exercise, we must not claim too much for it, for, '. . . it is a very serious mistake to suppose that the completion of a test and comprehension in reading are one and the same thing. How a student completes a test is an *index* of his capacity to comprehend; it is not the capacity itself and still less is it the comprehension itself. . . however realistic the exercise, it is still different from the real thing: reading for a purpose and understanding what one reads. In a comprehension exercise, the questions are provided for the pupil and his task is simply to answer them . . . Even the best tests of comprehension have their limitations, and such tests or exercises should not be used as the sole means of improving reflective reading.'[11]

Alternatives.

Why write the answers? If comprehension too often amounts to a writing exercise, only a quite conscious switch to oral responses will reinstate it as a reading exercise which allows valuable scope for discussion. Pupils will need to answer questions in writing in the examinations and the occasional written exercise will provide practice for this, but there are better and more interesting ways of allowing pupils to demonstrate their fluent and accurate command of the written word. We shall cover more ground less tediously if the response is an oral one, through question and answer with the teacher as guide and referee at the centre, or through small group work. This approach should demonstrate that some of the most valuable questions are those for which there is no single right answer and allow for immediate response from the teacher, whether reward or the analysis of a misunderstanding, rather than the belated hieroglyphics of the red pen. Great care will be needed in the choice of material and questions and the organisation of the task, if we are to override the objection that while the written test assesses each individual, however imperfectly, the oral exercise may not. It is unlikely that question and answer with the teacher as synthesisor at the front of the class will really draw a response from each pupil to a representative range of questions. Small group work is the obvious answer and there are a number of reading activities which owe their success in part to the autonomy invested in each group.

In *group cloze* procedure pairs or small groups of three to five are given a short passage or occasionally poem from which every nth word has been deleted, at its most difficult every fifth word, up to every tenth or twelfth. The pattern may be broken in order to delete key words which may promote discussion, or where ruthless numerical deletion may remove a large number of words of the same class, perhaps the definite or indefinite article. The task is made more realistic where pupils are given the preceding paragraph or verses so that they can acclimatise themselves to the writer's style and subject. It is made easier if the number of letters in each word is indicated or the first letter of the word is provided. While this may be valuable for the young, less able or inexperienced, the most useful cloze passage is one where no sensible suggestion is excluded, since it is the discussion which accompanies the initial selection which most valuably tests the quality of the comprehension. In many ways it is better if the teacher is as unaware of the original answers as the pupils so that personal predilection does not inhibit the pupils' responses. Unless discussion actually breaks down, the teacher should stand clear of the initial pair or group discussion and beware of excluding, however subtly, well-meant and feasible suggestions. In the plenary session, where the groups come together to compare their suggestions, the teacher will need to draw the threads together and establish a range of sensible answers. The successful cloze exercise will emphasize not the listing of possibilities but the justification for their selection, based upon contextual clues. Cloze procedure, with group-sequencing and prediction, should be seen not as a remedial strategy but as a basic technique to be used with all age and ability agroups. All can be made increasingly demanding, particularly where pupils must identify and accommodate the writer's style, as in the following example:

> Emily found the bench William had recommended with scarcely five minutes remaining. She was indeed fortunate to find it empty for an officious nanny had only seconds before gathered her skirts and her charges for the walk home through the park. The light was waning disconcertingly and Emily wondered whether William would ever find her, secreted in the darkness of the box hedge.
>
> She primly crossed her ——— and hid her fingers ——— in the splendid 'borrowed' ———. Slowly the library clock ——— the quarter hour but ——— consolation could not quite ——— her concern at William's ——— nor remove her fears. ——— a sound interrupted these ——— thoughts. A benign though ——— face appeared in the ——— surrounding the path. Although ——— by this apparition Emily ——— to regain her composure, ——— politely to inform this ——— of her proximity.
>
> 'Oh ———,' cried William, for it ——— he, 'How can you ——— my stupidity in not ——— a more fitting place. ——— you ever find ——— in your heart to ——— me?'

Group sequencing requires that pupils put a number of jumbled segments from a story, passage, set of instructions or poem into a sensible order, given the contextual clues. Once the initial decisions have been made the whole class or sub-groups reassemble in order to promote and justify their order. Comments such as 'But you wouldn't usually start a story with "Because . . . " ' suggest not just careful reading but a recognition of the job certain words do and thus an informal exploration of grammar. There is room for personal opinion and evaluation: 'But I wouldn't finish it off that way . . . ', and when the original is revealed (and here it should be) the group may well decide that their own version is a more rational and satisfying one. As with all group comprehension activities pupils should first familiarise themselves with the procedure and feel confident following it. It is wise to start a novice group on an easy and obvious example, perhaps best devised by the teacher rather than borrowed, as later, from a book, newpapers or worksheet:

> There was no friendly radio voice to assure Dolly that the usual familiar sounds would return soon. The window flew open and Dolly

jumped and clutched at her apron. The day was windless and yet the
peeling window frame was disintegrating before her eyes as it
crashed repeatedly against the brickwork. (5)

At first she thought it was another shrew caught behind the boiler
but the noise seemed to be moving around the kitchen and altering
its pattern, now three long beats followed almost immediately by
three rapid ones. (2)

Dolly knew with a gasp of recognition who it was and what she
should do next. She ignored the cold draught and the window and
apron, slippers and all she scurried down the hill to the centre of
the village. (6)

It was one of those mellow, glowing October days. Dolly came in
from the garden where she had been cutting the last dead rose heads.
The 'boys' had gone to work and she was alone, alone that is
until she heard the first faint but rhythmic tap-tapping. (1)

Suddenly the voices died. Dolly cursed the transmitter as she
swivelled the dial back and forth. There was nothing, nothing except
the tapping which gradually increased in volume and in confidence,
and now it seemed to be coming across the air waves too. (4)

Mrs Hurley, the vicar's housekeeper, stared at her flushed and
distraught visitor and informed her that the vicar was out.

'It was you I wanted,' said Dolly. 'We have a visitor, someone who
wants to meet you, someone you haven't seen for a long, long time.'

Mrs Hurley's eyes glimmered in the darkness of the hall. She didn't
need to be told twice. She had waited thirty years and this time there
would be no mistake. (7)

Dolly chuckled at her own nervousness; her fingers were clenched
tightly around the milkbottle she held. What would the boys say
when she told them of her superstitious twinges? The real world of
dirty pots and pans was staring her in the face. She tidied away the
breakfast things and tried to drown the sounds with the cheerful
chatter of the radio. (3)

Although this passage does have a concluding paragraph there is much that is left unexplained, and we might invite pupils to conjecture what might have happened in the past and predict what might happen next. Here sequencing and prediction are combined, but it is possible to devise an exercise where pupils are expected to use contextual clues in order to predict what will happen next. They are presented with the opening instalment of a story. When this has been exhausted as a basis for prediction it is replaced by the second instalment and so on. This is usually a more difficult exercise, if only because in the early stages there is so much scope for choice. The teacher needs to plant contextual clues carefully if pupils are to have sufficient foundation for constructive discussion and yet enough freedom to allow for different interpretation.

Crossed Lines

The gate clanged shut, the lights were coming on, and David felt that there would be no going back. Mrs Hatchett's corned beef sandwiches had wrapped themselves around his gloves. He wanted to throw her well-meant alms aside but they were, after all, a tiny memorial. Dinner would be a long time in coming, perhaps he should wait and find something constructive to occupy the time, but his heart sank at what lay ahead.

The emphasis was consoling; there was no one to shake his sweaty palms or notice his horrid nylon socks. He met the gaze of a passer-by. It was as if this stranger knew all about David's fears and hopes, so much fear and so little hope, all resting on the word of one man who would be quite unaware of all that lay in the past.

He heard footsteps coming along the passage. A young man with spiky blonde hair took a seat beside David and nonchalantly unfolded a train timetable. David wondered at the way such situations threw such a variety of people together. He was even more surprised to see a young woman emerge from a door to the right, she was smiling. He knew that women were supposedly equal but he considered that this was one field they couldn't compete in. They lacked the know-how and dedication ...

And so the story gradually reveals that David has travelled from Scotland to be interviewed by a panel of experts who are responsible for selecting those inventions and inventors to be featured in a forthcoming television programme. David has sacrificed family and friends to his invention and is pinning his hopes on this last chance for fame and fortune.

Group cloze, sequencing and prediction are all based on the extract or very short story. We might suggest that comprehension based on the class reader is far more meaningful and interesting when the prize is an understanding of a book that the class are currently reading and enjoying. Here the oral comprehension exercise will appear apparently informally, because the teacher has anticipated difficulties and earmarked issues or because a pupil's comments have invited analysis. A statement such as 'I think he was stupid to do that, Sir' can be sufficient to introduce a very worthwhile 'comprehension exercise'.

Why should the teacher always set the questions, even the passage? Pupils can prove very adroit at deciding which words or parts of a chapter are most crucial in revealing personality or in shedding light on the past or future. Having chosen, or been presented with, a story or poem or chapter they can provide shrewd and challenging questions for themselves or for other groups to answer. This of course presumes a precedent where the teacher has set shrewd and challenging questions in the past. The exercise is valuable in encouraging an active and enlightened questioning of the text, which is so vital in reading for learning.

Finally, why must the stimulus always be written? Agreed, this chapter is devoted to 'Reading' and comprehension of written material is obviously important, but our pupils spend a great deal of their time trying to make sense of oral stimuli: the staff and other pupils in school, and TV, radio and the family at home. Just as we communicate predominantly via the spoken rather than the written word so we need to *listen* intelligently if we are to make sense of this flood of language. If we can help our pupils to sift, deduce and evaluate as they listen they will find it easier to 'attack' a text in the same dynamic way. The gaps between the words will often be as significant as the words themselves, and our pupils will need to recognise news editing and the significant omissions from propagandist prose if they are ever to truly 'comprehend'.

Notes

1. F. Whithead, A. Capey and W. Maddren, *Children's Reading Interests*, Schools Council Working Paper, no 52 (Evans/Methuen Educational, 1974).
2. E. Lunzer and K. Gardner, *The Effective Use of Reading* (Heinemann, 1979).
3. The Bullock Report, *A Language for Life* (DES, HMSO, 1975).

4. F.R. Leavis and M. Yudkin, *The Two Cultures?* (Chatto and Windus, 1963).

5. The Newsom Report, *Half our Future* (Ministry of Education, HMSO, 1963).

6. *The Examining of English Language*, Secondary School Examinations Council (DES, HMSO, 1964).

7. *The CSE: Some Suggestions for Teachers and Examiners*, Secondary School Examinations Council (HMSO, 1963).

8. R. Lavender, 'Living by Fact or Fiction', in Grugeon and Walden (eds.), *Literature and Learning* (Ward Lock Educational, 1978).

9. K. Calthrop, *Reading Together* (Heinemann, 1971).

10. See 2.

11. Ibid.

5 WRITING FOR A PURPOSE

Good writing must spring from a desire to say something; it
must proceed with a superabundance rather than with a dearth
of something to say, and it must have within itself a clear
purpose other than that of fulfilling an imposed task. (The
Norwood Report, 1943)

Right 3B, I thought we'd have a look at holidays today. I've
put up a selection of holiday postcards that I've received on
the board and I have a few more to pass round. I want you to
look at them and think about your own holiday this year or in
the past and perhaps about a holiday you'd like to have. You're
going to do me a piece of writing with the title 'Holidays'. I've
put it on the board. I want you to make it as long and interesting
as possible and I want it finished this lesson so I can take your
books in and mark them all at once. Any questions?
Yes John, you can start a new page in your exercise book . . .
don't forget the date, and underline it and the title. I'll put
Tenerife on the board for you, Wayne . . . can anyone lend
Lisa a pen? I'm running out of space for all these spellings. Go
and get some dictionaries from next door, Nigel, and you can
share them out. I think we'll have a bit of hush now . . . you
have twenty-five minutes . . . if you don't finish? Well, you
must try to . . . I must take in the books this lesson or you'll
never get them back in time for your homework on Thursday.

A distillation, yes — but certainly not a gross caricature of the staple
introduction to many a so-called 'creative writing' lesson; for holiday
postcards substitute an old boot or a bag, a colour supplement, picture
or recording. There is no lack of 'stimuli'. Most pupils at junior and
secondary schools associate English (in common with other academic
subjects) with writing: 'Well, it's writing stories and poems isn't it?';
'We write notes and then essays about our set books.' The reason for
this association is simple; pupils will be continuously assessed and
finally examined almost exclusively on their use of the written word,
on a skill which when compared with talking occupies only a fraction
of their time and one which is even more complex and demanding than
reading and talking.

Many pupils find writing arduous because, as practised in school, it is so far removed from colloquial spoken English. In the latter we can rely, sometimes heavily, on the assurance of our listener's response, a nod, a smile, an interjection which will confirm us in our course or suggest a new departure. Our audience will normally tolerantly accept repetition, ambiguity, poor grammatical structure and frequent stabilisers and pauses, unless these threaten to obstruct the message. Pauses and repetitions will frequently be inevitable as we anticipate objections or strive to make our meaning clear. We will drop verbs, omit subjects, concertina sentences and sometimes use colloquialisms with a shared and private significance, reassured by a listener who can object if the meaning is not clear, and invite elaboration:

> She didn't really . . . you know/No?/Bill was there . . . told 'em not to . . . er . . . just like monkeys . . . /I could have told you . . . / . . . Not that I'd of . . . had the nerve to take them on just like that . . . without any warning . . . after her trouble with the lad too. / That as well? . . . You think that's it? . . .

Writing is very rarely simply a question of transferring spoken words to the page, as the above example makes clear. Nor is it simply a matter of knowing what to write about. Writing presumes discipline and will-power to prolong what is essentially an artificial and abstract activity devoid of the immediate feedback of conversation:

> Written speech is a separate linguistic function, differing from oral speech in both structure and mode of functioning. Even its minimal development requires a high level of abstraction . . . Writing also requires deliberate analytical action on the part of the child. In speaking, he is hardly conscious of the sounds he pronounces and quite unconscious of the mental operations he performs. In writing, he must take cognizance of the sound structure of each word, dissect it, and reproduce it in alphabetical symbols, which he must have memorised before. In the same deliberate way, he must put words in a certain sequence to form a sentence.[1]

Much that is left implicit and unsaid in conversation has to be made explicit in writing, which requires a tighter grammatical structure. Small wonder then if our pupils tell us more face to face than between the lines of an exercise book.

The focus for the writing has to be conceived and then understood in the light of all the writer's existing knowledge and experiences of writing and especially of writing for that particular audience. There are no clear dividing lines between planning, devising, revising and trusting the words to paper. These processes run concurrently and for the child who finds even manipulating a pen difficult the prospect of sifting through all the possible interpretations, regulating handwriting, checking spelling, making it 'interesting' and writing at length, and all in twenty-five minutes, may induce a paralysis which looks suspiciously like apathy or laziness to the teacher. He will not even have the 'reward', accorded to speech, of immediate response; with writing the feedback will be deferred, often so distanced by marking as to be almost meaningless.

Why Write?

If most written English is a complex and potentially arduous activity and 'The motives for writing are more abstract, more intellectualized, further removed from immediate needs', why insist on demanding end-less pages which require many teacher-hours of marking?

Writing is one aspect of literacy, and a literate society requires that its people should communicate effectively in writing. The written word is an instrument for representing, recording and exploring experience, opinions, ideas and facts. It provides opportunities for sustained thinking and reflection. More specifically, in the school context it is a means of recording completed work for future reference and a means of testing. The actual process of writing can be an aid to memory; it can clarify difficult ideas and provide a means of discovery as the writer stumbles upon ideas that were barely recognised and only crystallised on paper. Writing discloses what words can achieve and most important of all should be a pleasurable activity which leads to what the Bullock Report described as 'the sheer satisfaction of *making*, of bringing into existence a pleasing verbal object'.

When quizzed, teachers in general tend to stress the importance of writing as a means of recording, recalling and testing. The teacher of English typically emphasises the importance of writing as a means of self-expression and self-discovery. Fewer English teachers will publicly stress its importance as a means of practising the 'technical skills' of English, but an objective (and salutory) analysis of exercise books from first to fifth year would reveal how much writing is concerned with punctuation, summary, word-picking and spelling exercises. In the fifth and even the fourth year written work will generally be seen as a series of dummy-runs for the exams, or as another instalment in the CSE folder. This example, the output of an able boy in the second term of his fourth year, is typical; 'English: written output of about 6,000 words, but including seven punctuation, thirteen comprehension, two grammar and three multiple choice exercises, calling for little of the pupil's own writing.'[2]

Many teachers find a lesson without writing at best disconcerting and at worst a denial of the definition of 'teaching'. Writing for many, perhaps particularly the English teacher, is a means of validation and it is too temptingly easy to slot into the pattern of teacher's subject/class-written exercise/teacher assessment. We must have very good reasons for asking our pupils to write and for asking them to produce the types of writing they do. Both presume that we can categorise the range of writing we would wish our pupils to experience.

An Attempt at Categorisation

We can distinguish between types of writing in a number of ways: prose and poetry, factual and imaginative, personal and impersonal, objective and subjective. But, as James Britton and his colleagues working on the Schools Council Project on Written Language discovered, none of these polarisations are sufficiently defined to categorise the range of writing which we should expect of our pupils in school, and they certainly do not recognise that a single piece of writing may serve several purposes. The report of the project distinguishes between language in the role of participant and language in the role of spectator:

> In a very general way the distinction between the roles of participant and spectator is the distinction between work and play: between language as a *means* (to buy and sell, to inform, instruct, persuade and so on) and an utterance for its own sake, no means but an *end*: a voluntary activity that occupies us for no other reason than that it *preoccupies.*[3]

This distinction formed the basis for a scheme which attempted to answer the question 'What is this piece of writing for?', using three main categories which nevertheless recognised that one piece of writing might move between one category and another.

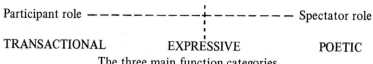

Participant role — — — — — — — — — —+— — — — — — Spectator role

TRANSACTIONAL   EXPRESSIVE   POETIC
The three main function categories

The differences between the three main functions can be summarised thus:

Expressive. Here it is presumed that the reader is interested in the writer himself, and thus the writer feels free to jump from facts to speculation to personal anecdote without the fear of criticism. The expressive form is the one most closely related to ordinary speech and provides a way of exploring half-formed thoughts and drawing tentative conclusions.

Transactional. Here the writer is presumed to mean what he says and thus can be challenged on a factual basis. This is the typical language of reporting, instructing, informing and theorising and is the type of language most used in school writing.

Poetic. 'True or false' is no longer a relevant question since the language is used not as a means but is to be relished as an end in itself. It is the language of the imaginative story, play or poem.

The project team came to see the expressive function as of crucial importance particularly in the process of learning. This presumes though that the reader and writer are on intimate terms. Their research showed that this was seldom the case in schools, where generally the teacher was the sole audience and significantly adopted the role of examiner and assessor. There was little scope for expressive writing and less opportunity for writing for anyone apart from the teacher:

> We think it likely that one reason for the great amount of inert, inept writing produced by school students is that the natural process of internalising the sense of audience, learned through speech, has been perverted by the use of writing as a testing or reproductive procedure at the expense of all other kinds of writing.[4]

This is obviously a general conclusion; we would hope to find that English lessons revealed a careful balance between transactional, expressive and poetic writing, with a bias towards the last two. Traditionally 'creative' and 'poetic' writing has been seen as the preserve of the

English department. It is hardly surprising then to discover that if English were to disappear from the curriculum so too would virtually all the pupils' poetic writing. It is more disconcerting to discover that its demise would probably cut a pupil's expressive writing by half.

The English specialist must, as a member of a school team, feel unhappy that 'the single most important use of writing in secondary schools appears to be as a means of testing and not as a means of learning' and that 'the more important function of writing — its potential contribution to the mental, emotional and social development of the writer — is being neglected'.[5] But before we can preach to our colleagues from our 'Language across the Curriculum' podia we must put our own classrooms in order, and here the Writing Research Team's scheme of classification provide us with a sensible matrix for ensuring that our pupils indulge in a range of writing, for a variety of reasons, and for more than one audience — the teacher as assessor.

The Scope of Writing

Writing in English lessons cannot be circumscribed by thoughts of the pupils' 'basic needs' to fill forms, write letters or cheques. Writing can and should be seen as a pleasurable and creative activity in its own right, as a means of developing a pupil's awareness of his own strengths, relationships and opinions and, while it is not a form of occupational therapy, it does provide a means of coming to terms with experiences. Pupils should try their hands at as many different kinds and tones of writing as possible: recording, describing, persuading, inviting, imagining, satirising, eulogising, criticising, comedy, tragedy, tragicomedy, farce, burlesque, science fiction, romance. They should meet and experiment with:

Prose. Letter, essay, story, diary, summary (though only where there is good reason for doing so), obituary, report, autobiography, biography, eulogy, advertisement, invitation, list, etc.

Poetry. Ballad, sonnet, lyric, ode, epic, Haiku, limerick, doggerel, narrative, epigram, lament, etc.

Drama. Dialogue, melodrama, the absurd, tragedy, comedy, farce, black comedy, revue, etc.

The range is enormous and we will emphatically not force all our pupils through all these hoops. This list serves as a reminder that English is patently not restricted to utilitarian prose, nor does it recognise our force-fed 3B incontinently scribbling stories in the 'creative writing' lesson.

Freedom of Expression

'Creative' or 'free' or 'personal' writing became particularly popular in the mid-60s in junior and secondary schools and came to be seen by some as the true test of literacy and the high point of creativity. In retrospect it is difficult to define 'creative writing' since it meant so many things to so many teachers and pupils. As its best it was one, important, part of the body of English writing and an antidote to the transactional-factual language that threatened to dominate the curriculum entirely. It gave free rein to a pupil's spontaneous expressive reaction to a stimulus and the results could be impressive, indeed exciting, revealing gifts that had been stifled by the formal essay, comprehension test and grammar exercises. The success of this approach led teachers to seek more and more ingenious stimuli for writing: the misguided student-teacher who lit a fire on the teacher's desk to 'bring the whole thing to life'; the course book which exhorted pupils to prick their fingers and then write about the pain; the rigged assault on the teacher in front of the jubilant class — 'Now write about what you saw/ felt/thought.'

The private individual's outpourings came to be seen by some as supremely precious, to be preserved free from red ink and spelling corrections. At its worst creative writing promised a merciful release for the teacher who came armed with a one-word stimulus, a pile of lined paper, and could legitimately insist on silence throughout the lesson. Little wonder if reactionary opinion jumped with glee on this apparent slide into inaccuracy, which equated spontaneity with recklessness and the uninhibited with the slovenly. Unfortunately the creative writing lesson, its very label prematurely destroying any notions of spontaneity, is still with us. 3B's experiences are typical; the pattern is horribly familiar. Both pupils and teacher have been through this many times before; the element of surprise has gone. Both are in a rut which has sapped initiative on both sides. The pupils are used to waiting passively for the teacher to impose a subject; the teacher feels little pressure to modify an arrangement which seems to be working, since there has been no objection to date and the whole class have been engrossed quietly while the brighter pupils have produced 'promising' work from all the stimuli. True, the slower and lazier pupils seem to spend too much time staring into space but perhaps that is to be expected. It hasn't occurred to either side that the pupils could conceive of their own subjects, or bring in interesting artefacts themselves, or that there is no god-given reason why all the pupils should be writing on the same topic or indeed all writing simultaneously:

> . . . the main stream of activity in the area of 'personal writing' should arise from a continually changing context, not from a prepared stimulus. This context will be created from the corporate enterprises of the classroom and the individual interests and experiences of the children, cumulatively shared with the teacher and the rest of the group.[6]

Given that there will be many occasions when the teacher, rather than pupil, will inevitably suggest the work to come, 3B's teacher is hardly jolting them into creative spontaneity by a mounted collection of postcards which the more perceptive pupils can see have been well used by several generations of 3Bs. Those at the back of the classroom can hardly see those pinned to the board and must wait in fidgety anticipation for the 'spares' to come round. The more able pupils may have little difficulty in producing a competent piece of writing from the cursory clue 'Holidays' and will have some conception of what 'long and interesting' means, since they will have seen this comment on previous pieces of work. For the average and less able pupil 'Holidays' may seem as great an abstraction as 'Charity' since even the helpful 'story' has not been hinted. With so many possibilities paradoxically they are stumped, a few panic, more capitulate. Since the bright ones are getting on with it there must be something missing in them if they cannot get the words mercifully quickly on to the paper. And what is most important? Its interest? Length? Or underlining – spelling – handwriting? 'What if I don't finish it?'; 'I can't write about holidays in general. She wrote, "Avoid essays which require general comments" last time and if I tell her exactly what we do on holiday she'll say it's boring . . . ' The teacher's introduction is a deadly combination of vagueness (' . . . a piece of writing with the title "Holidays" ') and rigidity ('You have twenty-five minutes.') The fact that 3B are considered 'average in ability' does not excuse her blanket treatment of them. This is not creative writing but a test where the pupils are left to their own devices to work in silence apart from the occasional fluttering of dictionary leaves. The teacher stands at the front, dutifully awaiting the enlightened questions which she has already skilfully deflected through her introduction and even her stance, position and gaze. Should pupils compare their work or ask each other a question this will be chatting since 'creative writing needs silence'.

'Some children have developed a knowing cynicism about the nature of "creative writing". They have become used to writing to order, used to reacting to the stimuli we offer them and accustomed to the teacher's concern with the finished product rather than the creative process which brought it into being.'[7] And, we might add, there is little hope of improvement where this is dependent solely on the pupil's ability to decipher the teacher's red ink. If we are to encourage writing of any sort and make the writing process stimulating, we must first decide on the conditions necessary to produce truly creative writing and not the narrow distortion represented by the rambling story. This demands an imaginative leap from the teacher: 'What do *I* require to finish a success- ful piece of written work?' For most the requirements will be three: incentive, time and confidence.

Incentive

Incentives come in many guises and it is important that we recognise that an incentive for one pupil is not necessarily one for another. It is easy to confuse an order or threat with a true incentive; 3B's teacher's 'I want you . . . ' is a thinly veiled order, with its own concomitant sanc- tions which hardly need rehearsal since the class are familiar with deten- tions, double homework and the like. Some pupils will no doubt inter- pret 'want you . . . ' as an invitation from a respected teacher, but others will see it as one more opportunity to challenge the teacher's authority and credibility and thus win peer-group approval.

Competition can be a powerful motivator, perhaps at its strongest in the lower school, though often re-emerging in the O Level set with a vengeance in the build-up to exams. Competition is the teacher's ally, but it should not be exploited in crude terms of 'Let's see who gets the highest grades this week, the girls or the boys'; 'You know you can do better than Tony, don't you?' There will be rare individuals who are not competing for the few prizes that schools award but who, irrespec- tive of the teacher's comments, are competing with themselves, oblivious of the teacher as audience and intent only on squaring any new product with a personal notion of excellence. More common are those who place their trust in the teacher's assessment system and are hoping to improve on the previous grade and comment.

We work best when we are working towards a goal and when there is a real chance that the finished product will not be derided or discarded but will serve a purpose, to delight, describe, or communicate a message. What matters at the time is that there is enough potential reward to make us persevere in a difficult medium. Although the occasional literary competition may promise tangible rewards for a few able pupils, the commercial rewards open to the professional writer are missing in the classroom. The professional writer can endure rejection slips since there may be alternative less damning assessors. For most pupils there is usually only one audience and assessor, and to fall out with that one is to invite a year's hard labour; far easier to find the lowest common denominator of the teacher's requirements. If we are to increase our pupils' motivation for writing well we must extend the possible audiences for such writing. At its simplest this may mean a veneer, 'Describe as if to someone who has never been there . . . ', or the real thing, 'John, if you want to know what it feels like why not write to someone who knows all about it?' More commonly it will mean investing in a group project, contributing to a script to be taped or acted, an interview, or a debate where the audience and adjudicator will be the group not the teacher. The audience may be the readers of the letter-page in the local newspaper, the director of a firm, the readers of the school magazine, those waiting in the dinner queue and those who share the classroom. At any rate the writing has a real chance of finding a real response, not the 'C+ Paragraphs!' at the bottom of a dummy-run letter, which totally disregards the content of the piece. There are other less obvious incentives for writing which are absolutely dependent on the audience's opportunity for response; making your readers laugh is one. Too many humorous plays, poems and stories are never rewarded by laughter since they only perform to the teacher's red pen. Persuasive writing is another; its effect should be judged by a 'live' response.

We are most committed, since our investment is greatest, when the writing is self-initiated. It is part of the skill of the English teacher to devise situations where the topic is suggested by the individual or group, and where the means of execution are revealed by discussion or the individual's planning and cogitation. This does not mean a flabby, 'Well, what would you like to write about?' approach but rather a nurturing of tentative ideas into life, where pupils can take risks without feeling that failure is irrevocable or derisible.

Time

If we are not to forget how painful writing can be when inspiration flags, we must make the time to write ourselves, and not just the factual ritualised prose of school administration. We would then realise that writing requires ample time since we need to rehearse the words in our heads first and the process will not stop there, since we can only judge a word's rightness by seeing it on the page. There are two implications here for the English teacher; we must respect the fact that different pupils and different tasks will require different periods for conception and incubation, and that pupils must be allowed every opportunity to modify what they are writing as they go along. There is not enough time, not enough talk and not enough rough-paper in most classrooms. The 'creative writing' ideal stressed spontaneity and many teachers still expect large classes to respond immediately to a single stimulus. No adult, and certainly no professional writer, would submit to such unnecessary pressure; we require time to think out our ideas for our best written work and we will require time to mull it over even when it is 'complete'. Even when we understand the task we will need time to devise ways of approaching it, to decide the right sequence and to compare the finished product with our original intentions. Time for scanning back is needed for corrections, improvements and for keeping overall control of the piece.

The manuscript of *Little Dorrit* is sufficient proof that even the greatest writers need to cross out and thus make an ugly mess of the first draft. Pupils of all ages deserve the sanctuary of rough-paper on which to improvise. Ideally it is this initial attempt which should be seen by the teacher or other pupils, so that suggestions can be made before the written work goes to press. Far too often we expect pupils to think and write 'in best'. We might object at this point: but won't only half as much writing be completed if much of it is tested in rough first? Undoubtedly, but then pupils spend far too much of their time writing, thus devaluing what should be seen as a special activity where the emphasis is on quality rather than quantity. There is no evidence to suggest that the sheer amount of writing has any bearing on exam success; far better to produce one or two successful and rewarding pieces per week than the routine and mediocre pile which suffocates the occasional good piece of work.

Adult writers demand both time and quiet; authors, even where they have little else in common, insist on the essential isolation of the writer. This of course is difficult to achieve in school, particularly since we will not always want our pupils to be writing simultaneously. The frigid silence imposed upon 3B may actually have inhibited inspiration for some, where a warmer silence generated by a general interest in the work will make writing easier for most pupils. The ideal of course is a classroom which is flexible enough to allow some pupils to work silently in a group or on their own, perhaps with their desks facing the wall, while others are discussing their work, reading it aloud or asking for help. There will be room for experimentation and different rules for different occasions and individuals: 'Discussion for the first ten minutes, then fifteen minutes silent work, then we'll all compare notes . . . '; 'I think you'd be best taking five minutes to plan it in rough on your own and then show it to me . . . ' There is of course a distinction between preliminary, ordered discussion and aimless chatter as pupils wander around the class trying to bully their friends into lending pen, ruler or paper.

Confidence

If we do not know why our pupils are writing then we can hardly expect them to guess our intentions. There is nothing worse than the suspicious feeling: well, even if I put all this effort into it what is it for? Where will it get me? Incentive and confidence are inevitably intimately related. We need to feel that however great the challenge success is a real possibility, and success is relative. There is no place for the English teacher who measures success in absolutes, irrespective of the circumstances and the individual. We shall not inspire confidence in our pupils merely by introducing the subject clearly, smiling glibly and saying, 'You know you can do it so get on with it.' 'Incestuous' writing, where there is no input from discussion, teacher, film, TV or recording is unlikely to be creative or confident. We should not feel squeamish about making suggestions, helping with spelling and in some cases planning the work with the pupil. All this should help to build confidence while leaving the pupil a great deal of autonomy over the remainder of the task. There is obviously a delicate balance here between interference and intervention: the teacher as vulture versus the teacher as consultant. A few pupils will resent any sort of suggestion from the teacher but will accept it from their peers; a few will try to lean heavily on the teacher's ideas. The guiding principle

must be: is this a suggestion that I, in the pupil's place, could understand — accept — act upon? Too often we suggest one thing to our
pupils and do another ourselves.

We write because there is somewhere a discerning and sympathetic
audience who will understand. All pupils are shrewd enough to see
through the trite and perfunctory approval, which is a line of least resist-
ance for the teacher who would like to think that he is actively encouraging good work while privately only bolstering his own self-esteem. Our
pupils will only trust our judgement, feel confident that a piece of work
marked 'excellent' is so, if we have shown that our standards are
rational and demanding.

This is particularly important for exam classes, where pupils will
inevitably be sensitive about their progress in relation to the exams and
must rely on their teacher's advice and assessment. The fifth-year exam
class should not require a special section in this chapter since their need
for time, incentive and confidence is as great as that of any other age
group. They may be even more impatient of the written task which is
apparently pointless, or which is insultingly relegated to the coursework folder with only a superficial comment. Their need for a variety
of written tasks will be as great, since there will be syllabus pressure to
confront only that written obstacle course presented in the exam paper,
nowhere more so than with O Level language and literature where
creativity may disappear somewhere between the formal essay and the
'What happens in Act IV?' literary question. If we are not very careful,
transactional writing, directed solely to the teacher as examiner, will
predominate and as Rosen's disconcerting research[8] suggests pupils'
written work may actually deteriorate during the fifth year. Such
research findings come as no surprise to those who have followed an
individual's progress from first to fifth year and have noted the decline
from the often vivid and original ideas of the first and second years to
the apparently suppressed and self conscious essays of the fifth year.

What Shall We Write?

It is all very well hoping that suggestions for written work will be generated by the pupils themselves, but it is the unusual pupil who preempts
the teacher's lesson-plan at the beginning of the school year. We may have
to work and wait for several weeks before pupils appear bursting with
their own ideas. Of course when they come they should, with very few
exceptions, be accepted enthusiastically: the homework which will form

the first chapter to a book, the poem which will become an ingredient in an anthology, a script for the Christmas play. But in the meantime we must plan and provide.

How can we show what words can achieve, make writing fun, challenging, rewarding, find an easy way in for those who find 'getting going' the hardest part of all? Through surprise and variety: we will not have an ear-marked writing lesson, nor a stereotyped homework pattern, nor will we turn up with monotonous regularity the course-book's suggestions for writing which follow the passage. We will not write about everything we read nor write every lesson. At times the writing will be open-ended, at others guillotined almost ruthlessly. It may be controversial, absurd, written for the writer alone or for a mass audience, on loose paper, part of a book, rejected at the initial draft, intended for performance, tape, set to music, acted out or chanted. The written work will reflect a whole range of language experiences.

Finding a Way in

> It appears that the title may play a part in finding a way to begin, and if a title is chosen, it has some effect on the way the writing proceeds, even if no title has been stipulated by the teacher.[9]

Titles suggested by the teacher are only to be criticised if they cannot be stretched to their limits and attacked by the writer. To stipulate a title such as 'The Meeting' for a piece of homework by a fourth year group without preliminary discussion would be asking for a stereotyped response: 'When my aunt wrote and told us she was coming back from Australia we were all very excited.'; 'I'd been looking forward to the disco all week because I knew Rod would be there.' But discussion, and better still improvisation, will disclose many possible approaches: an old lady unearthing the diary she kept as a young girl and confronting her old life and ideals; two lonely hearts, a vicar and his housekeeper, who quite accidentallly are brought together by a marriage bureau; kidnapper and kidnapped forced to revise their preconceptions by enforced intimacy. Some ideas will be shared, others will be possessively hidden by their instigators, and at times drastic action will be called for where a pupil is stumped. There are strategies, admittedly rather crude ones, for such occasions. A possible 'meeting' can be prescribed by twö or three sets of cards which literally throw characters together:

Arthur Bailey		Sonya Appleby,
age 68, retired		age 49, traffic
poultry packer,	met	warden, keen darts
poodle breeder.		player.

A few further questions (how? when? where? why?) will usually reveal an interesting skeletal plot or better still provoke a 'better idea' from the pupil. There is no need for the teacher to invent more than a few specimen cards since pupils can be very ingenious in producing their own. Gentle prodding will sometimes produce excellent work from the pupil who at first looks irretrievably at a loss, but there is seldom pressure for the group all to start at once. Time to think and look at the work of others, a distraction such as a reading book, may give sufficient breathing space for the pupil to settle upon his own idea.

A title, even a title accompanied by discussion and improvisation, may still leave a frightening amount of paper uncovered. A greater foothold may be needed: adopting another's beginning, middle or end, adopting a style:

1. It was the summer when the cat swallowed her bell, I took my exams and Auntie Freda ran off with Uncle Harry's apprentice. That's when it all started . . .
2. . . . If only I'd known . . .
3. . . . The creature outside was not Edward any more. His bloated fingers hung limply at his sides. His lank hair followed in strands the contours of his skull. His eyes were drained, his story done. He had lived to tell his tale.
4. The wind caught the last leaves and sent them spiralling upwards. The moon caught on the topmost elm twigs and slid into darkness. One last candle shuddered in the draughts through the turret window . . .

While this is obviously a parasitic approach it is potentially a very rewarding one for writer and audience, since it presumes an understanding of the characteristics of the original example.

All English teachers would dearly love to see their pupils experimenting more with imagery, plot structure, characterisation, but there can be no clear-cut schematic approach to these. There is no evidence for example that completing disembodied similes, 'As pretty as . . . ', or 'He sniggered like . . . ', produces a corresponding improvement in less artificial prose or poetry. The link between reading and improved

writing is unquantifiable but undoubtedly reading, and classroom discussion, provide the most effective way of introducing a wide range of
new vocabulary. It will however be the quality of the reading
experience as well as the motivation of the pupil which will decide the
extent of the cross-fertilisation between the two. If pupils are shown
that it is possible to discriminate between the good and the second-rate
then it should make possible a more healthy objectivity about their
own work and that of their peers.

'Extended Writing'

One example must suffice to demonstrate how a chance suggestion,
question, experience or reading can, if carefully exploited and
bolstered, provide a 'way in' to writing for the whole class:

They're mixed-ability first-years from six different primary schools.
One of the group, a West Indian boy, described a rather bizarre
dream he'd had about a mysterious Caribbean island for his homework. My response to the work was enthusiastic, partly because his
work in the first four weeks of the term was rather dreary, and also
because it was gripping stuff initially but came to a rather abrupt
ending, leaving a lot of questions unanswered. I wanted the rest of
the class to ask and answer these questions informally. That might
have been an end to Geoff's idea if it had not been for Wendy, who
with her partner took a rather precocious delight in belittling the
achievements of certain of the boys, Geoff included. On this
occasion she remarked rather querulously, 'His island's a waste of
time, it's not real.' This prompted a discussion about what 'real' and
'realistic' meant, particularly when applied to a fantastic dream.
When asked what she'd have done instead, Wendy was confused, 'I'd
need time to think, Sir.'

We got on with the lesson as planned but in the last ten minutes or so
we cleared everything off the desk and talked about islands in general.
Their experience seemed very limited but it was soon clear that
individual, idiosyncratic — possessive — ideas were already taking
shape: 'If I had an island it would be . . . ', and most promisingly, 'My
island *is* . . . ' The bell went and I promised that we'd return to the
island idea the next lesson. In the meantime I asked them to try to
draw their island in their heads — a rather unrealistic request.

I knew that there was no single definitive strategy for getting the whole thing going, only a number of possible starting points depending upon the interests and ability of the pupils. I started to plan:

The Island

Talking – Writing – Listening – Reading
Preliminaries: Routes to the Island

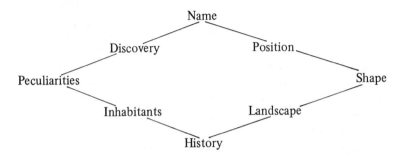

No doubt the more able and more imaginative pupils could have improvised upon the hints suggested here and would have realised that they could join the circle at any point, but what of the least able and imaginative? I produced a more prescriptive alternative which took the headings in an apparently logical order and provided more elaborate instructions. By this stage I was beginning to feel demoralised. The spontaneity of the original discussion was fast evaporating and it was only too obvious that any one instruction was going to strait-jacket the individual's initiative and imagination. Starting with 'Name?' might seem obvious but how important or possible was it to select a name at the beginning? After all, we usually name a puppy after we buy it, not before. The island might have several languages, one for each of the colonies inhabiting it, in which case their selection would have to come later. The very word 'Landscape' would suggest to some a conventional pattern of town-village-farmland, when its underground systems might be more important than superficial geographical features. A little consideration showed that my assumption that the most able would need less help and the so-called least able more was both simplistic and arbitrary. More than one possible approach would be needed but, with perhaps a couple of exceptions, the pupils could be trusted to adopt and adapt the pattern which most suited their own favourite approach. It was patronising to think that the 'least able' could not think for themselves.

We used my 'two routes' as the starting point rather than the finishing point for discussion. That is, they were put up as skittles to be unseated by better suggestions which were worked out on the board. Each pupil was then asked to devise his or her own basic programme which I then checked. This was continually updated as further ideas were added and ultimately became the 'Contents' page for the finished folder. I was concerned about the balance between talking, writing, listening and reading but felt that only the last ran the risk of neglect. I avoided the introduction of 'professional' descriptions or film of islands until the first crucial decisions had been taken. After this pupils were encouraged to make full use of a generous library loan and to bring the class's attention to relevant and interesting passages. We scanned the Radio and TV Times for promising programmes and explored existing video-cassettes. One friend of a friend came in to talk about strange goings on on a 'real coral island'.

Reaching the end of the preliminary 'Routes' took over a week of classwork and homework time. It proved expensive in paper but resulted in a magnificent display which spilled over onto the walls of the main corridor and Head's study. After the first week and a half I thought and hoped that I would be able to sit back and allow the wheels to roll. Pupils had already committed to paper possible starting points for extended writing, even if they couldn't immediately recognise them: clashes of interest over the use of the island, prey and predators, the arrival of newcomers, a change in climate. Some of their ideas I had already anticipated: letters to someone on the island, a holiday brochure's euphemistic panegyric on the delights of the island, an 'Island for Sale' inventory, the autobiography of the last inhabitant, a dialogue between a conservationist and developer, a one-act play based on an island myth. Other suggestions emerged tangentially; one collaborating pair fell out over the names of the colours of the felt-tip pens they were using. Yellow ochre and cobalt blue didn't mean much so they produced a long and fanciful list of alternatives of their own. This developed into an inquiry into the vivid names given to lipsticks and paint colours and again the pair suggested their own more enticing alternatives. We seemed to be wandering rather far away from the island but it prompted an enlightening look at metaphoric language.

One pupil wanted to start again, this time adopting the identity of an explorer whose descriptions of the island gradually unfold as he becomes more and more intimately part of the island and its inhabitants. Another pupil reversed the process, describing the island from the point of view of a prisoner who escapes from a life-time of incarceration to discover the island from the inside out. Both of these developed into annotated talks. Others, predictably, wanted to write an extended adventure yarn. I suggested that they should write it as if commissioned by the BBC so that the story fell into a number of sections, each of which posed a question in the final minutes in order to keep the viewers' interest. One boy wrote a spoof report for broadcast on April 1st concerning a new discovery in the archipelago. This was later taped, involving six or more pupils as roving reporters, officials, politicians, innocent bystanders and ranting objectors.

We could have prolonged the whole idea legitimately for another half term; for the first time even the least confident were not worrying, 'How long does it have to be, Sir?' Instead they were making their own decisions or turning to the group. The final word came from bemused and fascinated parents at a parents' evening who had been pestered for unusual spellings and probed for historical data. It occurred to me that it is not so much the title you choose as how you go about organising your inquiry.

Notes

1. L. Vygotsky, *Thought and Language* (MIT, 1934).
2. *Aspects of Secondary Education* (DES, HMSO, 1979).
3. J. Britton *et al, The Development of Writing Abilities 11-18*, Schools Council Research Studies (Macmillan, 1975).
4. N. Martin *et al, Writing and Learning Across the Curriculum*, (WLE, 1976).
5. Ibid.
6. The Bullock Report, *A Language for Life* (DES, HMSO, 1975).
7. M. Benton, *The First 2 Rs*, (University of Southampton, Department of Education, 1978).
8. H. Rosen, 'Progress in Compositions in the 'O' Level Year: Some Disturbing Evidence', *Use of English*, vol. XVIII, no. 4 (1967).
9. See 2.

APPROACHING POETRY

> It has to be acknowledged that poetry starts at a disadvantage.
> (The Bullock Report)
> What a poem means is the outcome of a dialogue between the
> words on the page and the person who happens to be reading
> it . . . (W.H. Auden)

The Bullock Report's stark statement requires some annotation; it is
suggesting that most people consider poetry to be odd and foreign, a
literary cul-de-sac which is divorced from real life and is both useless and
unintelligible. Poetry is a difficult irrelevance. This is certainly how
many pupils, particularly the older ones, see it. Student teachers are
not the only ones to hear barely repressed groans when 'poetry' is
mentioned. Yarlott and Harpin's research[1] suggests how many pupils
are thoroughly put off poetry by their experiences in schools.

There is, though, ample evidence that young children delight in
poetry, in listening to nursery rhymes and narrative verse and com-
posing their own. They have the true poetic flair for manipulating and
improvising with words, playing with them creatively and as a means
of emotional release. The junior school playground abounds with
poetry, the doggerel taunt, skipping rhymes and football chants. These
are not seen as foreign, difficult or sissy. Many thousands of viewers
enjoy Cyril Fletcher's 'odd odes' and Mohammed Ali's poetic boasts,
and respond with their own. In the eleven years of compulsory
schooling, something is going wrong, and in this case we cannot easily
blame it on the examination syllabus. It is possible to avoid the reading
of poetry until A Level and few pupils will have to write a poem in
order to pass CSE, O Level, A Level or university examinations. In fact,
the higher one goes the less encouragement there is to write any poetry;
thus a university lecturer, specialising in twentieth-century poetry, could
conceivably never have written a poem himself. If we cannot blame the
examinations can we find fault with the way poetry is sometimes introduced in the classroom?

Poetry becomes difficult when it is presented as something special
and potentially tortuous, when it is approched reverentially with kid
gloves. Many pupils see the species 'poet' as just as extraordinary and
eccentric as some of the poems we thrust upon them. Some must see
Milton as hand-in-glove with the A Level examiners and the *Four*

Quartets as a devious plot aimed at the unwary student. Too often, poets, Shakespeare included, are presented as slightly dotty and altruistic martyrs, sacrificing all to their vocation, oblivious of the demands of the market and happy to starve romantically in garrets in the interests of their art. This may have been true for some few of the nineteenth century 'romantics'; it is certainly not true where Shakespeare and the majority of poets are concerned. We cannot blame modern poets for this stereotyped view; Seamus Heaney, Vernon Scannell, Ted Hughes, Craig Raine and many others have gone out of their way to discuss and demystify the making of their poems, without in any way detracting from their power and magic. Nor can we blame the media which, aware of poetry's public reputation, go to some lengths to present it in as interesting and dynamic a way as possible. Pupils enjoy and remember much of the poetry which they hear and read outside the classroom, whether Pam Ayres reciting on a television chat-show or the lyrics of an Elton John song. It is poetry in the classroom which can be truly deadly; by the time we have picked through the poem's vital organs and dissected every last example of alliteration the victim is well and truly dead.

We may wonder whether poetry should be taught at all; could it not be assimilated subliminally without any conscious effort on the teacher's part? The answer is a fourfold one: a) given a suitable climate pupils enjoy reading and writing poetry; b) because of its neatness, its insistence that every word must work, poetry at its best can be memorable in a way that prose seldom is; c) far from being the preserve of the lone poet agonizing over his own innermost thoughts, poetry can be a participant sport and group activity — poems can be written in groups and discussed in groups; d) finally, children should be the best writers of poetry in the sense that they should be unselfconscious, unburdened by the weight of literary precedent, which tends to suffocate the inspiration of the older and more knowledgeable student. There are then very good reasons for encouraging the reading and writing of poetry. Unfortunately by the age of eleven some children, deterred by earlier depressing experiences, will have decided that poetry is at best just a mental obstacle-course. We can only hope to change this attitude if our own interest is obvious, if poetry is demystified, if poems are chosen carefully and for a number of purposes, and if our pupils are eased into the process of making sense of, and writing, poetry. Showing our own interest does not mean turning on a facile enthusiasm self-consciously whenever poetry is broached. After all, as Auden's comment[2] makes clear, appreciating poetry is a matter of taste and dialogue. It would be foolish to expect our pupils to like a poem because we do. It would be worse still to take advantage of our authoritative position and a malleable group in order to impose our tastes. There is a great difference between enthusiasm and crusading zeal; pupils must be allowed to discover their own enjoyment of a poem, to form their own relationship with it. They must not feel that the teacher has already tramped emotionally over the poem before prepackaging it for consumption like a supermarket chop. Far from showing our enthusiasm by concentrating obsessively on a rarified selection of 'excellent' poems, we should demonstrate it through the eclecticism of our tastes, showing that poetry can fulfil all the purposes of stimulating prose, and more. It can amuse, move, disgust, convince, teach and record.

Removing the kid gloves is not easy, particularly for the ex 'classically trained', English literature graduate who is still taught to classify poetry and pick over its origins before coming (if at all), to the vital questions: does it work? what do you think of it? Those of us taught to take weekly doses of poetry because 'it's good for you' find it difficult to reject this approach in the classroom, and make the fatal mistake of theorising first, thus starting at the wrong end. 'Read through this poem and try to decide for yourself what the poet seems to be trying to do' is preferable to 'I thought we'd look at a good example of a Petrarchan sonnet.' In the latter, form precedes sense and pupils are deterred from giving an immediate and honest response by the epithet 'good' and the assumption that this assessment comes authenticated by literary taste through the ages. It is a brave pupil who objects 'But it's a lousy poem.' Thus part of the demystification process requires that we make an imaginative leap and try to look at a famous poem from the point of view of a pupil who has not had the poet's greatness dinned into his head by a succession of teachers and lecturers. We must suspend our own academically angled ideas of 'greatness' if we are not to fall into the trap of 'We don't have much time to give to poetry each week, so I make sure they meet the classics.' The 'classics' are Shakespeare, Milton, Pope . . . but for a class finding its feet the best, in the sense of the most effective and accessible, may well be Belloc or Causley, riddles or Haiku. Perhaps we need to come clean about our own attitudes to poetry; what did we *really* enjoy at that age? What do we *really* enjoy now? We have a duty to facilitate our pupils' enjoyment of the great and the good. This is not the same as saying that we introduce them at the earliest possible opportunity irrespective of the cost.

Poetry *is* special, as the separation of this chapter suggests, but we should not make enemies by emphasising its uniqueness before pupils are confident practitioners — doers rather than theorisers. It is easy to waste precious classroom time and enthusiasm debating when a poem is a poem and when it is poetic prose, and attempting to draw a line between that and prosy poetry. These are unhelpful red herrings in most classrooms; a poem is a poem because of the way it is set out. We need go no further than this definition initially. Talk of metre and scansion, density of imagery and lyrical power can be introduced when appropriate, but only when pupils have had the chance to listen to and practise all of these unselfconsciously. It is unfair to ask, 'What is a poem?' Any definition must allow for the diversity of E.E. Cummings, Beowulf, Spike Milligan and Chaucer, and will thus be as necessarily generalised and inconclusive as the Bullock Report's suggestion: 'it is a man speaking to men, of his and their condition, in language which consists of the best words in the best order, language used with the greatest possible inclusiveness and power.' We must not climb poems just because they are there, imitate them just for something to do, nor see them as convenient components in a theme, or comprehension exercises where the 'good' poem is a dense one, full of comforting figures of speech, ambiguities and imagery. To insist on formally translating poetry into prose is to miss the point that poetry has its own irreducible way of saying something; I once witnessed a lesson where a group of thirteen-year-old pupils were busily trying to 'Put Hamlet's "To be or not to be . . . " speech into your own words'. The most obvious question to ask here is 'Why?'. There are far better reasons for introducing poetry than this. We do not need to analyse the difference between prose and poetry to realize painlessly that one short poem can convey a truth more effectively than pages of functional prose:

Streemin

Im in the botom streme
Which meens Im not brigth
dont like reading
cant hardly write

but all these divishns
arnt reely fair
look at the cemtery
no streemin there

(Roger McGough)

Unquestionably 'great' poems are ones that have passed the test of time and repay detailed and repeated study, but 'good' or effective poems such as this one have their own versatility. 'Streemin' could be introduced just because it is interesting and accessible. It could be seen as a starting point for discussion, a brief conclusion to earlier work, or introduced to give confidence to the pupil who protests 'But I don't know no long words and my spelling's awful.' 'I found this and wondered what you thought of it' shows the teacher's interest in poetry and his pupils, since he is paying them the compliment (rare in schools) of assuming that their views are just as valuable and justifiable as the teacher's own. Of course it is easy to slip from this position into 'But don't you think that that description is really rather good?' where the pupil feels duty bound to climb down in the face of the teacher's daunting knowlege and experience. We tread a precarious path here; our knowledge *is* valid and our pupils do look to us for guidance, but we are also looking to them to show intiative and discrimination, and if a poem is to be tested according to its power to communicate to a wide audience then it should not simply be bounced off the teacher. Pupils will need help with certain words, will need to know a little about the location and background to Wordsworth's 'The Prelude' or Anthony Thwaite's 'At Dunwich', for example, but this is not the same as inexorably steering the divergent pupil back onto the teacher's narrow rails. If a pupil pig-headedly insists on misinterpreting what is indisputable (a rare phenomenon since most pupils have been trained to accept passively) then it is better that a pupil discussion-group should examine these views.

If we are convinced that poems can do many things and be used in many ways then we will avoid the rut of the stereotyped 'poetry lesson': teacher arrives bearing a pile of slightly dated and shabby anthologies. 'Open your books at page thirty-three. There you will find a poem by Eric Smith. Anyone read any of Smith's poetry? No? Well, this is a poem about some antelopes that Smith saw on safari in East Africa. Anyone seen any antelopes or been to East Africa? You've seen some in a zoo — good. Well, let's read it.' The pupils are already laying mental bets on how long they have got before the inevitable 'Now we've looked at the sort of adjectives that Smith uses to describe the movement of these creatures . . . Now I want you to choose a creature, and describe its characteristic movement in verse, paying particular attention to the vivid adjectives which seem appropriate.' There is one disconcerting reference here which requires particular attention (I leave the reader to identify the remainder): how will these pupils interpret 'verse', a vague enough literary term at the best of times? Will they presume that their poem must rhyme, divide into verses, have a regular and identifiable rhythm, when none of these are obligatory?

This represents one approach to be avoided, but there are others; a favourite one is to produce a gruelling war photograph and invite pupils to write a poem dealing with any aspect of war. If pupils choose to write a 'war' poem because of a particular personal interest this should be encouraged, but it is unrealistic to ask a whole class to turn on feeling in this way, at a moment's notice, with inadequate stimulus and discussion, based on an issue which is not rooted in their own experiences. This is not to say that pupils can never write convincingly about unfamiliar situations, or as other people; writing poetic monologues for homework became quite the rage in a second-year class of mine after one pupil had chosen to write 'Thoughts of a Survivor', in this case of the Great Plague. Here the stimulus and input came as much from recent history lessons as discussion in English classes. The 'war photograph' approach encourages a stereotyped approach, so too does using a famous poem as the stimulus. (Keats's 'Ode to Autumn' was exploited in the past in this way.) Both the original and the pupil's interpretation usually suffer, and worse, pupils will tend to distrust the presentation of lone poems in case they have to repeat the procedure. While it can be claimed that pupils will aspire to the heights of the original, this approach is more likely to inhibit an honest and personal response or induce apathy as pupils realise that however careful their approach it will be mediocre in comparison with the model. This does not of course mean that we will avoid the reading of 'great' poetry, but rather we will see it as an unlikely stimulus for pupils' own work. What is needed is a more scrupulous approach to helping pupils to write about what interests them rather than what interested Keats and the poets of the past.

If writing is difficult (see Chapter 5), writing poetry can be doubly so. Unless we ease our pupils into the process of making sense of and writing poetry they will give up long before the revision stage: 'I can't think of anything to say, Sir'; 'Will five lines do, Miss?' When pupils ask such questions obviously something is amiss; perhaps we have pressurised them into writing quickly and spontaneously or have not prepared the ground thoroughly enough. The pupil who is not interested in what he is doing will be happy to produce the absolute minimum required to keep the teacher happy. Pupils need clear guidelines and reassurance; not knowing what to say is often the same as thinking what to say. Deliberation is part of composition. Poets do not on the whole receive a flash of inspiration and write down their thoughts rapidly and spontaneously in their final form. Pupils need to be shown the scribblings and crossings out of the 'experts'.[3] They need to be reassured that a poem comes to its end when the poet has no more to say on that subject for the time being. He may start another on the same or a different subject. He may return to the original to worry at it, try it out on a colleague, read it through to himself, abandon it or 'creep up' on it in order to attempt a more objective assessment. All of this takes time. It is unrealistic and unfair to set a class the same subject and then expect them to arrive at a final draft at the same time (though there are occasions when a guillotine may cut through agonized deliberations and make an individual put pen to paper, in much the same way as a publisher's deadline). Two excellent lines, good as far as the teacher and pupil are concerned, are always better than twenty mediocre ones, and those two excellent lines should be displayed proudly in the classroom, alongside longer work.

Poetry writing, and to a lesser extent reading, become easier if poetry is presented as a craft, a series of skills which can be taught and practised. As teachers we have to admit that we cannot *teach* originality, but we can catalyse our pupils into surprising themselves and each other by the unusual juxtaposition of words or originality of image. In the early stages at least we need to forget our squeamishness and sense of duty in the interests of making poetry interesting and accessible. With a class of eleven to twelve-year-olds this may mean returning to one of the best and most popular anthologies used in junior schools, *Junior Voices*. I have yet to meet a class that has not first turned the pages of these, and the more senior *Voices* anthologies[4] with a buzz of excitement. The teacher who insists that the class turn *immediately* to a specific page has forgotten his pupils and poetry in his selfish concern to 'get the work done.' Pupils should be given ample time to read poetry for pleasure; we should not feel queasy because they are apparently reading it with the same rapidity and enthusiasm as they would a comic or magazine. If we sometimes undo the harm done in the past by taking our pupils several steps 'back' to what they actually enjoyed reading in the past, we can also adopt this shallow-end approach to writing poetry. Pupils will feel more confident writing prose if only because they are more accustomed to it. We can build upon this familiarity and form the links between prose and poetry almost imperceptibly, presenting poetry as a game of substitution and accretion. Pupils should come to see words less as threats than as building bricks to be stacked, removed, replaced, split and juggled, capable of producing an infinite variety of responses.

The Shallow End: Writing Poetry

The aim here is to make poetry writing fun, to creep up on it so that
pupils are writing poetry almost before they know they are doing it,
and before the potential difficulties are registered. Substitution,
accretion or addition offer an enjoyable way in, since the task is defined
and localised and the pupil can lean on the context for help, and yet
the divergent thinker can stretch the context to its limits in order to
produce a highly original, yet rational version. Filling the gaps is not the
same as cloze procedure here, since getting close to the original is not
the point; instead the pupil is being invited to make his personal mark
on the original, to clothe the skeleton with his own thoughts. Mediocre
poetry usually provides the best framework and I usually invent my
own (though pupils are sometimes happy to produce their own frame-
works for their neighbours):

> The clock ——— three,
> The ——— have gone,
> And the staring ——— of ——— neighbours
> Glimmer suspiciously behind their ——— ——— ———.
> Where are the ——— to witness the ———,
> Why has the ——— not come ——— from the village,
> Who will listen to their ———,
> And who will clean up the ———,
> And put ——— ——— back together again?

Pupils can give their finished version an appropriate title and compare it
with those of the rest of the group. Since there is no definitive version
the teacher has quite deliberately resigned his claim to authority.
Indeed he should write his own version and be prepared to discuss it
alongside those of the class. The task can obviously be made more
demanding by increasing the gaps and making the context more
ambiguous.

Lists

Lists provide one of the most logical and painless ways into poetry.
Merely asking pupils to jot down in rough quickly any thought or word
connected with their chosen subject will spark ideas which would not

be revealed by the 'into the first line' approach. This can lead into the poetry-art collage where a title such as 'Rough and Smooth' can be interpreted through the textures of the materials used and through the words and images appropriately placed among these materials: 'Sleek damson cradled in the hand'; 'Kissing Grandad goodnight.; 'Dry tongue the morning after.; 'Stray perfect soapsud bubbles off to find the light'. There are several inspiring models, notably Alastair Reid's counting and naming lists, and traditional prototypes:

Counting One to Twenty

Yahn, Tayn, Tether, Mether, Mumph,
Hither, Lither, Auver, Dauver, Dic,
Yahndic, Tayndic, Tetherdic,
   Metherdic, Mumphit,
Yahn a mumphit, Tayn a mumphit,
Tethera mumphit, Methera mumphit,
   Jig it.

The possibilities should be discussed but it is usually best to remove the models, which may circumscribe the pupil's own imagination. Roy Fuller's poem 'Horrible Things' beings:

'What's the horriblest thing you've seen?'
Said Nell to Jean.

'Some grey-coloured, trodden-on plasticine;
On a plate, a left-over cold baked bean;
A cloak-room ticket numbered thirteen;
A slice of meat without any lean; ' . . .

John Clare's poem 'Pleasant Sounds' begins:

The rustling of leaves under the feet in woods and
   under hedges;
The crumping of cat-ice and snow down wood-rides,
   narrow lanes, and every street causeway;
Rustling through a wood or rather rushing, while the wind
   halloos in the oak-top like thunder;

These might inspire a communal poem, 'The horriblest thing I've ever

seen'; 'The most beautiful thing I've ever seen'; 'I like . . . '; 'I dislike
. . . '; 'Pleasant and Unpleasant Sounds'; 'Fear is . . . ', where each pupil
'consequences-wise' adds his line to the poem-list as it is passed round
the class. We can borrow Edwin Morgan's approach in 'A View of Things':

> what I love about dormice is their size
> what I hate about rain is its sneer
> what I love about the Bratach Gorm is its unflappability
> what I hate about scent is its smell

and can manipulate it in a number of ways; we can read the original
or not, amputate the lines for completion as the class thinks fit, drawing
the line after the penultimate word, or as far back as after the third
word. Pupils can be given the whole of the first line and invited to make
of it what they will, rather like an archaeological fragment which
imagination and experience must work upon. The list technique can be
elaborated, as in D.M. Thomas's 'Twelve Men's Moor':

> Who shaped me like a cromlech?
> Who holed me like a crickstone?
> Who rocked me like a logan?
> Who enchanted me like ninemaidens?
> Who blessed me like a holywell?
> Who bloodied me like a tinstream?
> Who lit me like a wrecker's lantern?
> Who blinded me like an engine-house?
> Who corroded me like an arsenic-flue?
> Who deepened me like a shaft?
> Who emptied me like a chapel?
> Who built me and left me like scaffolding?

or as in Robert Graves' 'Amergin's Charm', which begins:

> I am a stag: *of seven tines,*
> I am a flood: *across a plain,*
> I am a wind: *on a deep lake,*
> I am a tear: *the Sun lets fall . . .*

In form this poem is very close to another access route to poetry, the
extended riddle, since riddles are often basically lists where accumu-
lated clues point to the subject. Alan Brownjohn's 'Seven Activities for

a Young Child' and Jacques Prévert's 'How to Paint the Portrait of a
Bird' inspire many possible 'list' poems: 'Five things not to do in a
hurry'; 'Seven ways to eat spaghetti'; 'Eight things to find at the end of
the garden'; 'Six ways to annoy Aunt Elsie'; 'Five ways to spend a bent
half crown'; 'How to avoid washing up'; 'How to fail an exam'; 'How to
lose friends and make enemies'. Obviously pupils should ideally suggest
their own titles, which should be displayed for comment on the board.

The incubation period for a poem may well be a long one and the
stimulus should not always be produced only minutes before thinking
and writing is to begin; startling newspaper headlines and quotations
can be collected over several weeks and displayed prominently as the raw
material for discussion, improvisation and of course, writing as in this
pupil's poem 'The Main News of the Day', beginning:

> Glittering teeth of vacant smiles,
> NEW MISSILE DEAD,
> MAJOR LEAK FROM SECRET FILES,
> Refugees can't be fed.

Edwin Morgan's poem 'Off Course' provides the model for poems
which distort and manipulate the list idea to great effect. This idea is
explored less profoundly in this pupil's poem, 'Shoplift':

1 large white loaf	. . . Just something nice for me
Small pot of strawberry jam	To slip behind my hand
1 pkt. of chocolate biscuits	Hide within my coat —
¼ lb of ham.	Not as I had planned—
Large bag of sugar	Large white manager
¼ lb of tea	Full of strawberry jam
3 large lemons and	Leaning on the lemons
Something nice for me . . .	Spitting chocolate jam.

Playing with Words

It is important to take the pressure off pupils, to move away from the
idea that a poem must always be finished in a fixed time-span and then
fossilized 'in best'. Just as we can improvise profitably in drama (as in
music and art) so we can in poetry, and moving the words around in
both removes the assumption that there is one right way of saying
something. As with spontaneous improvision in drama the emphasis
is more on the *process* than any final product and one of the most
obvious ways to start is by improvising the raw materials — words.

Jeffrey Davies' 'The Washing Machine' suggests that:

> It goes fwunkety,
>   then shlunkety,
> as the washing goes around.
>
> The water spluncheses
>   and it shluncheses,
> as the washing goes around . . .

In which case what sounds does a depressed pendulum clock make or a
confused door chime, a lawnmower cutting wet grass or a
superannuated boiler? To put it another way: if 'ploft pluft plottle' is
the sound of plumping-up pillows what does 'plik-plak' describe, or
'scrit-scrittle-scritter'? If 'yiaowwl' is the sound a cat makes when you
tread on its tail, what sound does it make when it is locked in the
garage? Pupils, either singly or in groups, could compile a feline vocabulary, a list of domestic sounds, classroom sounds, or the sounds associated with a walk through a wood at night. They might look at sounds
from different points of view, that of a mouse, burglar, lodger or blind-
folded patient.

Words can be categorized: spiky words, whether real or imaginary,
to describe spiky subjects; weighty words; fluid words; airy words;
bland words; staccato words; fortissimo words; words to be savoured
and rolled around the mouth; words to be spat out, or whispered
furtively. Clearly Roget's *Thesaurus* can be a great help where real
words are concerned, though the sooner pupils begin to understand the
texture of words and use their imagination to make up their own the
better. Such compilations can result in a poem where the original juxtaposition of nonsense and real words produces disconcerting echoes and
images:

> The pain dribbed from the gutterals
> It was a lodely scene,
> When bruff knights teared in brimfuls
> When Arthur stilled his Queen . . .

Alliteration, onomatopoeia and imagery all open doors into poetry;
take a tongue-twister, 'Peter Piper Picked a Peck of Pickled Pepper.'
Variations on this theme might produce: 'Dapper Douglas dodged a
drove of doting dawdling damsels.' It is a short step from this to:

'Sadly, silently, she slid into her seat'; 'Feint fetid fog floated from the phantom'; 'Grotesque and gloating he greedily gored his grovelling guest.' Obviously this is an exaggerated form of self-expression which should be used sparingly, but pupils enjoy concocting their own lines and incorporating them in their own poems. They come to understand the power of alliteration (onomatopoeia or imagery) and increase their word power through practice in using a dictionary.

Edwin Morgan's poems, increasingly popular in modern school anthologies, suggest witty and vivid ways into poetry, techniques which demand not refined sensibility but a delight in what can be built with words. Perhaps his most quoted example is 'The Computer's First Christmas Card' which begins:

jollymerry
hollyberry
jollyberry
merryholly

Its sequel 'The Computer's Second Christmas Card' invites other suggestions, 'The Computer's First Menu' perhaps, or 'The Computer's Second
Wedding Invitation'. Building a poem along the lines of Edwin Morgan's
'Construction for Isambard Kingdom Brunel' has its parallel in man-
oeuvring bricks into place (or in this case girders). The bricks — words —
are laid out at random to start with, as builder-poet surveys the site and
the materials at his disposal, but gradually some sort of shape appears
from the chaos, certain juxtapositions work. The foundations are there
and the structure can rise around them. The best way into such poetry
is to ask pupils to collaborate on a subject and pool their 'materials':
'Jot down in rough quickly, every word, thought and idea that springs
to mind in relation to your topic'. These can then be supplemented
with the help of the dictionary, *Thesaurus*, teacher and other pupils.
Pupils may share and borrow ideas as the teacher thinks fit. Where
working in pairs is not sufficient stimulus the poem may become a group
effort using a suitably dramatic slide, large picture or piece of spontaneous improvisation in order to invite a collection of responses. The
last example is probably the most effective stimulus because of the live
action involved, which is frozen at a key moment or moments. An
improvisation dealing with a confrontation in a café might inspire the
following suggestions from the audience immediately: greasy leer,
gaudy lino, tea for two, scratching heads, fingering eyes, steamy
stare, 'He is wearing last week's paper,' shattered peace, torn menu,

filthy anger, clatter and crash of the door, ketchup on the floor . . .

Poems can be built with the help of a tape recorder, as in 'A Day at the Seaside'; the whole class reads a collection of poems which attempt to capture the sound of the sea. In small groups pupils experiment with their own onomatopoeic sea-sounds; when they have a realistic and easily reproduced sound it is listed thus: 'Scchlolush' is the sound of the waves lapping against a rock, 'sheeahh' is the sound of the waves sucking back from the shore. Different groups lay claim to different sea-sounds which will form the introduction to the tape. A 'collage' of sound is produced as different sounds gradually fade in, and become dominant before fading out again. Once the whole class is satisfied with the quality of the introduction pupils return to their groups in order to experiment with seaside noises (though one group will continue to provide a background of surf sounds): the screech of gulls; a baby crying; fairground noises; the ice cream van's melody; giggling girls afraid of the water; the beach picnic; dogs yapping. Again as one fades in on the tape its predecessor gradually fades into the background. When the mix is perfected pupils complete their list of sounds in rough, and this will form the raw material for an anthology of poems which will complete the tape. In addition the introductory sound 'collage' can be used as the beginning to a radio play.

Short and to the Point

Too many pupils associate the writing of poetry with the agony of trying to squash words into a fixed metre, finding words which rhyme, or trying painfully to scrape together the minimum number of lines required by the teacher. While we obviously do not want to encourage thoughtless and throw-away verse, nor the lazy pupil concerned to do as little as possible, pupils should come to see poetry as a collective term for an enormous range of responses; short poems can be as effective, even moving in their own way as longer, more ambitious poems. The following are examples of pupils' work, inspired by reading Japanese Haiku poems, William Carlos Williams' 'Short Poem', John Tagliabue's 'My Long Woollen Underwear', Michael Rosen's 'Father Says', Pam Ayres' 'I am a Witney Blanket' and a local gravestone epitaph:

Haiku
Tears that smear my smile,
Of parting – the sun connives
To dim our good-byes.

Short Poem
You broke your word
Oh but so kindly
I never saw the letters
Lying in the grate.

Sister

My	Now	Steals
small	she	my
quiet	makes	friends
Sister	scenes,	and
used	beats	jeans
to	me	
tag	up	
along —	and	

Gran Says
Gran says
If you don't — prod
Prod — eat that
All up you won't
Be invited again — and
Again and again.
Gran says — When I
Was young there was
No one to make a fuss
Of me, no Sunday tea —
Lucky Gran.

I am a
I am a jar of beetroot,
I've been left upon the shelf,
If they don't eat me by Wednesday,
I think I'll drown myself.

Classroom Epitaph
Here lies a great sinner
Always late for dinner
The first to lose his coat,
The last to bring a note.
Never quite caught on,
Now he's dead and gone.

I have quite deliberately omitted limericks since, although they make entertaining reading and are perennially popular in classrooms and course books, they are a very demanding verse form. Those pupils who understand the demands of the metre and rhyme scheme find it difficult to be really original, and the teacher is left suspiciously wondering whether the good examples are borrowed or not.

The Shallow End: Reading Poetry

Where the young or disillusioned pupil is concerned the priority must be to energise poetry, to demonstrate that it can present people, feelings and events uniquely as part of the fabric of communication, rather than as an extravagant irrelevance. Where reading poetry is concerned the emphasis must be on the immediacy of impact; deferred enjoyment ('You'll enjoy this poem when I've shown you what all the words mean') is out of place here, although this is not the same as saying that poems cannot be returned to for the enjoyment they give in successive readings. Certain poems, W.S. Gilbert's 'Nightmare', the ballad 'Sir Patrick Spens', Lewis Carroll's 'Jabberwocky', Charles Causley's 'Colonel Fazackerley', W.H. Auden's 'Night Mail' and Tennyson's 'The Lady of Shalott' cry out for group readings at least, if not actual performance. Final perfected readings with sound effects, where appropriate, can be recorded. This should demonstrate how much a good reading can contribute to the sense of a poem. Of course pupils should also be encouraged to read and record their own poetry. The group anthology, perhaps planned and edited in class and written in part for homework, is a sensible approach, particularly where the whole group takes its editorial responsibilities seriously and adopts the teacher's role of discriminator-in-chief.

While obsessive simile-spotting is fatuous if we really want to resuscitate poetry reading, one of our aims must be to encourage discrimination, at however informal or subjective a level. For this pupils will need a few basic tools. They will need to be able to make statements such as 'I like the way the poet compares A to B because . . . '; 'I like the way the poem takes it rhythm from the movement of . . . '; 'The verses run into each other so that the poem flows . . . ' Hopefully pupils will learn to take their cue from the teacher's own statements and from the careful introduction of basic terms such as verse, rhythm, comparison, vocabulary, description, contrast. The individual will only have the confidence to speak out, to nail his interpretation to the mast, if he is given time to think and is assured of a sympathetic and discerning audience and a teacher who is not, however inadvertently, intent on imposing his own interpretation. If the only way to prevent the teacher wearily filling the frigid silence with the official view is to divide the class into autonomous groups, so be it.

The Deep End

The principles and techniques of the shallow end hold true for the deep end too. That is, after a dynamic start in the secondary school, poetry should not become achingly dreary and demoralisingly difficult in the examination years. This is particularly important where set poets or anthologies are being studied at O and A Level. It takes a certain gritty resolution to set aside the O or A Level syllabus in favour of the class's own poetic output, but apart from the importance of self-expression in general we can justify this creative approach in terms of the syllabus itself. The sixth former who wrote the following pastiche of Shakespeare's Eighteenth Sonnet was learning that writing poetry can be challenging and fun, what it means to write a sonnet, a great deal about Shakespeare's style and qualities, and that it is possible to use a model unashamedly, and then kick it aside and recognise that a pastiche can have a life and quality of its own:

Shall I compare thee to a winter's night?
Thou art less cruel and far less unkind,
The stars within the heavens sparkle with delight,
But cannot banish fear from human minds.
Sometime the icicles dripping from the trees
Awake the sleepy shepherd from numbed sleep,
He shudders, frets his freezing knees
And turns in silent wonder to his sheep,
But thy shy purity shall not numb
Nor boast of lovers conquered, lovers flayed,
Nor thy proud innocence freeze the sun
When thy earthly course is once outplayed.
So long as men may hope, believe, aspire,
So long shall she warm man's hearts with her fire.

The same sixth former then went on to explore the difference between a pastiche and a parody through his own invention, beginning:

Shall I compare thee to a lump of cheese?
Ripe gorgonzola, bland Cheshire or homely Leicester red?
These sweat upon the slab, and invite a squeeze,
While you invite the milkman instead.
Sometime while out upon a jaunt you fling
All inhibition rashly to the skies . . .

Meeting living, working poets who are prepared to discuss their work
and its often humdrum origins helps to kill the idea that 'real' poetry
is synonymous with the 'set text' poets, Milton, Chaucer, Blake and
Pope, and that quality is synonymous with difficulty and obscurity.
Meeting a professional poet who candidly says, 'I don't know why I
put that' or, 'I'm not happy with that line now' helps to jolt the assumption that what is immortalised in print, in set books, must be right,
must be good. It encourages the essential impudence required to question
a poem and poet and to assert, 'If he can do it I can certainly have a
go'.

It is important that older students should be encouraged to write
their own poetry, but it is also important to realise that O and A Level
candidates will be required to demonstrate detailed knowledge of the
poems set for the examination, and that any capable English teacher
will have a good idea of the questions, whether textual or essay, which
they are likely to face. There follows a study of three representative
examples where the teachers concerned are helping their students to
prepare for such questions: the modern poet set for special study at O
Level, the unquestionably great poet set for A Level, and an approach
to unseen critical appreciation.

O Level Literature

The teacher met the group for the first time at the beginning of the
fifth year. They are required to study three poets in detail from a
modern anthology. The teacher describes the challenge thus: how, given
limited teacher-time, are we to preserve these poets from an O Level
mauling and yet give these students a fair chance of answering questions
such as, 'Select and analyse *one* poem that suggests the poet's ability to
perceive the apparently trivial and see in it something fundamental and
one that you feel effectively portrays an important experience in his
childhood or youth'.

Preliminaries.

1. The teacher and class have found out as much as possible about

the poet, in this case D.J. Enright, and his attitude to his work, though this amounts to little. The teacher has emphasised the fact that, in contrast to the well-annotated classics, here the class are on their own; any view that can be coherently justified is valid and the teacher is not privy to the right answers.

2. The class have, with the help of a variety of appropriate examples before them, discussed the following in small groups, before reporting back to a plenary session: is a poem necessarily good or poor if you have to look up many of its words in a dictionary or encyclopaedia? Is a poem necessarily good or poor if you understand all its words and apparently all its meaning immediately? does a poem have to have a 'message' in order to be effective? If it has a message should it be one with which we agree (i.e. could a poem with a corrupt message, for instance, supporting racial intolerace, still be a 'good' poem?)? The objective here was to help students into a position where they could come to terms with questions such as 'Is good-effective poetry merely a matter of taste?'; 'Can we differentiate between the effective and the great?'

3. The class have been asked to read through all the poems in the collection in any order as many times as possible for their first homework, and jot down their impressions in rough with the following sub-headings as a guide: subject-matter, style, poems which made an immediate impact.

4. These impressions were discussed in the subsequent lesson. The teacher found a pleasant way in through two short poems, 'Two Bad Things in Infant School', 'And Two Good Things'. These provoked a light-hearted look at personal memories, and students and teacher made a swift, fairly spontaneous attempt at writing their own short poems, given similar titles.

5. The class divided into groups to look at a small selection of D.J. Enright's poems which were connected in some way with memories of childhood and school. Each group looked at the selection as a whole but took special responsibility for a single poem. They devised their own questions which they then tried to answer. The groups reported back, in the hope that their answers and questions would be supplemented by those from other groups. This procedure worked well but the teacher decided that with a slightly more difficult poem, 'Ugly Head', it would be sensible to break the pattern and discuss it as a whole class.

UGLY HEAD

There seems to be a large gap
Somewhere about here.
If repression is at work
Then repression works efficiently,
In this sphere.

I don't remember learning about sex
In the school lavatories;
Though I remember the lavatories.

With a great effort I call up
Certain goings-on in the rear rows
Of the Physics class. I can't believe it.
That Welsh master was so sharp
You couldn't blow your nose
Without him glaring.

At one time or another
Some slightly special one or other —
But to kiss a girl
Would have seemed like criminal assault.
There was one called Pearl
Who would quote bits from Rosalind
In *As You Like It*, leaving me confused.
Once at a party I stepped heavily
On her hand, and was appalled.
In a strange way she seemed to like it.
I was glad to go home and study *The Prelude*.

It was homework and rugger; then
It was essays and walks to Grantchester.
Perhaps we were great Platonic lovers then.
Perhaps there is nothing to remember.

The class had five minutes in which to read through the poem
thoroughly in order to come to some conclusions about what it was
about. The teacher then read the poem expressively and asked for
their suggestions. The students' confusion was evident. Believing
that identifying the difficulties is half the battle, the teacher asked:

what was the cause of the difficulty here? Was it the words?

S1.   Not really — except 'Platonic' (This was quickly explained).
S2.   The words aren't difficult but you can't understand how he's using them here.
T.   Any examples? Underline them in pencil.
S3.   Well, 'repression', 'sphere', the last two lines.
S2.   And 'I can't believe it', 'Some slightly special one or other'.
S4.   And where does the 'Ugly Head' fit in? (The teacher then deliberately changed tack slightly).
T.   What did he get up to at school? (This produced an immediate list).
T.   What did he *not* get up to at school?
S5.   He didn't learn about sex in the school lavatories.
S6.   Never kissed a girl — didn't chat up girls.
T.   How would you describe the character who emerges from the penultimate verse?
S7.   A prude — a swot.
S4.   Confused and overcome.
S3.   Underconfident — shy.
T.   Look at the last two lines. Do you think he was a 'great Platonic lover' judging from the evidence?
S8.   No — I think he was scared stiff — stepping on someone's hand's pretty Platonic and he was appalled.
T.   What's the 'nothing' in the last line? What do you think he wanted to remember?
S6.   Sex?
T.   Let's try that interpretation on the first verse: what's he repressed?
S9.   Well, it's got to be sex hasn't it?
S10. No, because I think he would have liked sex — his memories have gone — they've been repressed. (General murmur from most of the class, apparently indicating support for this view).
S4.   What's the 'sphere'?
S10. It means 'In this area' — memories.
S11. He didn't have any sex — he has to try hard to think up anything going on in the back row . . . or it could mean that it definitely happened but he can't believe the sharp Welsh master let them get away with it?
T.   Could it be both?
S11. S'pose so.

S7.   But we still haven't sorted out the title – where's the gap?

S12. In his head?

S9.   A real one?

S12. No – imaginary.

T.   What's gone? What could have caused the gap?

S3.   Memories.

T.   Any advances on memories? Does that help with the title?

S6.   No – if he's got a gap in his memories why would his head
      look ugly?

S9.   It's not a *real* gap – you can't see the memories and you can't
      see the gap. (The discussion continued on these lines for
      some time).

T.   Perhaps that's not a vital point. Are we, do you think,
      supposed to take away something from this poem – a message
      – that might apply to us as well?

S1.   Perhaps he means that we'd all like to remember things we
      could show off about in the past, but they either didn't
      happen or if they did we only remember the embarrassing bits.

S4.   That's why he says 'Perhaps – Perhaps' in the last verse.

T.   Is that borne out by your own experiences?

The teacher, well aware that there was still a gap between this
question-and-answer session and a final intelligible record which
could form a basis for revision, asked the class to record their own
interpretations and justifications. The teacher was pleased with the
group's response and although only half had contributed orally felt
that this was a promising start, particularly since no one had been
prompted to speak. He was happy to adopt the role of facilitator
and questioner, but realistically suggested that this was only possible
because relationships were good between the pupils and between
pupils and teacher. In short, 'They've got to be interested and even
then they'll only risk making a suggestion, perhaps displaying their
ignorance, if they're not penalised for being wrong, and if they're
given credit for trying.'

A Level Literature

Following a series of skirmishes with a wide range of literature in the
lower-sixth year, this upper-sixth group were beginning the study of
the examination set texts, reading a nineteenth century novel and
Blake's *Songs of Innocence and Experience* concurrently. Their teacher
was only too aware of recent research suggesting that intensive study of

set poems at O and A Level could effectively put students off poetry altogether. He was determined not to allow poetry lessons to deteriorate into a predictable pattern, where the teacher talked like a textual annotation while the students busily and passively recorded his every word. His approach to Blake was typical of his approach to any 'examination poet' and consisted of juggling a number of approaches:

1. Group and teacher discover as much as possible about the poet and his time in the hope of presenting him as an interesting, gifted, fallible human being, capable of changing his mind, subjects and style: to what extent could he only have been what he was and written what and as he did because of the time in which he lived? The poet's work is compared with that of his contemporaries: to what extent does he appear to be derivative or innovative?

2. Group read as much as possible of the poet's work as quickly as possible in order to form first impressions, grasp subject matter and 'feel' the tone.

3. In order to win students over to the poet's side, group and teacher together approach the most accessible poems or parts. 'Analysis' is kept to the absolute minimum, allowing time for exploration through the students' own writing and through comparison with other approaches to the same theme.

4. Once students have found their feet the approach is changed for each lesson. The overall aim is to maximise student discussion and group or pair note-making, and minimise the amount of note-making straight from the teacher's mouth on the grounds that the teacher's words are an imposition which is easily forgotten, the students' less so.

Further suggested approaches

a) Read the poems for different reasons, e.g. immediate impact, rhythm, imagery, progression of thought, plot (i.e., don't always analyse everything).

b) Students individually or in pairs introduce a poem for discussion in any way they think appropriate; for instance, use of overhead projector and overlays, presentation from the point of view of a contemporary rival, or as the poet commenting on his own work.

c) Informal but prepared debate representing two different views or interpretations.

d) Pastiche in the interest of a greater understanding of stylistic technique.

e) Students left to their own devices with a difficult poem and a minimum of textual help.

f) Teacher plays devil's advocate, where the group is confident and informed.

g) The 'refresher' lesson: 'We've been studying a serious poet writing in the eighteenth century. I thought we'd have a change and take a look at a humorous twentieth century poet.'

Unseen Critical Appreciation

The teacher feels that this upper-sixth group need some pre-examination practice for the unseen 'Critical Appreciation' questions. The students know that they are likely to meet the following instruction: 'Read the following poem carefully, and comment on its subject matter and style and give your reasons for liking or disliking it.' The students are inexperienced and the teacher feels that she will need to give a lead and help them to find a model for such exercises. She wants to use this example to show how every word can be made to work in a poem, and how almost every word can deserve comment. (The students will be required to write for an hour about a single poem in the examination.) She wants to demonstrate how a poet can use these words to recreate the unfamiliar, to persuade, to object, and that the poet's view, the 'final taste in the mouth', may be the most memorable aspect of the poem. She wants to focus on a poem which comes unburdened by critical sifting, for which there are no right answers. To these ends she has chosen:

The Martyrdom of Bishop Farrar

Bloody Mary's venomous flames can curl;
They can shrivel sinew and char bone
Of foot, ankle, knee, and thigh, and boil
Bowels, and drop his heart a cinder down;
And her soldiers can cry, as they hurl
Logs in the red rush: 'This is her sermon'.

The sullen-jowled watching Welsh townspeople
Hear him crack in the fire's mouth; they see what
Black oozing twist of stuff bubbles the smell
That tars and retches their lungs: no pulpit
Of his ever held their eyes so still,
Never, as now his agony, his wit.

An ignorant means to establish ownership
Of his flock! Thus their shepherd she seized
And knotted him into this blazing shape
In their eyes, as if such could have cauterised
The trust they turned towards him, and branded on
Its stump her claim, to outlaw question.

So it might have been: seeing their exemplar
And teacher burned for his lessons to black bits,
Their silence might have disowned him to her,
And hung up what he had taught with their Welsh hats:
Who sees his blasphemous father struck by fire
From heaven, might well be heard to speak no oaths.

But the fire that struck here, come from Hell even,
Kindled little heavens in his words
As he fed his body to the flame alive.
Words which, before they will be dumbly spared,
Will burn their body and be tongued with fire
Make paltry folly of flesh and this world's air.

When they saw what annuities of hours
And comfortable blood he burned to get
His words a bare honouring in their ears,
The shrewd townsfolk pocketed them hot;
Stamp was not current but they ran and shone
As good gold as any queen's crown.

Gave all he had, and yet the bargain struck
To a merest farthing his whole agony,
His body's cold-kept miserdom of shrieks
He gave uncounted, while out of his eyes,
Out of his mouth, fire like glory broke,
And smoke burned his sermons into the skies.   (Ted Hughes)

The teacher believes that only a scrupulous and expressive reading
will help the students to find a way into the poem. She has already
underlined those words which seem to deserve special emphasis, which
should be relished or which should be spoken slowly and deliberately.
She reads it first for initial impact before students receive their copies,
and then again when they have read it themselves. Together they

establish what the poem is about and make the point that, while the
title sums up the subject matter in one sense, there is far more to the
poem than an account of a distant martyrdom, and the poet is hardly
an objective 'observer'. Students are asked to cover all but the first
verse and are asked not to write notes. The teacher's first question is
quite deliberately a move away from the 'Explain all the difficult
words' approach. She asks, 'What do we learn about the poet from the
first verse?' At first there is a bewildered silence as the students are
forced back to the words, but gradually they come to focus on 'Bloody'
and 'venomous' and recognize the ambiguity of 'can' and the poet's
controlled horror at what is being done in the name of religion: 'This is
her sermon'. The teacher asks them to look at what the flames are
doing, as they move up the body and the verse, and she makes the
point that there is little need for imagery, the description of events is
graphic enough. The sinews are shrivelled, bones charred, bowels boiled.
One student comments on the brutality of these verbs.

Together they uncover the next verse. The teacher reads it clearly
and carefully, bringing out the 'w's' of the first line and the horror of
'crack', deliberately pausing between 'stuff' and 'bubbles', trying to
reveal the power of those two central lines. She asks them to try to drive
everything from their minds but the sight of those sullen-jowled Welsh
townspeople who are watching the soldiers hurling on the logs, the
spectacle of that black oozing twist of stuff and a smell so ghastly that
it makes their lungs retch. She asks them to compare his silent sermon
delivered in agony with bloody Mary's own.

The teacher makes the point that the poet's voice cuts through the
smoke clearly at the beginning of the third verse. She asks them to
identify what he seems to be saying, and the most powerful words in
this verse. Together they notice the consistency in imagery in this, and
later verses. The next two verses are looked at together; particular attention is paid to the last two lines of verse four, the first three of verse
five and the pivotal word 'oaths'. The teacher asks, 'Where has the fire
come from?' The group agree that despite its hellish intentions the fire
is associated with heaven through its results. The teacher focuses
attention on the implications of the words 'fed' and 'dumbly' and the
allusion in 'tongued with fire'.

Having examined the meaning of 'annuities' and 'stamp' in the next
verse, the teacher asks the students to form small groups to discuss the
meaning of the following: 'comfortable', 'bare', 'shrewd', 'hot', and to
justify their interpretations to the rest of the class. Together they
confront the final and perhaps most difficult verse, relating it first to all

that has gone before but particularly the fifth verse, and exploring the triumph of the spirit over the flesh.

While the teacher hoped that the students would draw some initial conclusions about the poem's tone, she felt that this could only realistically be discussed after the group had tried to 'cut a path through to the poem's meaning'. She anticipated that the verse-by-verse, line-by-line approach might be charged with destroying the unity of the whole, but felt that this was the less evil alternative to a facile misinterpretation, and did at least provide a pattern for detailed analysis on future occasions. In order to 'reinstate and reunite' the poem the students were asked to read through the whole again, savouring and nominating any words or images which they found memorable. Group and teacher discussed whether or not 'Did you like it?' was a sensible question to ask in this case, and decided that 'like' seemed a rather trite term to apply to such a powerful and horrifying theme. Finally the teacher asked, 'Do you think our approach was the best way of getting to grips with the poem?' The group felt that it was in this case, but that such careful perusal would not have suited a simpler poem such as a ballad or song's lyrics. Not a word was written in the course of the forty-minute lesson because, as the teacher explained, 'They don't need a record of this, and more to the point when they're writing they're not thinking.'

None of the teachers who feature in these examples would claim that their approaches are particularly startling nor even original, but they do represent three realistic means to the ends of enjoyment and understanding. They recognize the demands of the examinations and the importance of maintaining a careful balance between teacher guidance and student initiative, if students are to be helped to make these poems and these interpretations 'their own'.

Notes

1. G. Yarlott and W. Harpin, '1,000 Responses to English Literature', *Educational Research* vol. 13, nos. 1 and 2 (1972, 73).

2. W.H. Auden, 'How can I tell what I think till I see what I say?' in N. Bagnall (ed.), *New Movements in the Study and Teaching of English* (Temple Smith, 1973).

3. R. Skelton, *The Poet's Calling* (Heinemann, 1975) which contains an interesting set of worksheets which show the evolution of a number of well-known poems.

4. *Voices*, The First, Second and Third Books (Penguin, 1968).

Other recommended anthologies

The English Project (formerly the *Penguin English Project*), WLE: a library of resource books containing short stories, poems, drama, fiction, non-fiction, pictures and drawings and catering for the age range 11-18, *Things Working* P. Blackie (ed.), from *Stage One*, age-range 11-13, is particularly useful.
M. & P. Benton (eds.), *Poems*, and *Poems 2* (Hodder and Stoughton, 1979).
C. Causley, *The Puffin Book of Magic Verse* (Penguin, 1974).
K. Webb (ed.), *I Like this Poem* (Penguin, 1979).
F. Finn (ed.), *Here and Human* (Murray, 1976).
C. Copeman & J. Gibson (eds.), *As Large as Alone* (Macmillan, 1969).
M. & P. Benton (eds.), *Touchstones 1, 2, 3, 4 and 5*((EUP, 1968).
R. Heath (ed.), *Theme and Variations* (Longman, 1965) for older students.

NB. These anthologies have been selected on the basis of their general usefulness; many other collections, course-books, BBC schools broadcasts and accompanying pamphlets contain excellent material. The reader is also referred to the list of acknowledgements.

Acknowledgements

The author and publishers wish to thank the following for permission to reproduce copyright material: Hope, Leresche and Sayle for 'Streemin', copyright © 1976 by Roger McGough from *In the Glass Room* published by Jonathan Cape; André Deutsch Ltd for 'Horrible Things' copyright © 1977 by Roy Fuller from *Seen Grandpa Lately?*; D.M. Thomas for 'Twelve Men's Moor'; Macmillan, London and Basingstoke for 'The Washing Machine' by Jeffrey Davies from *As Large as Alone* published by Copeman and Gibson; Bolt and Watson Ltd and Oxford University Press for 'Ugly Head' by D.J. Enright, from *The Collected Poems of D.J. Enright*; Faber and Faber Ltd for 'The Martyrdom of Bishop Farrar' by Ted Hughes from *The Hawk in the Rain*.

7 THE BASICS

> David's written work shows imagination and flair but his grasp
> of the basic skills is poor; on occasions punctuation is non-
> existent and his spelling is erratic. (Secondary school report)

Most teachers of English would understand the 'basic skills' to include
spelling, puncutation and syntax. That is, they would expect pupils to
construct, punctuate and spell their work correctly, or at least identify
and correct spelling mistakes with the help of a dictionary. Few today
would see parsing and clause analysis, the old Latinate interpretation of
'grammar', as a basic skill, and since syntactical errors are rare in any
pupil's work the emphasis is placed increasingly on spelling and
punctuation,sometimes obsessively so. The English teacher quoted
above is not unusual in implying a divide between creativity and the
more 'technical' aspects of English work. This is inevitable since it recognises the range within English, at its most functional in the teaching of
spelling and punctuation, and perhaps at its most creative in the
composition of poetry, at the other end of the spectrum. It is unfortunate that in describing such skills as 'basic' we may give the false
impression that they need to be mastered before progress can be made
in more imaginative, less routine, writing, when of course spelling and
punctuation, in common with any skill, need practice through as many
kinds of written work as possible. There is a temptation to feel that
since 'creativity' is too nebulous to be taught, since it does not lend
itself to sequential exercises, the teaching of spelling and punctuation
lends a certain security and respectability to the teaching of English.
Not only is this an area we can call our own but exercises are easily set
and marked and success is more immediately apparent — or so the story
goes.

Spelling

Do spelling (and punctuation) really matter, given that communication
is predominantly oral? In short, yes, in a society which values meaning
and accuracy and communicates formally through the written word. We
cannot turn the clock back to an Elizabethan golden age of erratic and
idiosyncratic spelling. Spelling is standardised and the hoots of derision

134

at the typographical blunders of famous national newspapers provide
sufficient evidence of the importance attached to accuracy. Spelling and
punctuation, like any other taken-for-granted skills, only become
important when you can't do them. Writing becomes an agony, a minefield, for the pupil who sees every word as a threat, as yet another mark
off. Spelling inability *is* a social disability, which may even bar pupils
from certain jobs. Experience and research confirm that pupils,
parents, teachers, employers and the public at large all consider spelling
important, sometimes as an indelible sign of care and discipline (perhaps
a hangover from the respect paid to the study of classical grammar as
a refiner of minds), and even as an indicator of intelligence and reliability. While poor spelling and punctuation *may* suggest carelessness
(though we must distinguish between ignorance and carelessness, an
error and a slip), the good speller is not necessarily a good scholar and
the poor speller may be highly intelligent. Indisputably, though, the
writer who misspells key words in an application form, however
excellent his credentials, is unlikely to be called for interview. Good
spelling is seen as symptomatic of the care and concern of the writer in
general. It is also a liberator, freeing the writer to use all the words at
his disposal, not just those which are immediately spellable.

There is a no place for a trendy negligence, no place for the *laissez-
faire* 'Well, I'm a bad speller and it's never caused me problems'. The
truth is teachers are not bad spellers, careless ones perhaps, but we
usually know when we are unsure of a word and know how to use a
dictionary. The bad speller will usually have a clear idea that he is bad
speller. He will probably have been told this many times, for several
years or more, but he usually won't know where he is going wrong nor
why. Before we can help him we need to attempt diagnosis of his
particular difficulties; why is he making these mistakes? The Bullock
Report suggests that 'Poor spellers may have lower verbal intelligence.
They may have difficulty in their visual perception of words and then
in recalling them through imagery. They may be weak in generalising
from the serial probability of letter occurrences.' Richard Lansdown,[1]
Principal Psychologist at the Great Ormond Street Hospital, suggests
that perhaps the poor speller may not be very clever, he may not be
able to see properly, or speak properly or hear properly; he may even
have brain damage. Both lists suggest how notoriously difficult
diagnosis is for anybody but the trained remedial teacher. The average
English teacher will not be able to diagnose brain damage, and among a
class of 30 may have problems picking out the pupil with undetected
sight problems. We might add to these suggestions another: the poor

speller may not have been taught, or may not have been taught properly, to pay attention to the structure of words; this is born out by research showing that pupils who miss significant amounts of school are also significantly poor at spelling.

Research into the teaching of spelling tends to produce confusing and sometimes apparently contradictory advice, but there are certain principles which should help to inform and enlighten the English teacher's approach:

1. Spelling competence is closely linked with pupil motivation and self-image. A pupil will care about spelling only when he cares about the task. If labelled a poor speller he will tend to conform to this label.

2. Any spelling instruction should have direct relevance to the pupil's own writing needs; only useful/interesting words should be taught.

3. Pupils with a history of spelling failure need short, regular periods of practice in order to build confidence through experience of success.

4. Spelling is best taught bearing in mind the particular needs of the individual.

5. Little and often is better than an exhaustive and sporadic approach.

6. Spelling can valuably be taught as spelling, and as an incidental offshoot of other activities.

7. Spelling lists are useful where they are based on words pupils have asked for, or contain common errors. Both teacher-devised and pupil-devised lists earn their place in the teaching of spelling, though the former may be more useful where younger and less able pupils are concerned.

8. Pupils should be encouraged to divide difficult words into syllables, and concentrate on the most difficult syllable, before reinstating the word as a whole.

9. Pupils should be encouraged to see the pattern in words, e.g. -tion, -or, -ible, ante-, post-, pre-, pro-, and understand the spelling and meaning of the commoner prefixes, roots and suffixes.

10. Spelling (and punctuation) are not normally caught from reading; only the most able and motivated are likely to learn a few words in this way.

11. Pupils should be taught the more consistent and thus most

useful spelling rules, e.g. 'i' before 'e' except after 'c', drop the 'e' before adding '-ing', formation of plurals, options for symbolising key sounds, e.g. s = s/c/ps.

12. Pupils should be encouraged to correct their own work where this is feasible. Adequate time should be allowed for revision and checking.

13. The occasional spelling test can be justified, but only where the pupil is competing against his own previous performance, rather than that of other pupils.

14. Mechanical copying, as with corrections, is usually ineffectual in teaching difficult words since the pupil is not encouraged to analyse the structure of the word.

15. Reading aloud can help spelling (and punctuation) because a clearer articulation of each word is required.

16. Spellings should always be given in writing, never letter-by-letter. Pupils should then be encouraged to look, cover, remember, say, write, and check the word.

17. While the inclusion of punctuation should be seen as an automatic part of the process of writing, correct spelling is not crucial in all circumstances. Priorities and objectives decide the technical accuracy appropriate.

18. Pupils should be given ample opportunities for practising new spelling (and punctuation) acquisitions.

19. Almost any systematic approach to the teaching of spelling (and punctuation) is better than no system at all.

This list includes the most useful and incontrovertible findings from a series of research studies.[2] Unfortunately, presented baldly in this way, they are likely to give most teachers at best an acute guilty conscience and at worst induce panic or paralysis. How does the English teacher act upon this advice, given a large mixed ability class?

Diagnosis is the first stage: what is the size and extent of the problem and what kind of spelling mistakes is the individual making, and thus what is the likely cause of the problem? In a mixed ability class of twenty-five or thirty we might expect the majority to be potentially good spellers. They may make occasional slips, need help with difficult words and confuse homophones (homonyms), such as there, their; stationary, stationery etc., but will usually make logical, if incorrect, suggestions for the symbols to represent the sound (*appeer* for *appear*, moap for *mope* etc.) and will be able to use a dictionary with minimal help. A few pupils may be trying to disguise a spelling problem by choosing the lowest common denominator of vocabulary in their written work, never using a difficult word where an easy one will do and thus rejecting words like absence, presence, definitely, recommend etc. If these pupils are not given immediate help in learning these problematic and useful words then written work will remain flat and inexplicit, and may give the false impression that the pupils have a generally impoverished vocabulary. Perhaps as many as half-a-dozen pupils will be 'remedial' spellers, spelling as many as one word in six wrongly, finding even copying genuinely difficult, producing highly unlikely spelling forms (wrk for week, qwine for queen etc) and confusing certain letters (droab for broad, frist for first etc). These are all serious errors, signs of ignorance rather than carelessness, which should not be greeted with the quite useless 'Watch your spelling!' They can be distinguished from the potentially good speller's slips, which careful proof-reading may well reveal. Remedial spellers need immediate and intensive help, which the teacher of a large mixed ability class will not be able to provide. They should be receiving remedial help, but of course this will not solve the English teacher's problems, since they are likely to be present for most, if not all, of their English lessons, remedial extraction or not. Their needs must be acknowledged in any teaching scheme:

There are five major options for the teaching of spelling (and punctuation):

1. An initial intensive programme for all pupils.
2. Division within the class, i.e. poor spellers given intensive help as a group.
3. Correction of spelling mistakes but emphasis on spelling 'caught' from reading.
4. Prearranged weekly/fortnightly spelling lessons for the complete class throughout the year.
5. Help given sporadically, as needed, to individuals, small groups, the whole class, as appropriate.

Stage two requires a policy decision: which option should we adopt? Of course these approaches are not mutually exclusive and we might perfectly feasibly combine 1 with 3, 4 or 5, but this list represents the most easily discernible teaching patterns. Option 1 might mean a spelling (and punctuation) week or fortnight at the beginning of the autumn term when the main spelling rules and patterns would be explored and practised, not necessarily through interminable spelling exercises and tests but through imaginative writing, where the emphasis would be particularly on accuracy, and through flash cards and word games. This would at least recognize the importance of spelling and punctuation and demonstrate that both are skills to be learned and practised. Unfortunately it would also, wrongly, present them as skills which could be learned *en bloc* and *en masse*. The process would almost inevitably be boring, might demoralize the poor spellers further, and would give the false impression that English is all to do with accuracy, rather than creativity and originality. There is a danger too of concluding that spelling and punctuation have 'been done' for the term ('Now I want you to learn these rules carefully because we won't be coming back to this for some time') and that subsequent lapses are the pupil's fault, rather than the result of inadequate and insufficient teaching.

As soon as we single out a minority, as in option 2, two problems immediately arise: the self-image of those singled out as defective in some way, and how best to stimulate the remainder who are not being given the special treatment. This is true whether the poor spellers are given an initial intensive course or whether they are being singled out regularly throughout the year. There are obvious dangers in the 'keep the majority quiet and engrossed' idea, and the success of the remedial group approach depends upon this. The majority may have to suffer routine and unstimulating exercises and the minority may hardly benefit given that whatever help they receive is likely to be sporadic. But, in defence of this option, the poor spellers, whether they sit together or not, do form a discernible group and this fact will become immediately obvious when the first piece of written work is taken in and marked. This group will need special attention and help, and it may well be worth the effort and the compromise occasionally to set a reading task for the majority while the minority are being given some extra practice. It may well be that some of their problems are shared to a greater or lesser extent by the rest of the class, and occasional revision might not harm or bore the 'average' pupils at least. The danger of course lies in seeing the class as two groups, the good and the bad spellers, both of which respond to blanket-treatment. The advantage of the small and select group approach should be that it makes it easier for us to respond to the *individual's* problems.

Option 3 is the least useful strategy, most obviously because research and experience suggest that it is ineffectual, and both agree on the importance of a rational and systematic approach to the teaching of spelling and punctuation. Only already capable and motivated spellers will 'catch' the occasional word from reading, and competent readers can prove to be poor spellers. 'Correction' and 'corrections' can be defined in several ways, but the common interpretation involves crossing out the wrong word or punctuation and replacing it with the correct one and then asking the pupil to write this out one or more times. There is no evidence to suggest that this alone improves a pupil's spelling, even though it provides a reference point for future work. The pupil must be encouraged and be given the time to look at and dissect his mistakes if there is to be any improvement. Copying out the corrected versions is unlikely to help the pupil, since copying is not the same as reproduction from memory. Too often corrections are merely a routine chore, interest and motivation are at their weakest and this results in copying mistakes, a bored class and a frustrated teacher.

Option 4 at the very least sees spelling as a course of study which requires a definite time allocation; it guarantees that it will be taught and it is a refinement of option 1 in that it guarantees regular reinforcement. There is always a danger with this approach that it will degenerate into the convenient routine of Week 1, learn a list of spellings, Week 2, sit a test on them, but if 'spelling lesson' is interpreted imaginatively to include a variety of approaches geared to a variety of individual problems it will be a lesson that both teachers and pupils look forward to, and which demonstrates that spelling and punctuation practice is not rule-bound and test-bound but can be interesting and fun.

Option 5 offers a compromise in that it recognises the differing needs of individuals, at different times and in different contexts. Unfortunately compromises can be notoriously weak, and if the 'as needed' is interpreted unsystematically as, 'when the pupils actually ask for instruction', and if spelling is seen as merely incidental, then pupils will be confused and lack a basis for improvement. But if we can define what the help might consist of, this is undoubtedly the single most valuable option. Since looking at individual words carefully will help all spellers, irrespective of their reasons for their problems, this is probably the best place to start. The potentially good speller is often triggered into correcting a word because 'it doesn't look right'. All pupils need to be able to generalize about the probabilities of certain letter-combinations. They need to know that *q* is always followed by a *u*, that no English words end in *i* (cf. Italian macaroni, spaghetti); that *si ci* and *ti* all make the sound *sh* in the middle of words (mansion, ancient, station). A large number of words are best learnt as part of a pattern (*drop, dropped, dropping, stop, stopped, stopping; knot, knotted, knotting; useful, cheerful, until, skilful, fulfil*). With younger

pupils in particular it is sensible to emphasise the pattern rather than
the rule, whose terminology may well only confuse the issue: 'Where a
word has more than one syllable and ends in a *t*, preceded by a single
vowel, and where the accent is on the last syllable, the final consonant
should be doubled, e.g. admit, admitted; but visit, visited.' There is
little point in the poor spellers dutifully copying this rule, unless they
are absolutely sure of the meaning of *syllable, preceded, accent,* and
consonant. Since this is highly unlikely, and since instruction in the
meaning of these words will only further confuse the issue and hold up
the lesson, the teacher must, if he feels the pupils need to know this
rule, bring attention to the pattern via the board and discussion and
only then find suitable words to generalize: 'What do *admit, permit,
regret* have in common? How do they differ from *visit, benefit*?' He
will need to bring attention to the difference in accent through his own
clear pronunciation and should suggest that pupils say difficult words
clearly aloud to identify syllables and key vowels and consonants.
Pupils will only look carefully at words when they have little
alternative, so the rapidly scribbled dictation exercise is of little use here,
as is the highly competitive spelling exercise where the emphasis is on
finishing quickly. The best way to encourage each pupil to look carefully is obviously to sit beside him, use flash-cards, and make sure that
he is concentrating on the word for ten seconds. This is obviously
impossible in a large class and the teacher will need to compromise
through careful board-work where the pupils can be seen to be concentrating, or through the use of 'pair' flash-cards, where one pupils asks
his partner to pronounce the word clearly, look at the word on the card
for ten seconds, remember the word, and then write the word down
from memory before comparing this version with the original. Such
work is obviously best seen as a part of a 'spelling' lesson rather than as
an annoying interruption in another piece of work. On other occasions
spelling practice may be brief and spontaneous, a response to a query
from a pupil, 'How do you spell your name, Miss?'; 'Are there four
es in *eerie*?' Though circumstances will sometimes force us to rush to
the board, or the pupil, to deliver the goods immediately, this is
obviously not the best response, since the teacher will become little
more than a walking, but much more accessible, dictionary. Guides to
the teaching of spelling can suggest alternatives:

1. Write the words on the board or on paper, perfectly legibly.
2. Pronounce the word clearly and distinctly, using your normal voice.
If you have a regional accent, do not attempt to change it to standard

English. Draw attention, if necessary, to the fact that words may not be pronounced the way their spelling suggests they will sound.

3. The child pronounces the word. Make sure he has pronounced it distinctly. Do not correct any regional accent he may have.

4. Give him time to look at the word. Draw his attention particularly to any difficult parts, by underlining, or merely pointing.

5. Ask the child to write the word himself from memory. He must not copy it letter-by-letter: erase or cover the original word.

6. The child now turns the paper over, or covers his first attempt, if it was not right, and writes it again from memory.

7. If he made a mistake, repeat stages 2-4.

8. Make sure that he uses the word again soon in his writing, but naturally.[3]

This is excellent advice — for those dealing with a small group of pupils. It tends to leave most class teachers gasping, or grinning suspiciously. Far more useful is the distillation of this system: look — cover — remember — write. Or, as the Bullock Report suggested, 'It is a process of look, read, visualize, reconstitute, and reproduce.' But we will not have the time to stand over each pupil to enforce this system; our only hope is to train pupils to use it habitually and to reinforce the process by asking pupils to learn their 'corrections' in this way. Even when the 'look — cover — remember — write' approach proves unrealistic there are better alternatives to the 'I'll put it on the board for you' response. One is, 'Have a good think, have a go at it in rough, put your hand up and I'll come to have a look.' The pupil may have the satisfaction of getting it right, or at the very least the teacher will have a clearer idea of why he is going wrong and how best to help him to remember the word for the future. Another approach might be, 'Think of the first three letters, write them down, use them to find the word in the dictionary. If you can't, having looked carefully, then try to find another way of spelling the beginning of the word.' This second approach will not work with the very poor speller who may not be able to make a sensible guess at even the first two letters. It presumes some understanding of the symbolic alternatives for certain sounds, and of course a knowledge of alphabetical order.

The most useful spelling aid for the potentially good speller is a dictionary. Initial introduction to its use, followed by regular reinforcement and guaranteed access to a selection of dictionaries, including hopefully the pupil's own, will help all pupils. If introduced carefully, dictionaries are both useful and fascinating but it is important to see their use as a skill to be taught and learned. The pupil, if left to his own devices, will soon give up, bemused by the odd symbols and abbreviations and apparently contradictory definitions. Looking up a simple word such as *nice* demonstrates the problems. The *Pocket Oxford Dictionary* gives:

> nice, a. (-cish). Fastidious, of critical taste, punctilious, particular, delicately sensitive, (must not be ~ about the means; a ~ ear, judgement, &c; a ~ observer; weighed in the ~ st scales); requiring precision or care or tact, subtle, fine, minute, (a ~ question, point, negotiation, distinction, shade of meaning); (*colloq*. agreeable, well-flavoured, kind, friendly, considerate, satisfactory . . .)

The pupil who genuinely wants to know how to spell *nice* is dependent on the definition to confirm that he has hit on the right word. Here he needs the tenacity to find his way through the whole series of unusual meanings before lighting upon the familiar 'agreeable, well-flavoured, kind . . . ' which is presented as a colloquial after-thought (which of course etymologically it is).

How can we help a pupil through such mazes? Ideally we can provide a dictionary which is suited to the pupil's ability and understanding, but even where this is possible we will still need to train pupils in the use of 'adult' dictionaries. We can emphasise the importance of thinking carefully before consulting a dictionary: what is the word's likely spelling? What are the most sensible spelling alternatives? What meaning(s) will we expect to find? If pupils ask for the meanings of *adj*., *prep*., and *syll*. we will repay their interest with a brief explanation and refer them to the 'Abbreviations' list, but we will not use this inquiry as a pretext for a formal grammar lesson (though this can provide an interesting trigger for an informal look at the parts of speech with older interested pupils). It is more important that pupils should understand how the dictionary indicates ways a word can be modified or incorporated in common phrases or idioms, thus: *commit*: -tt i.e. *comitted*; -tal i.e. *commital*; -ment i.e. *commitment*; ~ to memory, i.e. commit to memory. Pupils should also understand that they should usually look initially for the simplest form of the word; *debate* rather than *debatable*, attractive rather than *unattractive*.

Simple competitive games can make dictionary-use more fun: 'Think of as many words as you can which begin ex-, inter-, ab-, post-. Spend

five minutes on each. Then add to your list with the help of the
dictionary. Make sure that you know what the words mean!' The
teacher can then invite pupils to suggest the meaning of these and other
common prefixes, and suffixes. Where pupils are making do with the
rather flat *nice, nasty, big, small,* because they know none better, or
can spell none better, the dictionary, or better still Roget's *Thesaurus,*
can be used as a basis for a lesson on synonyms and antonyms. I have
met many sixth-formers who regretted the fact that they had not been
formally introduced to Roget earlier, since they found the book to be
both invaluable and fascinating. Roget suggests five key meanings for
nasty, selecting just *one* of these we find an enormous list which
includes the following: *vile, base, gross, irredeemable, wretched, measly,
shoddy, ropy, punk, fetid, rotten, vicious, intolerable, wanton,
pernicious, dreadful, beastly, horrid, scruffy, putrid, obscene, execrable,
diabolical . . .* ' We can bring attention to the spelling of these words
but we can throw the net wider to examine the derivation of some of
them, their 'relations' (beastly, *bestial, vile, vilify*) and the nuances of
meaning (wanton, pernicious, wretched, diabolical). The inclusion of
punk might single-handedly inspire a discussion concerning the way
words shift their meanings historically or geographically, the way words
come into and out of fashion, and youth culture in general.

For many adults and pupils spelling at school was and is extricably
associated with spelling lists and spelling tests. For those at the
receiving end feelings seem to be mixed about their worth. Many of my
own pupils and students have told me that they quite enjoyed them, but
felt that they did little to improve their spelling; others, notably the
poorer spellers, found them worthless and extremely painful; a few
found the spelling tests and lists a very useful part of their English work.
It seems that they are not alone in this. Graham Banks[4] writes:

> In the comprehensive school where I taught, the English depart-
> ment issued a questionnaire to their pupils at the end of their first
> year, when they were fourteen. The last question asked what they
> would like to see added to their English lessons, and we were
> astonished when about a third requested spelling tests.

Most spelling authorities feel that spelling lists are justified where they
are compiled on the basis of pupils' needs and interests, but are divided
as to who should compile them, teacher or pupil. Freyberg[5] suggests
that where younger and less able pupils are involved (and these will
account for most of our spelling concerns) it is probably better if the

teacher compiles the list. Any lists should be fairly short, no more than a dozen words to be learnt at any one time, and should be based predominantly on words which the pupils ask for and words which are commonly mis-spelt. The most useful starting point for compilation is an analysis of the mistakes made in a week's class work and homework, and then a selection from among these, so that only one or two problems are examined in class time, perhaps confusion of *they're, there, their*; or *able* and *ible* endings. There is no need for a subsequent spelling test as long as this learning is reinforced, however informally, at intervals. The next piece of formal written work is probably as close to a test as the pupils need to go, for the problem with the spelling test is both organizational and academic; no one test is going to suit a whole class, since lists should be geared to the needs of the individual, or at least the sub-group. At least three different lists would be necessary and the organization problems for the teacher testing these would be obvious. It is more sensible to ask pupils to devise a list of their own mistakes from a series of corrected written work and to test each other in pairs, using flash cards or the 'look — cover — remember — write' procedure. Testing a partner can sometimes be as great a help to the tester as to the tested, and the testing can be reversed so that the test is based on the tester's mistakes. Though research seems to suggest that spellings should always be written down if learning is to take place, there is nothing wrong with the 'mini' test at the end of the lesson where individuals are asked to spell out words which have been causing them problems. It is obviously more difficult to spell aloud, so pupils could try out the word in rough first. It is important of course that the difficulty of the word is related to the individual and that the teacher's and class's attitude to mistakes is a sympathetic and supportive one. Mistakes should be analysed, not just corrected.

Spellers are not irretrievably good or bad; poor spellers will improve if they are given sufficient reason for doing so and if the pressure is taken off, and they realize that it is possible to earn praise and high marks for poorly spelt (as opposed to carelessly) spelt work. This may appear contrary ('Surely if we don't punish spelling mistakes they'll never see the error of their ways') but such punishment soon loses its effect if every piece of work earns a demoralizingly low mark and disparaging comment. The pupil may well give up, ignorant of how he might improve and why he should improve, but if the piece of work has a purpose, to reach a wider audience though display or publication, there is more incentive for getting it right. Once again rough paper and first draft writing will be important, for while pupils can cope with punctuation as they write, many find it difficult to write quickly and imaginatively and avoid spelling errors. The first draft should be devoted to the content, to getting the sequence of ideas down on paper. This can be revised and proof read; collaboration can be a great help, for even good spellers find it difficult to proof-read their own work and may pass over slips which are immediately apparent to a colleague. Reading aloud will often help to identify spelling and punctuation mistakes, particularly the latter.

Punctuation

The emphasis here has inevitably been placed on spelling; teachers and pupils and the public have always considered correct punctuation less crucially important, though its absence may distort the meaning even more than poor spelling on occasions. Although there is more latitude for personal taste in punctuation, as Shaw and Dickens demonstrated, there are certain rules which should be taught: the function of the comma and full stop, ways of joining sentences, paragraphing, the punctuation of direct speech, and certain uses of the apostrophe (boy's, boys, its, it's; there's, theirs). All of these are of use to the writer and reader. The exploration of single quotation marks and possible uses of the colon can be deferred almost indefinitely for most pupils. Punctuation must be seen as an ally, as a series of signposts each with a quite rational function, and it should be taught as such. As with spelling, pupils should be encouraged to look at correct usage in context, rather than merely copy a list of definitions, such as 'A comma is used to . . . ' etc.

The comma, semi-colon, and full stop are often taught, at least initially, as indicators of pauses of different lengths, and despite Michael Marland's[6] reservations this makes more sense than rote recitation of the rules. They are also taught to younger pupils as having different strengths, light-weight, middle-weight, and heavy-weight. Again, as long as this is elaborated through practice, there is nothing wrong with techniques which at least try to bring the potentially tedious to life. Pupils should be encouraged to read their own and their friends' work in order to test the rationality of the punctuation marks: 'He's asking something, you have to lift your voice at the end so you'll need a question mark'; 'You've gone on to something different here — what about a new paragraph?' Informal analysis of the way professional writers use punctuation is more useful than wading through the course-

book's examples, which may make sense to the teacher but totally confuse even the competent punctuator. Even the best course books are
open to abuse by the inexperienced or unsure, and it is easy to take
their invitations to pupils to 'Study these rules carefully and practise
them on your own' at face value and leave pupils to do just this,
without careful mediation and annotation by the teacher. For there is
nothing wrong with rules where they make sense but they are best
introduced and reiterated in relation to the pupil's own work, rather than
in a sporadic punctuation blitz. As one English teacher remarked, 'It's
not worth punctuating until you've got something worth punctuating.'

Judging from the request made to innumerable student-teachers on
teaching practice, 'Please could you concentrate on inverted commas',
'They need to revise the use of speech marks', these seem to cause more
problems than any other punctuation marks. There are five basic rules
for their use, beginning with 'Put the words actually spoken inside
inverted commas' to 'Each new speaker needs a new paragraph'. Unfortunately, however carefully these rules are phrased, their terminology will
tend to confuse the issue: 'If direct speech is interrupted by a verb of
saying, the remainder of the statement does not require a capital letter,
e.g. "If you're late", she said, 'we'll both be in trouble" ' It is more
sensible, though admittedly less explicit, to explain that if you wish to
put 'he said, replied, whispered etc.' in the middle of a sentence then it
does not make sense to have two capital letters, since the sense runs
on. But the examples will always be more enlightening than the rules
themselves and they should be made memorable; 'John said, "I'm going
to school now" ' is eminently forgettable; but humorous (though not
libellous) examples, particularly those involving local personalities, are
likely to make more impact. Most course-books state the rules for
punctuating direct speech, give the pupils a few perfunctory examples,
and then ask them to complete the exercise. Those who have always
known how to punctuate direct speech will do very well in the exercise; the majority will use the examples as a temporary template and
then return to their usual mistakes in their next piece of written work.
There is nothing wrong with short exercises used for diagnosis purposes,
as long as the teacher takes the time and trouble to help each pupil
who is having difficulties to see how and why he is going wrong. There
is little point in any case in demoralizing the least able, who have
problems with full stops, by rubbing their noses in inverted commas.
More useful punctuation practice, perhaps a short piece of imaginative
writing, could be used as an alternative.

While asking poor spellers to correct poor spelling will probably confuse them, there is nothing wrong with asking pupils to add punctuation marks to an unpunctuated passage. This assumes that the teacher is prepared to allow discussion and justification since, if nothing else, it should demonstrate the range of options in punctuation and what the alternatives imply about the meaning. Experience suggests that unless we move quickly from rule and example to the pupil's own writing we shall be repeating both *ad nauseam* year in year out. Perhaps it doesn't matter anyway? Punctuation, like spelling, certainly does not matter on all occasions and an obsessive emphasis on either should not be allowed to inhibit content; 'Teachers whose sole standard is correctness can dry up the flow of language and shackle creative and imaginative writing before it is under way.'[7]

The conclusion to be drawn from all this is that spelling and punctuation need to be taught and, according to research, taught systematically. Although research studies and handbooks make logical, if impractical, suggestions, it is inevitably up to the teacher to decide on a system which takes account of the context and the clientele. Great care is needed, because if 'system' is misinterpreted we shall be back to the deadly Monday morning spelling-test and the sequential course of punctuation lessons, culminating nonsensically with inverted commas in the summer term. It should be a system built upon the principles listed at the beginning of the chapter and upon a sense of priority; 'Should I really be teaching a class lesson on this when half the class aren't ready for it?'; 'If I bring attention to the lack of paragraphs will I give the impression that the content is poor?' It will be systematic in stressing the importance of looking at words, breaking them down into phonemes, into syllables, and selecting only the most useful and interesting examples. It will use all the spelling and punctuation aids available, dictionaries, reading books, displays of words and of work, and will allow opportunities for collaboration, discussion and revision. It will always relate the importance of correctness to the nature of the task; informal letter or job application, first draft or publisher's manuscript. Finally it will make sure that there is a good reason for careful spelling and punctuation.

Grammar?

We cannot quite dismiss grammar as casually as the opening paragraph of this chapter suggested, for it seems that while formal functional grammar has disappeared a new and many-headed monster may have taken its place. As the Bullock Report noted, 'In our discussions with teachers it became obvious that the term was often being used to include sentence construction, precis, paragraphing, vocabulary work, punctuation, and more besides.' Here grammar is quite incorrectly equated with 'language work' in general. Her Majesty's Inspectors demonstrated what this can mean at its worst:

A term's programme in English for one fifth year non-examination group . . .

1 Sep.	Phrases and sentences (e.g. 'As cold as ice' is a ————).
3 Sep.	Idioms ('They fought tooth and – to repel the invader').
8 Sep.	Sentences (In spite of his tiredness he could not –). Choice from the list.
8 Sept.	Comprehension.
10 Sep.	Common mistakes. Vocabulary ('New College is at –') ('Dr. Spooner was a – of this college').
15 Sep.	Comprehension.
17 Sep.	Letters (copying a model – painting a house). Proper and common nouns (Plymouth, plumber).
22 Sep.	Letters. Another Model.
24 Sep.	Proper nouns (' – College is the oldest in Oxford').
29 Sep.	Singular and plural (potato, tomato, piano . . .) (One answer – 'potatoes, tomatoes, pianoses . . . ') etc.

Implicit in this programme are a number of false assumptions: that non-examination groups require a functional model of English (sometimes called a 'survival' course in the 'mechanics' of the language) in order to fit them for the world outside school, and that such frills as reading for enjoyment and imaginative writing are inappropriate here; that expertise in the use of English can be built incrementally as one element (pronouns or idioms) is grafted on to its predecessors (adverbs or irregular plurals). This programme also assumes that the pupils are benefiting from such a scrupulous scrutiny of their language. In one sense they probably are, since many pupils (and teachers) enjoy the security that such exercises provide. They are easy to administer and encourage harmless competition and look, at least to the uninformed outsider, as though these pupils are getting somewhere. Unfortunately they probably are not, since there is no evidence to suggest that such exercises actually help to improve pupils' writing elsewhere. The very pupils who brightly suggest, 'Miss, can't we do some of them exercises again?' are also likely to be those who fail to see the connection between these and their own creative writing. Unfortunately, as with all educational bandwagons, there has been a tendency on the part of educational commentators to throw the baby out with the bath water and dismiss all exercises as worthless. Many teachers know better and despite the grim warnings continue to set exercises, though now with qualms and guilty twinges. Are we suggesting that these popular manuals providing a basic course in English should not be allowed into schools? No, only that the warnings of the authors of such books should be heeded: these are no books to be worked through from 'The Phrase' to 'Onomatopoeia', for to do so would be to disregard totally the needs and interests of the individual. An occasional exercise used to focus attention on a common problem, which is immediately explored more meaningfully through imaginative prose or poetry, *is* justified. What is not is the assumption that an exercise done is a principle learnt.

How much does each pupil need to know about his language? Or, to put it another way, does correction of a mistake like 'should of' necessitate reference to grammatical terminology? The answer is inevitably pupil-and-context related; the majority of pupils will only be confused if we introduce the word 'auxiliary' to explain the function of 'have' in 'should have'. Conversely, where words and their uses are explored in an interesting, sometimes humorous way, pupils, irrespective of ability, do remember that 'conjunction' is the best possible description for a word like 'and', and that adverbs often end in 'ly'. There is a certain arrogance in not divulging such adult secrets to those who show an interest in how language works, and what its moving parts are called, particularly when these same pupils display a great deal of knowledge of fishing, riding, stamp-collecting and football terminology. But we must be opportunists, pragmatic rather than dogmatic, ready to exploit the cloze test discussion, or analysis of the poet's style, in order to plant a word and an explanation which will make the pupil's job easier; 'What sort of word will fill that gap?'; 'What do all the words you have just listed for us have in common?'. Knowing that the name of a person, place or thing = noun is a convenient shorthand, an aid, particularly when time and precision are at a premium, as in the A Level Practical Criticism paper. Knowing what a noun, verb, adjective, adverb, pronoun, preposition, conjunction do gives a more able pupil, at least, a feeling of confidence and satisfaction. Many O Level, A Level and undergraduate students bemoan the fact that they were only introduced to the basic parts of speech and most useful literary terms late in their educational careers. If we are going to penalise an examination candidate for writing imprecisely, 'Hughes' use of words to

describe the most important things in this poem is unusual . . . ' then
we are duty bound to teach the parts of speech, however quickly and
informally.

An occasional glance at grammar should not be onerous or tedious.
We can borrow the gap-filling techniques of cloze procedure to show
the relative powers of different parts of speech. Pupils enjoy making a
piece of writing their own by replacing first adjectives, then verbs, then
probably most dramatically, key nouns. We can demonstrate that
English is now a largely uninflected language, where word order is vital
to meaning and understanding, by building sentences like construction
kits:

THE — ADJECTIVE — NOUN — VERB — A — ADJECTIVE — NOUN

DEFINITE ARTICLE — NOUN — ADVERB — VERB — INDEFINITE ARTICLE — NOUN

CONJUNCTION — VERB — POSSESSIVE ARTICLE — NOUN — ADVERB

We can also use a dictionary to demonstrate that a word like 'place'
may function as a noun, verb, and even an adjective, and ask for other
suggestions. We can look at recent headlines to show the versatility of
certain words: 'Radical Front Backs Grounded Wing'. Such 'games'
must be fun, their aim must be simply to familiarise pupils with these
terms and their most important uses. They will not be fun if they
are not apparently incidental to the more important reading, writing or
discussion, nor where pupils are still struggling with simple sentence
formation. They should never be followed by a test; instead the famil-
iarization process will continue if the teacher uses these terms quite
naturally, though amplified at appropriate moments; 'What is the effect
of using all these conjunctions, *and, but, so* and *or* . . . ?' The principle,
as with spelling and punctuation must be: does the pupil need to
know this, am I introducing it in a way which will help him to know
this, and am I giving him useful and interesting practice in using this?

Notes

1. R. Lansdown, 'Children with Spelling Difficulties', in *Child: Care, Health and Development*, (1976), pp. 353-64.

2. *The Teaching of Spelling: A Research Brief for Teachers*, prepared by the Centre for Educational Research and Development (University of Lancaster, 1979) summarizes the most useful findings of recent research into the teaching

of spelling.

3. M. Torbe, *Teaching Spelling* (Ward Lock Educational, 1977). A very useful guide.

4. G. Banks, 'A Broad Approach', *English in Education*, vol. 14 no. 3 (1980).

5. P. Freyberg, 'A Comparison of Two Approaches to the Teaching of Spelling', *British Journal of Educational Psychology*, vol. 3 no. 34 (1964).

6. M. Marland, *Language Across the Curriculum*, (Heinemann, 1977).

7. The Newsom Report, *Half Our Future* (Ministry of Education, HMSO, 1963).

8. *Aspects of Secondary Education in England* (HMI, DES, HMSO, 1979).

8 ENGLISH AND ASSESSMENT

No examination is serving a useful purpose for schools,
candidates, employers or the outside world generally if it
encourages pupils to adopt a form of examination room
English instead of seeking to express appropriately what they
have to say. (The Lockwood Report, 1964)

I wanted to ask the class what they thought of our lessons
— but I didn't dare. (Student teacher)

External Examinations

It is understandable that those seeking standards and support in classroom assessment should turn to the example of the external examinining
boards; the eight GCE and fourteen CSE boards together examine
eighty per cent of pupils and eighty-two per cent of pupils are now
entered for an English examination at sixteen, either CSE language and
literature, or O Level language or literature.[1] O Level language, in
particular, is seen by many pupils, parents and employers as *the* stable
test of literacy and accuracy in an apparently unstable world of slipping
standards and widespread permissiveness. All these examinations are
flawed and fallible and yet they are the terminus for our teaching. We
cannot ignore these realities; but we can hope to build upon their
successes and reject their mistakes.

Despite most English teachers' belief in the indivisibility of English,
the O Level Boards continue to examine language and literature separ-
ately. 'After thirty years many teachers of English in secondary schools
. . . still strongly object to an examination arrangement which suggests
that "English Language" can be treated as the medium in which "English
Literature" happens to have been written, and that the medium has an
existence independent of what is written in it . . . '[2] These objections,
dating from 1967, seem to have fallen on deaf ears, judging from this
typical and current O Level language syllabus:

Paper 1.1½ hours
(a) A composition chosen from a number of topics. The subjects may
be factual, descriptive, imaginative or controversial. Emphasis will be
placed on the orderly arrangement of the subject matter.
(b) An exercise designed to test ability in the more practical aspects

of expression. Emphasis will be placed on lucidity, relevance and precision.

Paper 2.1¾ hours
A summary of a prose passage of 300-350 words. A comprehension test based upon a second prose passage. Questions will be asked on the general content of the passage, and on the meaning of particular words and phrases. Questions may also be set on English usage, for example, on direct and indirect speech, the correct use of parts of speech, and idiomatic and metaphorical expressions. Formal exercises in parsing and analysis will not be set.

Quite distinct from this is literature:

Candidates will be required to answer 5 questions taken from *at least three* of the following 4 sections; not more than 2 questions to be answered from any one section.
Section 1 — Plays
Section 2 — Poetry
Section 3 — Novels
Section 4 — Other Prose. (AEB)

And A Level? Despite recommendations[3] this remains an examination of English literature. The London Board's approach is typical:

Paper 1 (3 hours): Chaucer and Shakespeare.
The paper will consist of a compulsory question on the texts of the prescribed Chaucerian works and of the play by Shakespeare which is to be studied in detail.

Paper 2 (3 hours): Candidates must answer one question on each of 4 books chosen from numbers 1-23 below . . .

Paper 3 (3 hours): Comprehension and Appreciation.
The paper will consist of passages of verse and prose on which questions will be set to test the candidate's ability to elucidate their meaning, and to show appreciation of their literary form and content.

The characteristic pattern begins to emerge: O Level language: essay + summary + comprehension exercise. O Level literature: 3-4 set texts which will almost inevitably include a Shakespeare play. A Level: 2-4 'greats', followed by a selection from the 'not quite so great' and an exercise in critical appreciation. While this is the pattern, some would say rut, that most English departments have adopted, it is not an inevitable one. Things have changed, however slightly, in response to the frustration of English teachers and the boredom of their pupils. GCE boards commonly offer a 'General Syllabus' as an alternative to the 'Selected' O Level literature syllabus. The former requires reading of a greater range and number of texts. The AEB and JMB have taken this one stage further; the AEB offers an O Level English syllabus which includes both language and literature work, spoken English and an extended essay on a subject of the candidate's own choice and a corresponding A Level English language and literature syllabus. The JMB pioneered the O Level English Language, alternative D syllabus (Internal Assessment):

> This alternative is designed for centres which wish to avoid the constraints of an external examination paper in English Language and seek the freedom to draw up their own course of study and to use appropriate criteria for judging their pupils' performance. The assessments are carried out by the teachers themselves on written work that candidates produce as a series of assignments during the final year of the Ordinary level course.

Unfortunately not all the changes have been as far-reaching and enlightened as these: criticisms of the O Level language precis question led to the introduction of the summary. Both are typical of the testing device which is a great help to the examiners since it can be simply set and neatly assessed, but which is a totally meaningless and artificial exercise for the candidates. The replacement of the formal precis by the often equally formal summary has made little difference, since it has failed to relate the selection of material to a realistic context. The move from the conventional comprehension exercise to the more 'reliable' multiple-choice exercise produced as many complaints as it stilled, not least the observation that it failed to discriminate between true comprehension and lucky guesswork, between a skill and a knack. Criticism of one-word essays such as 'Loneliness' or 'Relations' led to ostensibly more interesting requests for personal experiences and opinions, 'If I never had to work again . . . Explain how you would spend your free time.' Although the deadly 'Estimate the value of the education you have received so far and indicate how you plan to extend it.' (AEB)[4] may have disappeared, candidates are still invited to debate,

'To what extend do young people of today have more freedom than their parents?' Teachers have been warning pupils for decades, 'Don't do the "Discuss" ones unless you're really confident. Stick to the ones which invite you to tell a story.' This is not perverse advice, since candidates do seem to cope less well with discursive subjects: 'A further criticism of essay subjects is that whilst much care is evidently taken to ensure a reasonable choice, there is not sufficient recognition of the fact that some are more difficult than others and require a different type of skill . . . '[5]

If O Level is aimed at the top twenty per cent of pupils, the CSE, introduced in 1965, is designed for the top sixty per cent, with grade 1 CSE loosely seen as an equivalent to a pass at O Level. In fact the CSE, as the statistics would suggest is taken by all but the least able ten to twenty per cent. It is ironical that where O Level and CSE are concerned, as so often, the more enlightened approaches are reserved for the less able pupils; while only three O Level syllabuses involve a coursework component, thirteen CSE syllabuses make coursework compulsory and it is optional in five others. All CSE boards include an oral component in their syllabuses; in GCE syllabuses it remains a rare option. There are usually three parts to the CSE examination: course work; written examination (essay, comprehension, informative prose); and oral examination (formal or continuously assessed). Since the examination involves both language and literature one grade is usually awarded for both. Pupils are encouraged to select a variety of writing, some based on set books, some transactional, some imaginative, for presentation in their course work folders. The list of suggested texts is usually long, even with Mode I syllabuses (where the board decides the syllabus and sets the examination papers). The SREB is typical in suggesting (1982 syllabus) sixty or more books, from *Pride and Prejudice* to *Shane*, Robert Louis Stevenson to Leslie Thomas.

How much guidance do these quite disparate approaches provide for the teacher in the classroom? The emphasis on the formal comprehension exercise and summary in the O Level language examination is a cautionary tale; bad enough to assess a general capacity to use language in this way at the end of the fifth year, let alone throughout the five years of compulsory schooling. The CSE's course work folder, although it may only account for a third of the marks, is surely right in acknowledging that the final, formal examination is an unrealistic and unrepresentative indicator of the pupil's ability to use language in a number of ways, and in a number of circumstances. Such examinations examine little but the candidate's ability to write under pressure; their formality is scant guarantee of reliability. Worse, they have an almost inevitable back-wash effect on the teaching in preceding years:

(a)   by setting a premium on the power of merely reproducing other people's ideas and other people's methods of presentment (*sic*), thus diverting energy from the creative process;

(b)   by rewarding evanescent forms of knowledge;

(c)   by favouring a somewhat passive type of mind;

(d)   by giving an unfair advantage to those who, in answering questions on paper, can cleverly make the best use of, perhaps, slender attainments;

(e)   by inducing the pupil, in his preparation for an examination, to aim rather at absorbing information imparted to him by the teacher than at forming an independent judgement upon the subjects in which he receives instruction; and

(f)   by stimulating the competitive (and, at its worst, a mercenary) spirit in the acquisition of knowledge.[6]

Some will see here a remarkably accurate summary of some of the worst excesses involved in teaching towards a traditional O Level literature examination.

Far from looking to the example of the examining boards, those teachers who cannot look forward to the freedom of a Mode III syllabus (school set and assessed) will have to determine their own assessment policy *despite* that implicit in the board syllabuses. They will have to ignore the demands of the traditional O Level English syllabus until the last possible minute, and will need to assess those components that O Level language and A Level literature so obviously omit to: oral language and imaginative writing respectively. The Lockwood Committee[7] came close to recommending the end of O Level language examinations; some English teachers believe that English should not be examined at all. Undeniably, external examinations in English are a fact of life for the foreseeable future, and to abolish them would be to invite even more mediocre replacements, devised piece-meal as 'literacy' tests for work or further education. Teachers can vote with their feet of course, by changing syllabuses or devising Mode III examinations, or by putting pressure on examining boards to devise syllabuses which put the subject and the pupil first rather than convenience or the demands of industry. What this amounts to is a move away from the end of course examination towards continuous assessment and course work. There is a cost of course and it is one which both boards and teachers may not be prepared to pay. The boards may see this as a whittling away of their control and authority, teachers as further extravagant use of their time spent in moderation meetings and extra marking. Undoubtedly, though, a move away from the formal written examination would, and does, remove a great deal of confusion and frustration and provides teachers with invaluable experience and a coherent pattern of assessment.

There is a postscript; in February 1980 the government announced its decision to set up a single grading system for GCE and CSE, to entrust control of standards to the GCE boards and to determine national criteria for marking. A small number of examining boards had anticipated this development by developing joint syllabuses in a limited number of subjects. In response to the Waddell Committee's recommendations (published as *School Examinations 1 and 2*, 1978) a number of schools sought to bring O Level and CSE syllabuses closer together. This proved easier in English than other subjects, but in many schools the split between the two remains only too obvious. It is difficult to predict what the new 'single system' will mean in practice; obviously if it consists of little more than a re-vamped grading system a great opportunity will have been lost.

Internal Examinations

Irrespective of the external examinations, the English department must decide for itself whether tests or examinations are needed at the end of each term or year. Such tests are justified for diagnostic purposes, as examination practice close to the real thing and perhaps for dividing a year-group into examination sets. 'Because we've always done it' or 'Because it's expected of us' is not sufficient justification. Internal examinations are valid only where they are related to predetermined standards. There is no room for half measures since moderation should be scrupulous if the results are to be made known to pupils, other staff, parents, or filed on record cards. Unless all the pupils in a particular class or year have been following the same course (clearly ridiculous where mixed ability groups and English are concerned), standardisation of questions and results will be impossible, in the examining of English anyway. Where English departments use such examinations they are usually of the 'lowest common denominator' O Level variety: essay + comprehension exercise. Where all the pupils sit the same examination predictably the very able do very well and the least able do least well, as we knew they would. There are two options here; confirm the least able in their lack of ability by a scrupulously 'objective' grade E or ten per cent, or tamper with the marks and assess them subjectively in relation to their 'usual' performance. They might then rise to a grade C or fifty per cent. More to the point, at the end of the examination they will probably be no nearer improvement in subsequent examinations than they were before. Apart from this sinking of pupil morale, these examinations are expensive in other ways, notably in time, particularly if the teacher wants to prepare pupils for the experience. Like all examinations they too can have their 'back-wash' effect as the teacher, perhaps unconsciously, begins to practise only those skills demanded by the end of year examination. They are often a waste of time, particularly where the teacher's continuous assessment is contradicted by a 'freak' examination result and the latter is rejected in favour of the usually far more meaningful and complete profile.

Classroom Assessment

We tend to use the terms 'assessment', 'evaluation', 'correction' and 'marking' rather loosely and interchangeably to describe what we do to our pupils, and in particular to their written work. Assessment is concerned with a more generalised, overall view of a pupil and his work. It may be formal; the twice yearly report, a termly record sheet for the head of year or departmental file, the deputy head's sporadic review of 'standards'. The English teacher will be particularly concerned with the pupil's reading, writing, talking and listening abilities, and thus with all the subordinate and associated skills explored in the rest of this book. We shall also be concerned with such general qualities as initiative, tolerance, co-operation, perseverance, conscientiousness and enthusiasm. Assessment will also be informal, everything from the approving grunt to the ironic 'Oh, so you decided to come in to school today . . . ' Here pupils come into their own, they may not have an opportunity to assess staff formally, but even the most docile and apparently passive class will find ways and means of indicating their assessment of their teacher. We are all being assessed all the time.

How pupils are assessed and the result of the assessment will depend on who is assessing, why, when and how, as the following examples suggest:

NAME: Graham Wilkins FORM: 3E

SUBJECT: English DATE: February 1981.

EFFORT C- ACHIEVEMENT: C

Graham is a lively member of the group. He has made some effort to improve the presentation of his work but his accuracy is somewhat erratic. He must learn from past mistakes if he is to succeed in the future exams.

TEACHER: P.W Briggs.

NAME: Graham Wilkins FORM: 3E

SUBJECT: English DATE: February 1981

COMMENTS

Good 'O' Level		
'O' Level		
'O'/C.S.E.		
C.S.E.	✓	
Poor C.S.E./ Non-Exam		

Vivid imagination but careless mistakes spoil most written work. Too happy to submit the minimum. Easily distracted. Likely grade 3 - 4 CSE candidate.

TEACHER: P.W.B.

RECORD CARD

ENGLISH DEPARTMENT

NAME: GRAHAM WILKINS FORM: 1A

DATE: ENGLISH

Quiet and conscientious: fluent reader, eager to please, and has written some interesting and detailed work.

SIGNED: PWB. 2:12:78

11th March 1984

Dear Mr. Jones,

re: Graham Wilkins

I have known Graham for five years and have always found him to be a conscientious and articulate student. I would expect him to do well in the forthcoming exam since his English work is ...

.... It surprises me that Graham finds the lessons boring Mrs Wilkins .. he takes such an active part in lessons ... Yes he has the necessary ability to get a creditable grade at C.S.E. He could work harder but I see no real...

.... It wouldn't surprise me if Graham was involved, he's been hanging around with Tony Hughes and he's been pretty evasive recently .. He's been playing up Mrs B. as well .. That gump seems to have a lot of money to ..

Quite good story, but please check for careless mistakes and write up to the margin.

(B-)

MARK BOOK:
C (careless)

Well yes Graham but that's not really what I had in mind ... perhaps Brian can give us a clearer idea .....

MARK BOOK:
Oral ability : tendency to say the first thing that comes into his head.

One teacher is the assessor throughout, but how do the circumstances of each assessment differ and what effects do these circumstances have on the results? How useful and reliable are these assessments? It is unrealistic to talk of true objectivity and reliability where fallible human beings are involved, though this is not an excuse for a lax approach to assessment. Any form of assessment must help the reader or listener, whether parent, form teacher, or of course pupil, to understand how the pupil can best make progress. It is not just a historical record but is a blue print for the future. Thus we may wonder how helpful the assessment quoted above and delivered at a parents' evening will be to Mrs. Wilkins or her son. Just as we must inquire of any activity in English, 'Why am I asking this pupil to do this?' so when assessing we must ask, 'Will this assessment help this pupil to improve – to learn from past mistakes and build upon past successes?' If the answer is 'no' then the assessment is worthless.

Any classroom assessment does not end with the pupils, the 'receivers'; we must assess our own achievement. This is ritualised in the teaching practice file through the formal 'Lesson Evaluation'. In full-time teaching it is easier to forget our own responsibility for the course of the lesson: 'The trouble is they're dim – they can't appreciate real literature'; 'First thing in the morning I can't get a word out of them . . . ' Assessment, or evaluation here, is inextricably linked with objectives; if our objective is to help pupils to enjoy and understand an example of highly metaphorical poetry then we will focus our attention on the extent to which each pupil has done so. In the course of this we will also evaluate the means we have chosen to achieve this end; was small group discussion the best approach? Did the poem chosen fit the pupils and the circumstances? Were written comprehension questions the best way of reinforcing the discussion? Was a mark out of ten the best response to the written answers? These questions alone should suggest that a rigid assessment policy is unrealistic and inadequate. In the classroom at least it is inappropriate to propose some mythical norm and relate all assessments to it, particularly where notions of originality and creativity are involved. An examination moderation meeting is sufficient evidence for many of the ranges of interpretation of these two terms, and of the inevitable personal bias involved. A rigid policy will fail to take into account the starting point of the pupil; true it will have the stony impartiality of the formal written examination, but it will also have its artificiality and, like the examination, will not help its failures to improve. Some teachers respond to this by relating a pupil and his work to that of others in his class, or year, group, but even here problems can arise, particularly where the assessment is made public:

A	Robert's work is extremely poor. His handwriting is untidy, words are mis-spelt and he cannot form sentences correctly. He seems incapable of learning from his mistakes.

All no doubt true when related to other pupils' achievements and when compared with notions of excellence, but what will Robert and his parents make of this? How will it help him to improve? There is no mention of carelessness or laziness so there appears to be no 'moral' failing in this sense, and yet the final comment seems to lay the blame squarely on Robert. His mistakes have obviously been brought to his attention, probably forcefully and repeatedly. Robert obviously knows something is very wrong but, if this report is typical, he does not know why, nor how to put things right. Given that the teacher obviously intends him to feel guilty, and since there is no indication of a sign of hope, no success to commend, however slight, Robert will probably give up altogether. We can compare this report with two alternatives, both describing the same pupil:

B	Robert has shown that he is capable of producing a range of interesting and detailed written work and has been an active and perceptive contributor to class discussions. He continues to have problems with his spelling but he has made progress and is now taking a greater pride in the general accuracy and presentation of his work.

C	Robert is a friendly and entertaining pupil with plenty to contribute. He should do well if he learns to check his work carefully.

If report A is the result of rigid self-righteousness then C is the result of culpable negligence. If this is typical of the teacher's attitude then Robert is probably being under-stretched and under-stimulated. Robert's parents probaby know that he is generally friendly anyway, and the 'He should do well' is probably fooling no one. He is in the bottom set, and the only hope is that extra attention will help him to make progress in those skills which he finds most difficult, and yet the teacher seems to suggest that proof-reading will cure all his problems. If that was the case he would not, should not, be part of a bottom set. Report B takes a middle path between the two extremes. It recognizes the reality of a situation that all concerned know only too well. Robert does have problems but he is responding to treatment; he is trying and, most important, he has interesting ideas and potential. B relates Robert's achievement to his previous record and does not, like A, compare him with an ideal. Until the exams loom close this is the only sensible way of assessing pupils.

Assessments always give away something of the teacher, not just the surface features, length, accuracy and vocabulary (see Graham's assessments), but something of the relationship between teacher and pupil and the concerns and skills of the former: A's concerns are clear;

honesty whatever the cost. C wants an easy life and probably wants to be liked, whatever the cost. B seems to have encouraged a range of written work, has assessed it initially in terms of ideas and interest, and has encouraged discussion. Behind the report is a teacher who is actively encouraging the pupil, not trying to ignore him or lambast him. But even with B we will require elaboration. No report slip will allow us to say all we would want to and ideally it should be seen as the culmination of a whole series of 'meetings' between teacher and pupil, teacher and tutor, and teacher and parent through written comments, conversations and the occasional note home. It is worth adding here that so often we only contact the form-tutor or parents in order to criticise a pupil's behaviour. Given that parental encouragement and support is vital in determining pupil progress, an approving comment, a congratulatory note, can achieve remarkable results. It is an axiom to English teachers, as to all others, that the parents we really need to meet at parents' evenings never come, in which case the report, duly received and signed, may be the only communication between teacher and parent, and thus we need to ensure that it is both intelligible and informative. We need a rational but flexible approach to assessment which is pupil and context related, which recognises the importance of immediate response wherever possible, which is readily understood by all interested parties, and which recognizes the difference between responding to an idea and assessing it *and* the speaker.

A Policy for Individuals

At its simplest this would mean that we might penalise a bright fourteen-year-old for mis-spelling a difficult word and ignore the same mistake in the work of an under-confident speller of the same age. At its most obvious it would make allowances for illness and family problems, though not to the extent of embarrassing or insulting the pupil by singling him out in this way. For certain, particularly older, pupils peer group approval is far more important than teacher approval; fulsome public praise from the latter may well only embarrass the pupil into avoiding such success in the future. A low-key remark in passing, a written comment, might be more effective. All pupils, but especially the least able, need opportunities to shine, to show off, and we should not only engineer such opportunities but should be seen to be taking them into account in any general assessment. Conversely, pupils need to feel that they can be 'at ease', 'off duty' at times, that they are not constantly being assessed on every possible count. As the Bullock Report recommended, 'If a pupil is progressively to develop control in his handling of language he needs the opportunity to experiment with new forms, and to do so with security'.

It is important that the criteria for assessment and success are made clear before the task is begun: 'I am looking for . . . ' or better still, 'What do you think you should be aiming at . . . ?' For many tasks general instructions will be supplemented by guidelines for the individual: 'Try to vary your vocabulary, as you did last time . . . '; 'Don't worry too much about the length —concentrate on finding the best possible words . . . ' If individual pupils are unaware of the criteria for success then any task will be little more than a stab in the dark, or as one pupil put it, 'He keeps telling us to think before we write anything — trouble is we don't know what to think about'. We will need to reiterate these criteria, if only to explain our marking policy, when work is returned. Take the case of a third year mixed-ability class in the process of compiling a wide selection of work prompted by the theme 'Childhood Revisited'. At any one time different pupils will be writing poetry, responding to reminiscences from literature, drafting their own memoirs, listening to recordings of grandparents' memories and discussing the tensions of the parent-child relationship. Some are working in pairs, some small groups and two or three pupils have chosen to develop their own approach alone. The teacher is circulating slowly, helping, listening, reading, occasionally reprimanding, but all the time observing carefully. For he is assessing the *process* as much as the *product*. He is assessing progress in a number of fields; personal relationships, co-operation, organization of materials and reference skills, use of time available, ability to seek and act on advice, perseverance, discrimination, as well as the more obvious factors associated with the product — originality, accuracy, delivery. This does not of course mean that the teacher will grade each pupil formally on these and record each grade in the mark book, but he will have some idea before the task is begun what he is looking for from each pupil and he will intervene at the first draft stage, where mistakes can be corrected and assessment is constructive and painless. It is one thing to say, 'It's rather boring so far' while there is still time and room for revision, and another to write it on the finished product when there may be no opportunity for suggesting how the pupil might have made it more interesting.

At the end of the week the teacher takes in a wide range of work which has little in common apart from its impetus, 'Childhood Revisited'. How does he assess it? To what extent does he take account of the individual and the process, which resulted in the product? He picks up the first piece of work:

<u>Children should be seen and not heard</u>

I chose to write about this because my Gran used to say it ~~when~~ before she ~~did~~ died. She died in February and then I didn't care but now I can see she wasn't so bad really, at least not as bad as she sounded She used to keep those old-fashioned mints in a little tin she was always going on about independistion and nagging my Dad about his fags. She was a teetotaller. I used to think it meant she only drank tea because that's how her teeth went brown but Uncle Jack said it was why she wouldn't go to the pub She had a little dog called Sandy who barked at anything which moved. My brother Robert used to say that Gran's chin was as hairy as Sandy's and why didn't she shave. Gran had some good points, well one or two, she always gave us a cheque for our birthdays, only trouble was it never went up and we all got exactly the same amount even though I was the eldest. Dad and Gran never got on. I think she liked Uncle Jack best because he had his own business. She was always talking about Uncle Jack's and Aunty Paula's holidays and she once said to Mum, 'You could learn a thing or two from Paula. Her kids are always turned out well.' My Mum was furious. I couldn't imagine her ever having had my Dad though I could imagine her spanking him I think secretly she was frightened of us children perhaps because as we got bigger she seemed to shrink. She hated modern music and modern clothes If she'd had her way Robert and I would have ended up sleeping in the caravan behind the garage ...

The teacher-as-examiner would find a great many faults here. The link between the title and account is tenuous; it is too short to do justice to the subject; there are several spelling and punctuation errors and the vocabulary is rather obvious and infantile. The whole thing is rather rambling and ill-organized and the lack of paragraphs and punctuation gives the impression that it was written without careful thought. An objective assessor would probaby correct the mistakes and add a rather damning comment and grade or mark:

What has this to do with the subject?
Check spelling and punctuation.
Paragraphs?
Try to vary your vocabulary. Far too short — abrupt ending. $^4/_{10}$ C-

This is no doubt a 'fair' assessment when related to the output of the rest of the class or to notions of excellence, but the teacher is here reacting as an examiner, expecting and correcting mistakes, rather than as a reader who cannot disregard the starting point, the process and the individual. Adam, the writer, a quite conscientious but not particularly imaginative pupil, missed the first two sessions and 'borrowed' the title from his partner. The teacher suggested that he should treat it in any way he wished. The two pupils discussed possible interpretations for some time, finally settling on different approaches. When the teacher reminded the class that they had ten minutes in which to finish and check their work Adam started writing. Aware of all this, the teacher corrected inaccuracies almost as scrupulously as the objective assessor, since he felt that they were the result of haste and carelessness, rather than ignorance. He wrote the following comment but deliberately did not grade the work: 'useful class discussion: an interesting first try. Find a more sensible title and take this further in your next homework.' These comments were supplemented by remarks near the beginning of the following lesson. Adam was asked if he understood the teacher's corrections and was asked to suggest improvements.

We could repeat this process many times over, substituting a different pupil on each occasion; if a bright but occasionally lazy pupil had written the account the teacher might well blame himself for not intervening in class, and might simply write 'Please see me' at the bottom. In this case the teacher ensured that there was sufficient time in the following lesson to follow up successes and failure. He deliberately tried to reinforce good practice and tried to 'reward' as many pupils as possible, by asking them to describe how they had arrived at their conclusions, by reading or asking pupils to read out their own work, and by recommending work for display, making the criteria for selection quite clear, whether originality of subject, approach, or effective presentation. Thus all, including the least able, were given a chance to rise above their inaccuracies as their work was read out or rewritten correctly for display.

A Policy for Different Contexts

While the individual and his progress will most directly affect our approach to assessment, *what* we are assessing will also decide the form the assessment takes. Thus we will not assess the informal discussion in the same way as an examination essay. We may be looking for the same essential qualities, but to different extents. How the work is assessed (grade, verbal comment, written comment or reference to a third party) will be decided by the task. The first draft play-script will be assessed by those pupils who are asked to read parts but it will only be truly tested when it is performed in front of an audience. Many teachers feel naturally squeamish about marking poetry, and just as many pupils feel their work is devalued if close attention is not paid to it. A mark out of ten for a very personal and lyrical poem seems rather ludicrous; it would seem more sensible to make our comments explicit, bringing attention to what we like in the poem and why, suggesting where re-writing is necessary.

Certain work, notably drama and talk, is best assessed by its audience through pertinent questions and constructive comments. Any devolution in this sphere is bound to be valuable since, if we can encourage our pupils to devise criteria for assessing each other, we will provide a basis for personal assessment and improvement. The successful pupil is after all one who does not rely on the teacher constantly looking over his shoulder to weed out every mistake. Experiments using pupil assessors have shown what many have long suspected, that if pupils are allowed to use their initiative, and where they can follow the example of an effective teacher-model, the assessments are both shrewd and helpful. Asking pupils to correct and comment on their partner's work is not irresponsible; it is sound common sense in a classroom where the teacher is divided thirty ways. The fact that pupils do not normally wince at every spelling mistake is a positive advantage since, unlike teachers and proof-readers, they will tend to look more closely and fruitfully at the content and meaning of the piece and its effect on a contemporary.

There is one context which, despite our complaints, requires particular attention; the class preparing for an imminent exam, whether O Level of CSE. Here a flexible, pragmatic assessment policy which suspends ideas of the 'norm' in the interests of the individual's progress and morale is out of place. Pupils should be given a clear indication of their progress or lack of it in relation to examination assessment. Comments such as, 'If you maintain this standard you should do very well in the final examination' are out of place in the first three years, and probably the fourth as well, but examination candidates do want and need to pace themselves, and grades should be related to the 'real thing'.

A Policy for Marking and Correction

'Marking' is usually used to describe both the allocation of a mark or grade and the correction of work, although it would be perfectly possible to do one without the other. It is a necessary and time-consuming task, which unless we are careful can quickly become a demoralising and counter-productive treadmill. To take in a set of work from each of six classes once a week, and spend only two minutes on each book, would require a minimum of six hours, or well over a whole school day on marking alone.

It has become fashionable to suggest that since English is an expressive, creative subject that marks and grades are totally inappropriate. Such categorical statements conveniently ignore the reality of teaching in most schools, which are hierarchical institutions to their bones. Schools grade and categorise pupils implicitly and explicitly from the moment they arrive, and, where they are not drawing distinctions, our pupils are busily grading each other in ways which are often more stringent and ruthless than our selfconsciously 'enlightened' ones. The mark that we put at the bottom of a piece of work is more than a fairly random mark; many pupils see it as a sign that the teacher has at least looked at the work long enough to assess it formally. And at best it is an indication of progress or lack of it in relation to previous work. Ideally, if examinations did not exist and if our written comments and verbal assessments were more detailed and scrupulous, we should not need marks or grades. In the meantime the school, pupils and parents expect them and they must be awarded coherently, which means that all three should know what they mean. Marking policies must be discussed at departmental level but more locally, we must explain our approach on first meeting a group, and reinforce this by relating grade to comment when work is returned. Thus C to a first year pupil might mean 'This is just a pass, but you are capable of much better work, any worse than this and work will have to be repeated.' A fifth year CSE pupil might interpret C as 'This is just worthy of inclusion in your final folder . . . potential grade 3'. A single mark placed baldly at the end of a piece of work, without comment, is useless, whether it is an A or an E, since either way the pupil does not know how he has acquired it and thus how to learn from failure or success. Many teachers would suggest that one mark is inadequate anyway, that if we are to come to terms with mixed ability groups, we must award a grade for effort and one for achievement. Even this unfortunately does not solve the problem of differences in ability; what is the less able pupil to make of an A for effort and a D for achievement? It is no answer to object that such pupils should not be graded. If we grade the work of the rest of the class, ignoring the less able is an insult and a blind that deceives no one. We may have to resort to two sets of marks, one of which, the more encouraging, will appear at the end of the work, the other, the more objective, will go into the mark book (though most teachers will hardly need such a formal reminder of the difference between the two). Pupils should have opportunities for questioning their marks; 'Well, I understand your comment but if that's true why did I only get B-?'; 'You gave me A- last week. This one's much longer but I only got B'.

What are we marking, particularly where the story and composition are concerned? Content and accuracy, the what and the how, most obviously, and some teachers reflect this by giving a separate mark to each. These can be subdivided. Content: relevance, range, originality and organisation of ideas and vocabulary. Accuracy: spelling, syntax, punctuation, presentation. Agreeing on 'the what' seldom causes problems, to what *extent* may well. What weight do we give to these attributes when marking work: is spelling inconsequential when compared with the interest and originality of the piece? Is sticking to the title more important than paragraphing? Inevitably we can only find a solution by relating the weighting of marks to the task, and ultimately the individual. Relevance may seem more important in a discursive essay than in a first-person narrative, and careful organisation more important in a formal speech than in an anecdotal account. We can make our 'terms' clear when setting the work and then reflect these in the way marks are apportioned. We will not give a mark for the same reason on every occasion, nor will we strenuously mark or grade every piece of work.

Mistakes are an inevitable accompaniment to learning and yet it is easy to see them as an aberration, as a deliberate attempt by the pupil to insult the teacher. We have all seen work where the teacher has apparently blown a fuse, slashing through whole paragraphs with livid

red lines, obliterating the original with 'Rubbish!', 'Nonsense!' or
worse. Sixth formers may be able to surface after the ducking and learn
from the experience, but younger pupils, particularly those who have
tried, may well go under. The pupil who has made many mistakes will
not learn from them all, all at once, and time pressure alone will mean
that we shall have to select only the most basic and correct these.
'Correction' is an unfortunate term in the same way that 'criticism' is;
both seem to imply that the teacher's business is to delete, deface and
decry rather than to encourage what is promising and commend what is
good. An enthusiastic 'Yes!', 'Good choice of word' or interested
question in the margin may well be more effective than frantic and
confusing swipes of the pen. These 'corrections' can be unintelligible
since the symbols used may have a significance for the teacher alone.
What is the pupil to make of *txfed depided   recommend*
or *plain*? Is a straight line under a phrase a sign of approval, or the
opposite? Does (E) mean 'excellent', or 'poor English'? Does '?' mean
'What does this mean?', Is this true?', I can't read this' or 'This requires
a question mark'? We habitually tell our pupils to cross out the *whole*
word when they have made a mistake and rewrite it above or alongside.
We then break our own rules. Far better than the confusing *their'n*
or *their's* is the legible alternative or explanation in the margin or at
the bottom of the page.

A Policy for Survival

Teaching full-time implies at least six hours of marking a week for
39 weeks in a year. This can be a heavy burden for any teacher, but so
much seems at stake for the English teacher since, 'If we don't set an
example who will?' This is a laudably conscientious attitude but an
impossibly demanding one, for if we mark every piece of work in the
same punctilious fault-finding way our pupils, lesson preparation, social
lives and enthusiasm will suffer. So, in the interests of survival, we will
not continually set long and demanding pieces of written work which
require long and demanding hours of marking. We will vary our demands
and therefore our marking and arrange to take in work to match our
free time, pacing this marking load through the week; one set perhaps
on Monday for marking after school, one set on Tuesday before two
free periods in the afternoon, and so forth. It is only commonsense to
ensure that projects, extended essays and examination marking do not
coincide. But however well-organized we are, illness or domestic
problems may cause a marking jam, in which case honesty is always the

best policy, 'I'm sorry I didn't have the time to read your work carefully, so rather than just ticking it I prefer to take it in again . . . ' Where we see a class on consecutive days the pressure is obviously on to return work immediately. Here loose-leaf folders provide a flexible solution, and an inexpensive one if exercise book paper is used and pupils make or buy their own wallet files. Marking is a sensitive issue for pupils, parents and teachers, but particularly the latter. We feel exposed when our exercise books are inspected by another teacher; we secretly fear the accusing parents' evening question. 'Accountability' should not be a dirty word in teaching circles. If we believe our pupils are accountable for their mistakes we must be accountable for how we respond to them.

Notes

1. B. Bloomfield *et al, Ability and Examinations at 16+* (Macmillan, 1979).
2. J. Petch, *English Language: An Experiment in Assessing*, Second Interim Report (JMB, 1967).
3. Notably Randolph Quirk's proposal, appended to the Lockwood Report.
4. For other, equally dreary, early examples and alternatives see *English Examined: A Survey of 'O 'Level Papers* (NATE, 1965).
5. The Lockwood Report, *The Examining of English Language,* Eighth Report of the SSEC (DES, HMSO, 1964).
6. 'Report of the Consultative Committee on Examinations in Secondary Schools', quoted in B. Hudson (ed.), *Assessment Techniques: An Introduction* (Methuen, 1973).
7. See 5.

9 ENGLISH AND DRAMA

> Drama brought a new kind of thought, talk, writing and atmosphere into the classroom and I was shocked to discover how much initiative and ability I had suppressed for so long. (English teacher)

> Drama is when you learn things by doing them for yourself. (Secondary school pupil)

This chapter cannot hope to explore drama in education, nor even to define the links between English and drama in education in detail. Rather, it hopes to demonstrate that the English teacher with little or no drama training can borrow techniques from the drama specialist in order to illumine the teaching of English. But first some justification and definition is required: why should English and drama be so commonly associated? Why for example are so many drama teachers also teachers of English? Drama and English are often linked because they both obviously have plays in common, although there the association too often ends, since a perfunctory desk-bound play reading has little in common with the dramatic performance which is the true *raison d'être* of the play. In fact the relation goes deeper, for both share a more fundamental concern for language, particularly the spoken word: 'Spoken language develops through social interaction and is one of the prime media of dramatic expression'.[1] Drama provides opportunities for pupils to use a variety of language registers, in a variety of situations and for a variety of purposes. Not least, it provides a realistic context for talk which seeks to debate, deduce, plan and persuade, and thus for the types of language most rarely found in the classroom.

This is not the place for a full-blooded attempt at a definition of drama in education; this can be found elsewhere.[2] Suffice it to say that a concern for language (some would take it further and suggest a concern for life) would inevitably link drama with other curricula subjects, notably the humanities, but drama should not be seen simply as a learning medium for other subjects. Drama in education does not need the prop of its more academic relations. It has its own identity and integrity and is capable, like others, of taking from and contributing to other curriculum areas. But if we are to get closer to this identity we must distinguish between drama and theatre, that is between process and product, activity and performance. Drama in education is not synonymous with the school play, with a self-conscious dressing-up and learning by heart, nor with the academic 'theatre studies' course. All these are aspects of drama in education, part of its continuum, but drama brings to English more valuable gifts, mime, movement and particularly improvisation. Most authorities would agree with John Allen that 'there is no definition of what constitutes an improvisation; it may be a single exercise, done once and forgotten; but it may equally well be an episode that is built up over days and weeks to the formality of a full-length play. Nevertheless, improvisation begins with an idea which is developed and dropped at the will of the participants.'[3] All attempts at definition emphasise the spontaneity of the response to the stimulus, the autonomy invested in the group or partnership, and the responsibility and commitment demanded of each participant to the group and to the idea. Improvisation allows much-needed opportunities for pupils to make relationships with each other, to learn from and about each other. Almost any stimulus can spark improvisation but the association between improvisation and literature is a particularly fruitful one since, as the Bullock Report noted, 'The written word can provide origin and stimulus for improvisation, and improvisation can illuminate the written word'. More specifically drama techniques, and particularly improvisation can

1. Make the easily forgotten memorable.
2. Throw new light on the familiar and clichéd.
3. Cut a path through the unfamiliar or obscure, see improvisation as an approach to the Shakespeare play.
4. Demonstrate communication in its fullest and truest sense through the use of gesture and intonation, mime and movement.
5. Breathe life into tentative or unvocalised ideas.
6. Provide a stimulus for writing.
7. Encourage active and discriminating observation and listening.
8. Allow the less academically-able potential scope for success, which may inspire greater confidence generally.
9. Encourage a more sensitive awareness of the human relationships at the heart of literature, and thus hopefully of life.

For many English teachers the opportunities for drama work are obvious when a class is concentrating on a particular idea, theme or book. The problems are associated with the transition from stimulus to lesson plan, from idea to development. The teacher of drama might, with the greater time at his disposal, choose to follow this theoretical model:

Movement ⟶ Mime ⟶ Improvisation

That is, he might start an inexperienced group on simple movement
work, and move on at an appropriate pace to mime and from there to
improvisation. This transition might take place in a single lesson or over
several weeks. He might combine this with another model:

Individual work ⟶ Pair work ⟶ Group work

where movement and mime are first explored individually, then in pairs
before moving on to group improvisation. The individual lesson might
well begin with an exercise or series of exercises (not necessarily
involving vigorous movement) to relax the class, introduce the theme
of the lesson however superficially, and focus attention on what is to
come. This might be followed by the teacher's introduction, recapitulation and presentation of the stimulus (whether pupils' or teacher's)
and initial whole class, group or pairs' discussion of the idea. The
ensuing practical work would bring a response from the group, whole
class or teacher, sometimes all three, and this evaluation, however
informally expressed, might prompt further refinement of the original
idea or extension or a move to something new.

General introduction and exercise(s)
↓
Introduction of stimulus and class discussion
↓
Initial practical work and response
↓
Refinement / extension / new stimulus
↓
Performance

'Performance' may imply further polishing for the benefit of the
performers and the teacher, but most pupils will feel disappointed if
they are not given an opportunity to show off successful work, however
infrequent these chances may be. Performance means that audience as
well as actors are put to the test. Watching and listening should
encourage discrimination; pupils' evaluation of the work of others
should provide a touchstone by which to measure, and ultimately
improve, their own work.

These are generalised guidelines; most drama teachers use different models for different lessons, different themes and different pupils,[4] but they do at least provide a possible framework (from which to diverge) for the English teacher who rightly wishes to avoid the chaos of the unstructured drama lesson or sequence of lessons. For the drama lesson, perhaps least of all lessons, can not be left to chance. Partly because of its lack of definition and lack of status in the eyes of some pupils, parents and teachers the drama lesson has to be more, not less, structured and disciplined than the conventional academic lesson. Suddenly those pupils who were securely strait-jacketed by their desks and circumscribed classroom territory are let loose in a space which seems, at least where younger pupils are concerned, to invite exaggerated noise and movement. Despite the freedom drama allows pupils to act out their feelings in an honest and uninhibited way, any sort of group work in an undivided space calls for a great deal of tolerance and self-restraint. Pupils have to listen attentively to the teacher and to each other. They have to follow instructions exactly, much like actors in rehearsal. In order to help them to do just this we must define, justify and if necessary illustrate our expectations clearly at the beginning of the first drama lesson: what should pupils do if they arrive at the drama area, whether cleared classroom or hall, before the teacher? Wait quietly outside or change into plimsoles and then sit on the floor? Which are the no-go areas? For example, the stage, chairs or PE equipment. Which signals can the pupils expect the teacher to use? For example, 'Freeze' where pupils must instantaneously but safely freeze in the position in which they find themselves. What are the routine arrangements for performance to the rest of the class? If any performance is to mean anything it must be seen as an important and disciplined occasion which approximates as closely to theatrical performance as is possible on a hall or classroom floor without curtains or wings. Thus imaginary demarcation lines between audience and performers must be drawn and kept to. The performers must know when they are on and when off stage, and when the audience is sufficiently attentive to make the performance worthwhile. A count to three followed by a firm hand-clap is usually enough to alert audience and actors to the imaginary raising of the curtain. It is only when these organisational 'details' have been dealt with, and only if they are reinforced from lesson to lesson, that the real work can begin.

English into Drama: Practical Approaches

There are obvious and immediate stimuli for drama work. The Shakespeare play, in particular, needs the drama lesson if it is ever to be more than an irrelevant and archaic examination obstacle-course for many of our pupils. But I will side step the whole inviting question of Shakespeare and drama work since this has been ably explored elsewhere.[5] I will perhaps surprise some by ignoring the pupil's written play. Younger pupils in particular will be eager to 'do' their own plays and will often have grandiose ideas of stage performance in full costume and, although this may not occur to them immediately, this will require duplicated copies and pupils who care enough to learn their lines. This is one aspect of drama in education, but it is a costly one. It will correspond to many pupils' ideas of 'drama' in terms of the school play and occasional trip to the theatre. It is usually more sensible to distil the idea at the heart of the play and develop this through improvisation, freeing pupils from the tyranny of learning by heart and cues and choreographed movement. For a scripted play is a complex and demanding undertaking since it is only worth doing if it is done well, something which will not be possible in the sporadic drama lesson which this chapter has in mind. It is far better to work well on a smaller canvas where success is realistic and realisable, on the interpretation of an extract or short poem, a moment frozen from the set text, specific and localised approaches to a thematic abstraction such as 'Survival' or 'Conflict' or the examination essay. We might rework a writer's approach using the different medium of drama, Pope's treatment of vanity in 'The Rape of the Lock', Golding's debate from *The Lord of the Flies*, for example, or attempt to understand more about a literary character, by placing him or her in a situation which is not explored by the book, play or poem. Almost any aspect of English work can tilt into drama almost effortlessly. This chapter can only describe a selection of examples which aim to demonstrate how different teachers working in different contexts have used the drama lesson to develop understanding of their chosen stimuli:

The Extract

Context: This medium-sized class of quite able fifth year students have been reading and writing dialogues. They have looked at examples of irreverent conversations from the plays of Plautus, at Shakespearian repartee and the absurd dialogues of Ionesco and N.F. Simpson. They have also listened to examples from record and radio. Using this prelim-

inary exploration as a stimulus the teacher at first gave pupils a free
choice in writing their own extended dialogues but soon realized that
such a wide choice was disconcerting and was likely to produce rather
facile responses. The task became more challenging, but paradoxically
more tractable, when the choice was limited to a situation in which
two people find themselves in an enclosed space; while they may be
quite content with their surroundings neither is happy with his or her
companion. The teacher and class first tried to stretch this framework
to its limits: what sort of enclosed space? A prison cell, sauna, space
craft flight-deck, diving bell, lift, kidnapper's cellar, television news
studio, doctor's consulting room, bank vault, tomb, waiting-room for
Miss World finalists, whale's stomach. Into these spaces they imagined
the characters, at first conventionally; the graverobbers in the tomb, or
thieves locked into the bank vault by the security guard, but then
(and herein lies the essence of the dramatic event or the successful news
story) they introduced the unexpected. The unusual space stowaway
who appears on the flight-deck, Jonah who has settled happily in the
whale's stomach, entertains a twentieth-century 'visitor', the patient
who comes to treat the doctor. The students planned and described
their ideas in rough but before these were developed in full the teacher
promised the class an opportunity to explore and interpret an example
of dialogue in some detail. She deliberately did not mention 'drama' or
acting since she did not want to raise false assumptions in a group
which last had drama lessons in the first year. The lesson was planned to
take place in a large classroom, with the desks moved to the back,
leaving the chairs placed around the sides of the classroom. This was
considered less inhibiting than the echoing space of the school hall.

Teacher's Objectives:

1. To put students in a position where they will have to use their
   voices to full effect.
2. To make the point that the words on the page are only the first
   step towards meaning, that behind them and between them lie
   other, sometimes more humorous, sometimes more sinister
   meanings.
3. To put the students in the actor's position of having to entertain and maintain the momentum through their interpretation of
   the text.
4. To encourage a more discriminating concern for the construction of dialogue, for making each word count.
5. To ease a rather inhibited 'academic' group into improvisation

from a safe literary base.

The Lesson: The students are asked to sit in pairs on the chairs, at
a slight angle to each other. They are given the extract, in this case
from Pinter's *The Dumb Waiter* and are asked to read it silently,
in order to try to decide what appears to be happening. The entire
extract, which begins with Ben's instructions to Gus, and ends
with Gus's impassioned series of questions, is divided into two parts
by the teacher and printed in such a way that any one part can be
conveniently isolated for particular attention. The teacher invites
answers to the introductory question, and accepts any suggestion
that takes into account the key clues. Without further preamble
students are asked to read the first section aloud, each taking a
part.

The teacher asks, 'From what you have just read what do we know
about the two men, and in particular what do we know about the
relationship between them?' This produces the suggestion that Ben
seems to be the dominant partner, and teacher and class then seek for
the corroborative evidence and the most appropriate adjectives to
describe the two characters as they appear in this section. The students
return to read the first section so as to reflect their interpretations of
the roles and personalities of the characters; generally this means a
rather tense, quiet voice for Gus and a louder and more assertive voice
for Ben. The teacher and class listen to the interpretation of one pair
and the teacher asks, 'Would it be possible to read this differently while
still making sense of the situation?' One student suggests reversing the
voices, using a generally loud, belligerent voice for Gus and a hushed
and cautious whisper for Ben. Another suggests giving Gus an
intelligent sounding voice and Ben a far less intelligent one. Different
pairs try different interpretations and discuss their impressions. A
representative selection is heard. The teacher asks, 'What effect do these
different readings have on our interpretation of the relationship?'

The students are asked to pick out the parts which they find most
difficult to read. Most select the most repetitious speeches, particularly:

Ben: He won't know you're there.
Gus: He won't know you're there.
Ben: He won't know *you're* there.
Gus: He won't know I'm there.

The teacher uses this example as an excuse for an experiment in varying intonation, tone and emphasis. Each pair is asked to say the quartet of lines in a monotone, then as automatically as a robot might. The class then suggest all the many alternative 'tones' which could be used; sarcastic, wistful, angry, weary, absent-minded, uneasy, impatient. They add to these, variations in volume; a conspiratorial whisper, a nervous whisper, a frustrated shout, a triumphant shout, and mark with a pencil the interpretation they have chosen for each line. The teacher and students then return to the lines to select any words for particular emphasis, beginning with the obvious example in the third line. They enjoy stressing different words in turn in order to gauge the effect. Each pair agrees on a final interpretation and a number perform this for the rest of the class.

The class uncovers the next section, beginning with Gus's observation, 'You've missed something out' and ending with his exit. The students are asked to look particularly at the speed at which these lines should be said and to decide on and justify the length of pauses between lines and between words. Each pair tries out its interpretation aloud. The whole extract is approached by pairs of pupils who combine to make several foursomes, where each couple acts as audience and commentator in turn to the other. In order to define the task more clearly the teacher acts as discriminating audience to one pair, asking them to describe their interpretation of the characters before beginning, and relating this to the finished performance.

Development: Here the lesson ends but the teacher can see many possibilities for development. The teacher as theatre director might ask the students/actors to work on two different scenarios, half the class working on the first and half on the second. In the first Gus is seen as weak and mentally dull while Ben is more ruthless, single-minded and intelligent. Both are repellent. The second sees Gus as the one-time senior partner whose conscience and scruples are beginning to show. He is now considered weak by Ben who is incapable of seeing the alternatives. Thus Gus is seen as the more sympathetic victim trapped by his past sins and his brutal partner. Alternatively more attention might be paid to plotting the movements of the characters, particularly if the script is discarded and the students improvise on a situation which they now know well. In this case the teacher sent the students back to their own planned dialogues and asked them to complete their scripts and then, working in their original pairs, to assess them for performance, improving and modifying if necessary as a playwright and director might. All this was intended as preparation for the next drama lesson which would be devoted to the interpretation of pupils' own scripts and improvisation based upon these dialogues.

The Theme

Context: A number of this mixed-ability second year group have been, coincidentally, reading books or stories based upon street life. This has prompted animated description of the characters, sometimes eccentrics, to be found in the pupils' own streets. The teacher is eager to tap this interest but feels that a great opportunity will be lost if pupils make a premature and accelerated move from discussion to writing. Drama seems to provide the obvious medium for discovery and clarification and the teacher books the hall for two fifty-minute periods at the beginning of the week.

Teacher's Objectives: To explore the make-up of a particular fictional street, its relationships and tensions; to provide a prelude to written work by encouraging discussion and role play; to encourage pupils to bring their own experiences to the fore-front of discussion, in order to exploit them creatively and constructively.

Lesson 1: introductory exercises. These are intended as a painless and enjoyable way into the theme and as an introduction to possible personalities in the street. Pupils are asked to plan and imagine carefully before launching into any movement but the teacher feels that stereotypes are inevitable and are not to be condemned at this stage. He is more concerned with the concentration and commitment that is demonstrated. Pupils are asked to mime appropriate movements for the following: the postman on his rounds; a boy or girl being taken for a walk by the dog; running for the bus having over-slept; a businessman on his way through the railway station; an old person attempting to cross the road; and suggestions from the class. The teacher draws the pupils together in a large group at his feet. He tells them that the street will have a fictional name, which the class will select at the end of the lesson, but will be based on real streets in their own town. He tells the class that the street can be as long as they like and then asks, 'What buildings shall we have in our street?' Pupils suggest a long list of different types of homes, shops, public amenities and institutions. The teacher then asks, 'But who shall we have in our street?' This again produces a long list which becomes more interesting as pupils are forced to move from types to distinct individuals. The teacher informs the class that for this lesson they will become one special personality.

The boys are sent to collect a blue card, and the girls a red card from the stage, where they are laid out face down. Pupils pair off in order to read their cards to their partners, discuss their identities and prepare answers to the questions at the bottom:

> Name: Malcolm 'Muscles' Springer
> Age: 22
> You work as a nightwatchman for a large firm but your great interest is building up your muscles (even though your girlfriend Sandra says she likes you as you are).
> *But*: Tell us about your family and where you live, and about your hobby and why it appeals to you.
> Do you have any other interests? Do you ever feel lonely or frightened at work? How do you see your future?

The teacher picks up a spare card and illustrates how each pupil might prepare a first-person introduction to the character, initially for his partner but ultimately for the rest of the class. Pupils are encouraged to suggest interesting and relevant information and approaches to this 'filling out' of each character. They are warned to be prepared to answer requests for further information from their audience.

The teacher circulates, encouraging pupils and occasionally planting a question to aid the process of revelation. The planning session is guillotined. Pupils are asked to rehearse their informal monologues to each other. The teacher selects a few examples for presentation to the rest of the class. He is supportive and sympathetic and reinforces the point that these are not formal speeches but informal introductions. The audience is encouraged to pose supplementary questions: 'You said that you don't get on well with your Gran. Have you always felt like that about her, or is it only since she moved in with you?'; 'What do you think you'll do if the factory closes and you're made redundant?' The teacher asks the class to suggest how these introductions could be generally improved, and pupils return to work on vocabulary and tone, in particular.

These roles are tried out in simple situations, as the partners meet in the street, or at the bus stop, or in the post office or fish-and-chip shop. The pupils gather so that the teacher can take them forward to the next English lesson where they will be asked to prepare their own role play cards and develop their introductory monologues on paper. These will form the first contribution to the 'My Street' folder. It is clear that many pupils have already fixed enthusiastically on their role and will want to elaborate on these at the earliest possible opportunity. It will be the teacher's task to channel this enthusiasm and ensure a range of personalities.

Lesson 2: introductory exercises. 'Down our Street'. This starts as an exercise in careful mime and ends as an energetic game as the movements are speeded up. The teacher, in role, introduces the class to four residents from the street; Mrs. Maisie Birt, a cleaner, Miss Anthea Higgins, a keep-fit instructress, Johnny Mullins, a school-boy who is currently playing conkers, and Eddy Tomkins, a council gardener. As the teacher calls these characters' names pupils are asked to perform appropriate movements as realistically as possible.

'The Knock at the Door': using their own role cards pupils are paired. A will keep his card identity, B will assume a new one. A will answer the door, a carefully defined door, to an unexpected visitor on the doorstep who will surprise or shock A. Possibilities are discussed before pupils move to their work areas. A and B discuss and develop the scene and then change places, and as before the visitor's identity is concealed from his partner until it is revealed in the scene itself. A few examples are seen by the class and again the audience is invited to commend and to criticise constructively.

This idea is extended. The teacher asks, 'What other doors might we open in our street, in order to see what happens next?' Pupils suggest the doors of the doctor's consulting room, the police-station cell, the corner shop, the parrot's cage, the cellar, the mysteriously locked room, the attic and the burglar who is breaking in. Pupils return in fours to work on their chosen door in any way they wish. In some cases this involves a narrator who provides a running commentary for the action, which is mimed or acted out with minimal vocalisation by the rest. Other groups improvise a series of short scenes in which the door plays a leading part. One group shows how a single door can be seen and treated differently by different individuals.

Developments: the teacher asks pupils to suggest where they might take their drama work from here and specifically what other scenes from street life they would like to explore in future sessions. The class suggests a long list which includes: the street party; noisy neighbours; the the water off; the day the Queen drove by; market day; th customer; the accident; locked out; moving house; the hav unexpected arrival; the election; and the fair. The teacher feels that the improvisations could ultimately contribute to a play on the lines of Thornton's Wilder's *Our Town* where the street's identity is seen as being the sum of its parts and a little bit more, and where, at a more sophisticated level, characters are seen to show different facets of their personalities in different contexts. Alternatively, or concurrently, pupils might return to their English lessons to exploit some of the incidents and relationships revealed through drama in scripted plays, poetry, prose, newspaper reports, or tapes.

The Text

Context: This group of twenty fourth-year pupils are half way through their reading of the novel *Billy Liar*. While the class still appear interested, the momentum is flagging and the novelty of the subject and its narrator is long gone. Earlier in the year the pupils explored 'Interviews' through role play and many have expressed their eagerness to 'do some more drama, Miss'. The teacher is aware that not all the class are equally keen; there is a group of retiring and conscientious girls who are quietly horrified at the idea of having to move from their chairs to do anything remotely physical, particularly anything associated with the endearing but boisterous lads from the back row. The teacher's relationship with the class is a good one, but she is aware of the need for care and tact if any approach to drama is not to jeopardise this hard-won co-operation and respect. The first lesson after lunch has been earmarked for this 'drama' session and the desks have been pushed to the back of the large classroom.

Teacher's Objectives: To breathe new life into the class's reading of the book; to make central characters and incidents memorable and to fire discussion of the issues raised, however humorously, by the book.

The Lesson: The teacher has already made a provisional list of the scenes from or associated with the book, which lend themselves to improvisation and which should help pupils to understand the characters and their own attitude to them a little more. Pupils are asked, in groups of four or five, to choose from these options:

1. Apply your brand of Number 1 thinking to your future career, or to your family.
2. Look ahead ten years. Imagine what married life would be like for Billy and the Witch. Bear in mind a) their personalities as you

have seen them so far; b) their family background; c) their probable financial position; d) their surroundings; e) their career and family aspirations, the Witch's desire to start a family etc.
3. Judging from what you have learned of the characters concerned imagine the scene if Billy brought the Witch home for tea and declared that he was going to marry her.
4. Choose any one incident from the book that you think would make a promising scene for dramatic interpretation, and discuss your choice with the teacher.

The teacher realizes that it is unfair to ask an inexperienced group to turn on improvisation with little more than a list of options for stimulus. Each group's approach will have to be structured more carefully, to take into account the abilities and inhibitions of individuals, if the work is to be sufficiently rewarding to justify the session in the eyes of teacher and pupils. The teacher first considers the most potentially intractable problem, five girls who are happy to write and imagine but are frightened by the slightest thought of performance. The teacher is prepared to be prescriptive here in order to relieve these girls of the initial decisions. She asks them to re-read certain pages which focus on the relationship between Billy and his family and to use these as a basis for the third option. As an alternative to spontaneous improvisation the teacher suggests a compromise where each pupil contributes individually to a whole; the group discuss the likely course of events at the tea party and then choose a role (Billy, the Witch, Gran, Father or Mother) and describe their own part in what happens, as a preparation for a first-person account which aims to show how self-interest colours the perception of the occasion. The group are allowed paper and pens only when it is clear that group discussion has disentangled their individual contributions, and the teacher intervenes to suggest appropriate styles of narration for each character. The girls seems to react well to the realization that their approach is unique, and do not demur when the teacher suggests that the finished accounts are good enough to be taped or performed.

While most of the class are happy to plan and discuss with minimal interference from the teacher, one other group need particular attention: the lads from the back immediately settle to the first option but are content to blunder in without sufficient thought. The teacher tries to discipline their approach by returning them to the text in order to define the distinction between Number 1 and Number 2 thinking, hoping that in the process they will realize that Number 1 thinking has much in common with the often glamorous image presented by advertising. The group chooses which of their number will play the central part and choose to focus on his future career, since he hopes to work in a bank. Having decided that the scene will begin with the reality and routine of the bank cashier's day, they gather and pool information about working in a bank and then plot the stages in the cashier's meteoric rise to the top, a knighthood and a royal marriage.

Although the classroom has been cleared for drama the teacher is quite happy to allow the whole of the forty-minute lesson to be taken up with discussion, as long as progress is being made and each pupil is given scope for contribution. There is no question, as perhaps with a younger and less inhibited class, of moving all the groups from discussion to improvisation simultaneously, although all the groups do make the move before the end of the lesson. The more extrovert groups are eager to show their work, and one example is seen, since the teacher feels that it is good enough to set a high standard and earn praise from the audience, and thus develop confidence in the group and class. The teacher encourages each of the characters to speak in role about their feelings for each other after the performance and asks the group to explain, out of role, how they have come to their interpretations and conclusions. Since other groups are eager to extend or polish their work, the teacher sets aside the next lesson for this, and suggests that they may wish to make a record, whether taped, narrative account or final script of their work, as the homework assignment for the week.

'Parts of Speech'

Context: This teacher of first-year mixed-ability pupils does not believe in formal grammar lessons but does feel that pupils can gain from and take some pride in identifying the functions of certain words. He feels that drama can introduce grammar in a fascinating and memorable way.

Teacher's Objectives: To introduce the functions of the more important parts of speech; to correct an overdependence on hackneyed adjectives and a reluctance to use a series of 'joining words' (not always strictly conjunctions) in order to avoid a staccato style.

The Lesson: The class sit in one circle. They are told that they are going to build a story but, unusually, rather than being a series of jerky sentences, it will consist of one single enormous sentence. Pupils are asked to suggest how this might be done; 'Joining words like "and",' says one. This provides the starting point for the exercise, and the teacher begins the story thus: 'Many years ago a rather frightening old man lived in his ruined mansion on the outskirts of this town *and* . . . ' Each pupil then adds to the story, passing it on to his neighbour with the final conjunction. When the story is complete the teacher sums up the extraordinary goings-on and then begins a new story which proceeds in the opposite direction. This time the task is elaborated and complicated since a series of joining words (and, but, then and so) must be used in turn. The teacher asks the pupils to provide the résumé this time and asks whether the inclusion of more joining words made any difference to the final product and the difficulty of the task.

The class splits into four smaller circles and repeats the procedure. They are then asked to recount what happened in any one story to the rest of the class. The teacher draws attention to the variety of plots, a variety often lacking in their written work. One pupil rightly makes the point that on occasions the stories became contradictory. This prompts further discussion. The teacher introduces the next part of the lesson as 'Charades, with a difference'. He has prepared piles of coloured cards which are laid face downwards on a table: Nouns, Verbs, and Adjectives. Each pupil in turn, from each of the four groups, collects a noun card, which might be labelled thus: 'NOUN (Common): centipede.' Pupils are asked not to disclose their cards to their neighbours but to describe the function of the noun with the help of the example before them. Each group then forms a semi-circular audience as each pupil acts out his or her noun. The teacher emphasises the importance of careful mime and attention to detail, since the aim is not to bemuse the audience unnecessarily. He stops the whole class on occasions in order to bring a particularly intriguing mime to their attention. The class quickly move on to the adjective cards, which are divided into an easy batch: tall, small, greedy, angry, miserable, tired, restless, itchy, and a more difficult batch: vain, arrogant, lonely, energetic, clever, bored, naughty, glamorous. Pupils are allowed to collaborate in pairs in a single mime for the latter if they wish. This procedure is repeated for the verb cards, the easy: run, cycle, eat, scratch, nudge, wriggle, fight, kick, steal, and the more difficult: wander, wonder, inquire, try, hesitate, submit.

The teacher draws a halt to the mimes in order to draw some conclusions; what is a noun? What is the difference between a common and a proper noun? Is it important to know the difference? What job do adjectives do? Who needs ajdectives? Why should a sentence need a verb in it? Finally each group is given three adverb cards. The whole group will plan a group mime for each. (The teacher will later use music in order to reflect the mood and the mime). A number of these mimes are performed to the rest of the class. The teacher compliments the performers on the quality of their mimes and the audience on the quality of their suggestions. He makes the point that many of the suggestions could well have been right: *proudly* and *arrogantly* for *haughty*, for example. This introduces the idea of 'synonyms' and 'antonyms' but the teacher is content to introduce the idea only on this occasion, since the terms can wait until a more appropriate occasion. As a 'test' that some learning has taken place among the atmosphere of competition and fun, the teacher asks each of the four original groups to prepare four sets of coloured cards for their own use or for use by other classes. Each pupil is provided with four appropriately coloured cards which are labelled noun, adjective, verb and adverb. They are asked to insert their suggestions in pencil initially so that it can be checked by the teacher as he moves around the groups. Pupils are encouraged to arrive at their selection with the help of the rest of the group, so that an interesting selection is arrived at which does not duplicate the teacher's original cards. Final selections are printed neatly and attractively in coloured felt-tip pen, and are displayed until they are next needed, on the classroom display board.

Developments: The teacher hopes to pick up the first exercise in order to explore other story-telling techniques in drama, but particularly stories which lend themselves to improvisation. He wishes to challenge pupils' abilities to make a story and a plot from an unlikely starting point, whether the opening sentence ' "Matilda, it's high time you learned to wiffle lugbits yourself," said Samuel.' or 'Harry had always wanted to meet a real live humanoid . . . '; or from the coming-together of unlikely ingredients: Grandpa, the tin of polish and the meter man; St. Peter, the train robber and the picnic hamper. He wants to demonstrate that starting points, even the most apparently limiting, can lead in an infinite number of directions.

There is not the space to describe possible dramatic approaches to the narrative poem, melodramatic plot, formal O Level language essay or traditional mummers' play and many more, but these examples should indicate something of the variety of approach and cross-pollination which is possible when English and drama join forces. None of the lessons described is particularly ambitious; none uses music, lighting, costume or make-up in order to achieve its objectives, although they well might. Not one goes far from the written word. All this is quite deliberate for all these lessons were taught by able teachers of English who, with their classes, were finding their feet in drama. In many cases pupils were renewing a relationship with a subject which had lapsed from their timetable some time before. All these teachers would agree that the effort involved, in lesson preparation and organisation, in locating a suitable space, in making every precious minute count, was well worth while in the interests of the redefinition and rejuvenation of 'English'.

Notes

1. L. McGregor *et al, Learning Through Drama,* Schools Council Drama Teaching Project (10-16) (Heinemann, 1977).
2. See 1, and G. Bolton, *Towards a Theory of Drama in Education* (Longman, 1979); J. Allen, *Drama in Schools: Its Theory and Practice*, (Heinemann, 1979); N. Dodd and W. Hickson (eds), *Drama and Theatre in Education* (Heinemann, 1971).
3. See 2.
4. See, for example, C. O'Neill *et al, Drama Guidelines* (Heinemann, 1976).
5. D. Adland, *The Group Approach to Shakespeare* (Longman, 1973); R. Adams and G. Gould, *Into Shakespeare* (Ward Lock Educational, 1977).

10 FINDING A BALANCE

> Language competence grows incrementally, through an
> interaction of writing, talk, reading and experience, and the
> best teaching deliberately influences the nature and quality of
> this growth. (The Bullock Report)

Despite concern over standards, the 'back to basics' lobby, regular
inspectorate surveys, expenditure cuts and examination demands,
teachers of English remain remarkably free to decide what is taught in
English lessons. Given over-pressed advisory staff lacking financial
muscle and busy heads of department, those most concerned with
monitoring teaching standards and content have few opportunities for
inspecting, let alone modifying, what goes on in classrooms from day
to day and hour to hour. Helping the underconfident teacher to
improve is often difficult, sacking the intransigent and incompetent
teacher often proves impossible. The freedom to blunder on, oblivious
to failure, is obviously deplorable; conversely freedom is valuable where
it enables a department or teacher to respond to the needs of pupils
in a particular context. Very few teachers of English would care to see
their aims imposed and resources decided by a centralised bureaucracy,
concerned with uniformity of syllabus and synchronization rather than
with local needs and expertise. But freedom is also disconcerting, if only
because he who makes the decisions must also carry the can. If the
price of freedom is accountability and responsbility then we will need to
become more self-critical and self-evaluating. If we have good reason for
doing what we do then as 'experts' we should have little to fear. We
need to think carefully and plan carefully: 'I am teaching in this way
because these strategies help to fulfil my objectives' rather than 'I am
teaching this way because that's how it worked out'.

Aims and objectives are vital preliminaries but they are also rarified
beings, insubstantial without a plan of campaign which will see them
put into effect. Unfortunately planning a series of English lessons can
be problematic just because English is neither a linear subject, nor one
which lays claim to a circumscribed body of knowledge. There are so
many possible starting points. Schools Council Working Paper 62[1]
rightly emphasised the importance of synthesis, of what it described as
'ways of weaving the elements of "English" into a continuous sequence
of lessons': 'We see the task as one of . . . helping the ordinary teacher

to plan a sequence of work'. Scarcely any English teacher would disagree with the Bullock Report's famous declaration, quoted at the beginning of this chapter. Who can doubt that the ability to use and understand language is a product of the interaction, of the synthesis, of writing, talking, reading and experience. Clearly we must find a balance between these four in any sequence of lessons, but the Bullock Report's statement is too broad to provide an immediate and practical framework for planning. We can identify the 'elements' which should be included, but in what order and in what proportions, and what might this mean in practice? It is not simply a question of balancing writing, talking, reading and experience. We must be sensitive to the balance between teacher and pupil talk, open and closed questions, teacher and pupil initiated activities, reading simply for pleasure and for information, functional and imaginative writing, first person and third person. We can only hope to maintain this series of balances with the help of a definite plan. Half the battle with planning ahead, as with taking any major decision, is identifying the options and their likely consequences. How might we approach the teaching of a series, whether week, month, half-term or term of English lessons?

Options

1. Separate English lessons whose content is decided by any of a number of factors; perception of pupils' needs, resources available, teacher's mood and interests.
2. Separate designated English lessons; basic skills on Monday, creative writing on Tuesday, reading and comprehension on Wednesday, discussion and debate on Thursday, pupil-initiated inquiry on Friday.
3. A scheme based upon the individual needs and interests of the pupil and not controlled by a specific theme or text.
4. A scheme based upon a governing theme, e.g. Adventure, Advertising, Narrative Verse.
5. A scheme based upon a literary focal point, usually a set book, but conceivably a poem or short story.

All these options work, in the sense that a gifted teacher will make the best possible use of each, just because good teaching will transcend the limitations of most schemes. Unfortunately few of us are gifted in this sense; we are the ordinary teachers of the Schools Council description who need to be alerted to the dangers of certain of these schemes.

Perhaps only the gifted teacher can really cope with the looseness of the first option and can find the right sort of balance almost
instinctively and spontaneously. Few of us really make a success of a
lesson where we arrive unaware of what will happen, content to hang
on to a general aim and to take our clues from the pupils' apparent
desires, the resources available or the whim of the moment. In the best
of all possible worlds we should be able to ask all our pupils, 'What do
you really want to do today?' and receive sensible suggestions, and the
appropriate resources. In the meantime our pupils will look to us for
direction. Indeed many classes will gleefully devour the inexperienced
teacher who arrives apparently unaware of the shape of the lesson and
its relationship to past and future work. Most of us need a structure
from which to diverge in the interests of flexibility. Without the structure 'flexibility' looks suspiciously like naivety and incompetence.

The second option at least guarantees that most of the elements are
represented, but far from encouraging a fruitful interaction it tends to
force them apart. Although the intention may not be simply to do
spelling and punctuation exercises in the 'Basic Skills' session, it is
dangerously tempting to concentrate on these since they are easy to
prepare and mark. This option may give the impression that English is
merely a rag-bag of disparate skills which never actually meet. It has all
the disadvantages and advantages, of any routine. Its supporters would
claim that at least 'We all know where we are', but the lessons may also
become boringly predictable, particularly if the sensible-sounding
lesson headings are reduced to exercises on Monday, stories on
Tuesday, written comprehension on Wednesday, teacher-dominated
question and answer on Thursday and copying from books on Friday.
It runs the risk of sacrificing the pupils' needs and interests to the
scheme, of actively discouraging protracted work born of an individual's
enthusiasm and spanning several lessons, because it breaks the 'rules'.

In contrast, the third option places the pupil squarely at the heart of
the course. It ideally demands materials and assignments to suit the
individual. Almost inevitably this implies a dependence on the worksheet or workbook and perhaps programmed learning via tape or film.
The individual's relationship with his material will shift the teacher's
role off-centre. No longer will pupils look to the teacher simultaneously
for guidance, instead the teacher will become a guide on a one-to-one
basis for much of the time. In its purest sense this scheme is rare for
obvious reasons. It makes enormous demands on the teacher who is
responsible for producing and monitoring a large number of individual

learning programmes. Since it sees the pupil, often valuably, as the unit, rather than the class or group, it can destroy social cohesion as pupils follow their own paths. There may be a guaranteed interaction between writing and reading but other valuable forms of interaction, between personalities and abilities, may be jeopardised.

The fourth and fifth options deserve particular attention because of their popularity and because of the combination of latitude and structure that they provide for teacher and class:

Teaching by Theme

This is a popular and convenient approach, in part because course books often organise materials thematically and thus save teachers some of the searching for appropriate stimuli. The theme at its best achieves a balance between the looseness and rigidity of options one and two, providing a sense of purpose, a circumference, and yet allowing a variety of interpretations of and responses to the subject. When deciding upon a theme there are several criteria for selection:

1. Will this theme provide a suitable vehicle for achieving my aims and objectives?
2. Is it likely to stimulate and interest as many pupils as possible? Am I interested in it?
3. Is it neither so broad as to be meaningless, e.g. 'Mankind', nor so narrow as to be unnecessarily limiting, e.g. 'Dragons'?
4. Can I, and my pupils, compile a selection of resource materials which will not involve the department in undue expense?
5. Does this theme have a particular significance for pupils in this locality, e.g. A Village Year, The Sea, City Days?

Some would say that where themes are concerned it is not what we do but the way that we do it. This is true up to a point though there are some themes that invite problems. I would never use 'Death' as a theme, although I would not go out of my way to squash discussion in other contexts. 'War' is likely to alienate the girls, while 'Conflict' with its broader connotation allows pupils to select issues of particular and personal interest. While 'Love' might seem an obvious theme for older pupils, it requires careful handling if it is not to develop into a single-tracked look at only one aspect of the theme. 'Advertising' and 'The Press' have become favourite themes for older pupils but it is easy to stumble into them in an indiscriminate way, without structuring lessons carefully, so all that pupils have to show for several weeks' work is a shoddy newspaper of their own and a collection of hastily-pasted colour-supplement advertisements. If we really wish our pupils to understand how the press and advertising work, and to respond intelligently to their messages, we should take them to a newspaper office or advertising agency or invite representatives into the classroom to discuss their work. We should start with these agencies as they are, rather than producing feeble imitations for no apparent reason, and they should be seen as commercial enterprises out to attract and capture their audiences. Once this point has been grasped the evidence is in the newspapers and advertisements themselves, and the more pupils discuss and analyse, compare and criticise the better.

A scrupulous regard for aims and objectives is necessary if theme and pupils are not to be subjugated to the teacher's convenience; 'We've got a lot of material for "The Generation Gap" so I thought we'd do that', where the materials may well be mediocre or quite unsuited to the class. The teacher's personal enthusiasm for theme or materials may blind him to the boredom of the class; 'I don't know what's wrong with you 4S — I've always found these stories fascinating'. There is the obvious danger of over-kill, epitomised by the oft-quoted remark from the junior-school pupil, 'Not blooming 'Daffodils' again!' The theme should not dominate every English lesson for several weeks. Out of six lessons four might be devoted to the theme, one might be seen as a chance for pupils to read their own books from the class library and one as a 'safety net', allowing comment on homework or misconceptions, planning for future sessions, providing a slot for improvisation or the televison or radio programme. Themes should continue for as long as they stimulate. As with the feast, they should come to a halt while pupils still have an appetite for more. Pupils should not progress from one teacher-imposed theme to another. Indeed there are very good reasons for allowing pupils to suggest their own areas of interest within an overall theme and develop these. The scope for cross-pollination of ideas is thus greater and this removes pressure from limited resources or a small library. This does not imply a 'project' since it is probably time we stopped fooling ourselves that individual self-initiated work, which too often results in a final folder of ill-assembled borrowings and routine copying, really deserves the name 'project'. Far better to aim for a carefully presented anthology representing the best of the pupil's work. The following is a list of themes that I have used or have seen used successfully by others.

Year 1 (11-12 years):	Myself	Adventure	Sounds
	Creatures	Exploration	Myths and Legends
Year 2 (12-13 years):	The Sea	Journeys	Memories
	The Five Senses	Grown-ups	Friendship
Year 3 (13-14 years):	Crime and	The Supernatural	Homes
	Punishment	The Street	Schools
	Machines		
Year 4 (14-15 years):	Conflict	The Press	Eccentrics	The World of Work
	Science	Advertising	Marriage	The Outsider
	Fiction	Satire	Melodrama	Television
Year 5 (15-16 years):	Childhood		
	Revisited		

Obviously these demarcations are to an extent arbitrary; many of these themes could provide starting points for different age groups, while others such as 'Satire' or'Myself' might be seen as particularly suited to one age or ability group. 'Myself' is a good example of a theme which can help to build a relationship between teacher and incoming first year pupils:

Planning a Theme: 'Myself'

Clientele. The teacher considers the class, in this case incoming mixed-ability eleven-year-old pupils from at least four different primary schools. This will be their first taste of secondary school English and the teacher wishes to make it interesting but not too startling, not too far removed from familiar junior school teaching methods (thus the need for liaison with feeder schools). The teacher wishes to make pupils feel secure and aware that they have much that is interesting and valuable to contribute, that their fingers are on the pulse of 'knowledge'. He selects a theme, 'Myself', and plans a programme of lessons which will allow him to discover as much as possible about the pupils' personalities and abilities and which allows scope for pupil initiative and choice.

Content. The programme of lessons will introduce a variety of reading, writing, talking and listening tasks in order to provide opportunities for assessment of individual pupils' abilities, and allow scope, however modest, for pupils to demonstrate how well they can initiate and organise their own work and co-operate with other pupils. Time: two weeks, more if needed; most of the twelve lessons will be associated with the theme.

Resources. The teacher wishes to broaden his pupils' literary horizons gently, without suffocating them under a mass of unfamiliar literature. He has made a collection of materials, some provisionally labelled 'Certainties' and others 'Probables', including short stories, poems, extracts, interesting pictures, one or two worksheets, reading lists and a set of 'Using the Library' pamphlets. He has assembled a display which he hopes the pupils will supplement, including copies of several inviting autobiographies and diaries. Above these hang two family-trees, one of the royal family and another of an ordinary and imaginary citizen, and a collection of photographs, among them one of the teacher as a baby. In addition: one tape recorder, several tapes, plain and lined file paper, sellotape and sheets of coloured sugar paper.

Finding a Balance

Reading. The teacher will try to balance teacher and pupil reading, silently and aloud, to the whole class or to smaller groups, for pleasure or assessment or information, reading pupils' own work or stories, poems, extracts, biography, autobiography, diaries and silent reading of pupils' chosen reading books.

Writing. The teacher first makes a list of all the possible writing assignments and then selects from these those that should be optional, and from the large group remaining those that seem more immediately useful and interesting. Since one of the aims of the course is to discover as much as possible about pupils there will be a bias towards first person narrative and expressive writing:

Introductory information:
My earliest memories.
Diary of my first few days at school.
A chapter from my autobiography.
I like . . . I dislike . . . (list poems).
Myself in 10/20/30/40/50 years' time: realistic/fantasy projection.
'Wanted' poster for myself and 'objective' description and
    photograph/ artist's impression.
As I would wish to feature in a newspaper report.
Ten things I would take to a desert island, and why.
Interview.

Optional:
Family tree (a complex task).
The family I would have liked to have been born into after my own
(this subject should *never* be made obligatory)

If I was reincarnated I would come back as . . . because . . .
A multiple choice questionnaire designed to reveal, e.g.:
Are you an indoor or an outdoor type?
What sort of student/friend are you?
My ideal home.

Talk. All written tasks will be preceded by question and answer. The teacher will take care to make the questions as open-ended and yet as supportive as possible, not 'What do you like doing?' but 'Tell me what you really like to do on Saturdays'. The teacher is wary of probing experiences that may still be painfully raw and of giving the impression that some memories, aspirations or experiences are somehow better than others. Some collaborative talk will be involved in planning taped interviews but since responses will be essentially individual ones there will be less scope for pair and group work and talk than with other themes.

Illustration. Diagrams, pictures, decorated borders, photographs, even illuminated lettering will be encouraged, since the teacher hopes to show how they can contribute to an understanding of written work and their importance as a sign of a general concern for the quality and presentation of work. They may also allow those pupils who have problems with spelling or handwriting to shine in one sphere at least.

A Balanced Approach: the Programme

Week 1: Lesson 1. Introductions and explanations; pupils registered, and issued with rough books, homework cards and check-list of materials they will need for lessons. Their use is explained and they are neatly and appropriately labelled. Initial questionnaire filled in on file paper: name, address, hobbies, likes, dislikes, pets past or present, magazines/comics, the last book I read/enjoyed was, what I'd like to be when I grow up (if known), two questions I'd like to ask myself. Pupils begin to make 'Myself' folders or opt to provide their own for next lesson.

Lesson 2. Oral review of questionnaire. Pupils begin diary of first few days at school, initially in rough to be filled in as time allows at the end of lessons. 'Wanted' poster; its function and layout are discussed. Teacher reveals possible framework for information on roller board/diagram. Pupils begin planning in rough and are asked to produce photograph/artist's impression for homework.

Lesson 3. Library lesson: pupils are introduced to the school library and its use and are issued with reading diary cards. They are asked to choose a book, fact or fiction, since the teacher wants to discover their interests. Pupils read silently, teacher circulates discreetly and talks to a few pupils about their reading.

Lesson 4. 'Wanted' posters completed. Photographs/drawings inserted in frames. Examples read out by teacher with the question, 'Who is being described?' (tactful selection).

Lesson 5. Pupils encouraged to take a careful look at posters, now displayed. Teacher introduces 'Memories', reads short first person accounts, e.g. Laurie Lee, Winifred Foley. Pupils are invited to remember first day at new school then taken further back into their past, by stages. Teacher introduces 'autobiography' and 'memoirs'. Ways of approaching 'My earliest memories' or 'A chapter from my autobiography' discussed. Work planned in rough. Teacher circulates.

Lesson 6. Teacher plays tape of old lady/gentleman remembering their childhood. Pupils continue with their chosen task, time allowed for completion as homework as necessary. Pupils complete brief diary entries for first week and read their own books silently. Teacher uses this time to look at some of the folders and discuss work with individuals.

Week 2: Lesson 7. Teacher enters in role as a famous personality and asks pupils to note two questions they would like to put to the guest. Teacher invites questions and attempts answers. Discussion of ordering of sensible questions. Pupils collaborate in drafting questions to ask each other as though guests on a television chat-show. Questions compared and checked by teacher and class.

Lesson 8. Pupils, facing each other, try out interviews in pairs. If satisfactory, interview and answers written up in best. Teacher and pupil read out a humorous example of an 'interview', e.g. N.F. Simpson. Comment invited. A few class interviews tried publicly, a few more taped privately.

Lesson 9. Library lesson: teacher again monitors pupils' reading.

Lesson 10. Pupils are given a worksheet which suggests how they might complete 'Myself' work, allowing a choice of tasks, and limited opportunities for collaboration. Pupils are invited to supplement this with their own suggestions. Since some tasks are more difficult than others the teacher pays particular attention to the selection made by the least able.

Lesson 11. Pupils continue with their chosen tasks. Teacher circulates, bringing the class's attention to interesting interpretations.

Lesson 12. 'This is what we did': Review and finishing off. Pupils are asked to check their work and that of their neighbour. Pages are ordered and numbered. Pupils complete a 'Contents' page and are asked to say which work they enjoyed most and why.

Evaluation

The teacher felt that this, albeit brief, programme had gone some way towards achieving the long-term aim of making pupils feel secure enough to risk contributing their own opinions and suggestions, and had allowed the teacher to assess a range of language skills. Although this theme is unusual in the relatively slight input from outside resources, the teacher felt that at this stage a heavy literary base was inappropriate and the emphasis on personal experiences and opinions helped to bring the class together as a unit, and counteract divisions in terms of ability, background or appearance. The teacher acknowledged the importance of careful preparation, organization and tact if this was to be achieved, rather than its opposite.

If 'Myself' is experience-intensive, at the other end of the spectrum comes a literature-intensive theme such as 'Satire'. The latter might well contribute to a series of themes introducing the lower-sixth form to the main literary genres or styles; comedy, tragedy, the epic, allegory, irony, etc. The chronological approach to 'Satire' is an obvious one, beginning with the classical satires and working through the centuries, but thus runs the risk of turning a literary theme into a series of literary history lessons, or rather lectures, as students make copious notes on some rather obscure names. It is better to start with what our students know, with writers and examples which demonstrate the definition of satire loudly and obviously. In satire's case this might mean analysis of a satirical television or radio programme and excerpts from *Punch* and *Private Eye*. This inductive approach requires students to devise their own provisional definition of satire given the evidence before them, comparing this with those provided by a number of dictionaries and other reference works, and trying their definition for size on a range of writing: Horace, Aristophanes, Chaucer, Dryden, Pope, Sheridan, Swift,

Austen, Dickens, Orwell, Bradbury. We would want students to hunt out their own exmples, using these expeditions as exercises in reference skills. We would hope to encourage discrimination both in terms of different examples and in the use of related terms: parody, burlesque, caricature, travesty, skit, and lampoon; sarcasm, irony, derision; deflate, debunk, mimic and imitate.

Using a Text as a Focal Point

While the theme is very popular, this final approach is even more so since the majority of external exam syllabuses focus attention on a small number of set books, often chosen as representatives or types, and therefore quite deliberately distinct from each other. The traditional O Level literature syllabus requires students to study a minimum of one Shakespeare play, a novel, a poetry anthology or poet, and a play. While the thematic approach opens out from its subject, there is a danger that the single text approach will close in on just that text, cutting its life-lines to its literary relations and historical context and leaving it floundering, devoid of any sort of context or relevance for its readers.

It is true that the gifted teacher can do wonders with an apparently unsuitable text, but most of us need to be particularly careful in choosing a text which may dominate English lessons for anything from three weeks to a term. We must take into account the maturity, ability and interests of our pupils; our own aims and interests; the relationship between the current text and previous and subsequent work; the time and associated resources available; the scope for choice and initiative which the text will allow pupils; classroom organization; development via homework; improvisation; other subjects; guests and visits; and the condition of the texts themselves. A complete set is obviously preferable to an incomplete one which forces pupils to share; a single version is usually preferable to several (although different editions of a Shakespeare play can provide an interesting range of interpretations and notes). A pristine set is obviously preferable to a shabby or mutilated one, but we should not be tempted to reject a set of dishevelled but suitable texts in favour of seductively undefiled but quite inappropriate ones. Pupils can come to ignore a book's demoralising appearance if the contents are introduced in a dynamic way. Nowhere is a dynamic introduction more important than where the examination set text is concerned, whether A Level, O Level or CSE. These examinations allow varying scope for choice to the teacher, although, even with the relative freedom of the CSE, students will be well aware that the associated written work is firmly anchored to a final qualification. It is easy, given pressures of time and the demands of the end-of-course examination paper, to forget aims, objectives and notions of enjoyment and creativity: 'I know this is boring, but these are just the sort of questions you'll have to face in June.' The Shakespeare play, set at A and O Level, causes particular problems for teachers and students, particularly where the latter are required to demonstrate a detailed knowledge of the text in answering the dreaded 'gobbet' questions. Equally challenging, if not so immediately daunting, is the CSE set text, often a modern novel, play or collection of short stories. The remainder of this chapter will be devoted to an examination of these two representatives.

'Saving Shakespeare'

Living writers wince at their appearance in exam syllabuses, only too aware of the mauling and desecration to follow. Shakespeare, we can surmise, must be at the very least saddened by the typical student's response: 'I s'pose we've got to do him — but it's so boring'. A recent *cri de coeur* from Colin Welland[2] brought a much-needed breath of reality back to the subject of Shakespeare study: 'The first thing that must be admitted about the Bard, acknowledged beyond all argument is that he is *boring* . . . The man's dialogue *is* three hundred years old and written in verse. And, the way it is often played today, its expondents could not make it more difficult if they pulled on stocking masks and stuffed their mouths with prunes . . . ' Shakespeare *is* difficult and parts of his plays are boring, something which we paid-up supporters must admit. The sooner we come clean and admit this to ourselves the sooner we can hope to demystify the Bard and thence help our students to discover the power and the beauty within. Shakespeare, of all writers, should not need the reverential kid-glove treatment. He succeeded as a popular playwright in a cut-throat commercial climate and he should be introduced to our students in this light, as a man out to entertain through his exploitation of admittedly unoriginal but engrossing plots, through the creation of characters who leap from the lines and who have their counterparts today, as in any age.

Introductions. So how do we start? Certainly not by introducing Shakespeare as our greatest playwright, still less by emphasising his importance in the syllabus. We won't necessarily begin at the beginning of the first scene. We must try to surprise our students out of the tension that just the mention of Shakespeare's name and the sight of the text may bring. There are several possible starting points:

1. The man, his life, profession, contemporaries and times; perhaps the best way to begin is with what our students already know and significantly do not know, or have misunderstood. A class of about twenty students will usually manage to pool a surprising amount of information, which can be supplemented with the help of a set of colour slides or film strip showing Shakespeare in the context of theatrical history; long playing records which use contemporary evidence to recreate theatrical scenes; and resource packs containing facsimiles of such evidence (see the *Jackdaw* series). Small groups can specialise in key 'research' areas; Shakespeare's life, the theatres, the plays, the acting companies, and the background to the play intended for particular attention. All of this should reinforce the point that Shakespeare was, like all actors, playwrights and citizens a prey to plague, poverty, the whims of the monarch, Puritan censure, an often unruly audience, pirating and the theatrical flop. Any inquiry, indeed any Shakespeare lesson, will require access to the resources of the school library and an ever-present class bookcase, containing all the Shakespeare companions and reference works that the teacher and class can muster from home and through an extended book loan from the local library.

2. We might equally well start, not with the man, but with his theatre and work out from there. Finding a local reconstruction of a typical Shakespearian theatre is usually difficult but models, diagrams and posters are available from educational publishers. Ideally these should be displayed securely for the duration of the course and for reference at appropriate moments: 'How do you think this scene would have been staged?'; 'Where do you think Hamlet was standing when he made this speech?' Students can justifiably make their own simplified drawings showing the apron stage, upper stage, inner stage, balcony, canopy, 'Hell', the 'Heavens', tiring house, trap door, and galleries. Contemporary accounts of stage properties, the behaviour of the audience, and theatrical reviews make interesting and often amusing reading and listening, and significantly demonstrate that Shakespeare was writing for all types and qualities of men and for an audience which was loud in its praise, rowdy in its disapproval, and sometimes the worse for drink, in fact very similar to many a football crowd. This point is worthy of emphasis since too often Shakespeare, and visits to the theatre, are seen as rather rarified

middle-class preoccupations.

3. Another starting point, though less obviously interesting than the previous pair, is the play edition itself. We tend to assume that students can find their way unaided around the prefaces, introductions, notes, abbreviations, appendices, bibliographies and glossaries of the typically scholarly Shakespeare edition. Students require specific initiation and regular guidance. It should be made clear that Shakespeare scholars need the help of notes, that this is not ignominious cheating but is the sign of the active and sensible reader who is prepared to dig out any suggestion that may help. Students should know that they do not need to read Hamlet in order to discover what actually *happens*, that the *Oxford Companion to English Literature* will provide a succinct summary of the plot, if that is what is required. In short, students should have immediate access to any commentary that might prove useful in throwing light on a disputed interpretation or unexpected query.

4. There is no reason why students should be threatened with the imminent arrival of the Shakespeare play. It can be approached obliquely and more subtly via a theme: crime and punishment (*Macbeth, Hamlet*); town and country (*As You Like It*); family conflict (*Romeo and Juliet, King Lear*); jealousy (*Othello, The Winter's Tale*). This approach should explore the options open to Shakespeare in his treatment of jealousy, political conspiracy or family feuding and should see this in relation to other more accessible writers' treatment of the same issues, thus avoiding the difficult leap from twentiety-century colloquial prose to sixteenth-century Shakespearian blank verse.

5. Starting *in media res* can work as well with a Shakespearian play as with an epic poem, or modern novel. This introduction works on the same basis as the film trailer; a dramatic and intriguing excerpt is chosen to whet the appetite of the audience, one which leaves as many questions answered as it answers. Improvisation offers an obvious way in; the teacher might translate the confrontation between Henry IV and Prince Hal, Juliet and her parents, Lear and his daughters, into modern terms and invite groups to discuss their reactions from the standpoint of different protagonists and then show their reactions in a series of angled improvisations. Where a lack of space makes improvisation impossible, students can discuss

these issues in their groups from a twentieth-century standpoint ('How would you react if . . . ?') and then make the imaginative leap back to an earlier time: 'Would your reaction be different if you were a contemporary of Shakespeare?'

6. 'Outside help' can be invaluable in getting the play off to a good start; the play in performance, film, television and local and national radio programmes should be exploited for all they are worth. We could debate whether or not it is best for students to see the play, whether on film or in the theatre, at the beginning, in the middle, or at the end of their study of the text. In practice such dilemmas seldom arise since most teachers must take the chance when they can. It is important though that students should have grasped the plot before watching a performance and a few simple questions will help to direct their attention. It is not true that *any* perform-ance is better than none, since a disastrous experience may put students off the play and theatre-going in general. Classroom improvisation or a filmed production may prove a better alternative. The local repertory company may well be happy to take parties around their theatre, and the comparison between twentieth-century theatre in the round, for example, and Shakespeare's Globe may prove to be an interesting introductory gambit. More specifically, a director's or actor's approach to the play may prove that examina-tion candidates are not alone in coming to Shakespeare inexperienced and untutored, and that any performance is only one corporate interpretation, any speech only one actor's and director's interpre-tation.[3] Actors are sometimes prepared to talk in role (and costume) about a part and answer questions from their audience. This is an approach that the enthusiastic teacher-actor can borrow; 'I've come here today from Illyria and I've been asked to tell you about some-thing very strange that happened to me several years ago . . . '

Some teachers will rightly object that starting-off is not the most difficult task since novelty will win our students' initial support. It is what ensues, the often dreary plod of reading from beginning to end, which may totally alienate the students from the play, Shakespeare and English. For those facing examination-questions there is no substitute for reading the play from beginning to end, for getting the feel of the language and grasping the plot. We must assume the worst, that even where students follow our instructions to read the play at home much will be misunderstood and most will be baffled. Understanding will only come as the result of a frontal attack with the teacher's help, in class time.

Reading. Probably the commonest, because the most obvious, reading practice is to take the play scene by scene using the class as readers. Though this works well where the class contains many enthusiastic and fluent readers, and where the text is read rapidly and decisively, it can become boring and confusing where too much time is spent on analysis between scenes, holding up the action and thus losing the plot in the process. This slow plod moves the emphasis crucially from performance and entertainment to paraphrase and note-scribbling, both important but not at this stage. It is also a predictable approach and students soon register that several weeks' lessons are likely to follow the pattern of 'Where have we got to?' – class reading – teacher explanation – class note-making. Though routine does make for security, we should be able to take up all the options, sometimes using the class as public readers, sometimes reading silently and occasionally using recordings. We can focus and inform students' initial reading of the text through questions which relate to plot and tone rather than to nuances of meaning: 'Is this the same man we met in the first act?'; 'What are we encouraged to feel about this character?' At the end of an act, having briefly checked off the events so far, the class can put themselves in the play-wright's position; 'All this has happened but what might happen next? What will you consider before laying pen to manuscript?' Only when the class knows who's who and what happens in the play (and this should be a rapid process) can we afford to return to a consideration of structure, characterisation, themes and, where the examination demands it, detailed paraphrasing. Even here we must gamble on scrup-ulously paraphrasing only key speeches and key scenes if we are to reveal meaning, rather than paradoxically destroying it.

Writing and Discussion. Since the initial reading for understanding should be as rapid and painless as possible it is wise to keep writing to a minimum of jotted notes and little more. After the first reading, writing, reading and discussion should go hand in hand. The challenge will be to find alternatives to the stereotyped written responses to Shakespeare at O and A Level, the dreary and interminable plot summary, the formal essay: 'To what extent is this a didactic play?'; 'This is a play without a hero. Discuss'; and the 'plot' question, 'Describe the course of events that leads to the fight in Act 2'. Exam-ination candidates will need a summary of the plot for revision purposes and it is usually not enough to direct them to the teacher's version or the one which usefully accompanies the text. Students will need to make sense of the events in their own way if they are to be remembered. We should avoid asking a class to summarise each scene as an individual task. This can profitably be a group activity where each group concentrates on an act, discusses its contents, is made responsible for preparing a summary of a predetermined length, and explaining it and its relation to neighbouring acts to the rest of the class. Since a useful plot-outline is necessarily succinct this is a valuable exercise in note-making and summary work generally. After the teacher and class have assessed each group's work orally, the former can duplicate and disseminate the finished summary. This is the simplest alternative but there are more interesting and challenging ones: each group looks at the events through the eyes of a different character, contrasting several different perceptions of 'reality'; Friar Laurence, the Nurse, Romeo, Lady Capulet and the Prince in *Romeo and Juliet*. The task can be localised by concentrating on the second-rank characters, often the most perceptive spectators; Nerissa and Lancelot Gobbo in the *Merchant of Venice*, a courtier and Lady Macbeth's gentlewoman in *Macbeth*. These views can be presented as a chapter from an auto-biography, as a newspaper obituary, or as an interview or interrogation. These last could profitably be recorded with others to provide an enter-taining and invaluable revision aid. Commercial tapes exist which do just this[4] but students, once introduced to the model, can learn a great deal in producing their own series of interviews with leading characters in the play.

All Shakespeare's plays, packed with incident and intrigue as they are, lend themselves to the group newspaper approach, particularly if we envisage a special edition devoted to the goings-on in the play. This simultaneously becomes an investigation into journalistic style; thus we might compare the popular tabloid paper's approach to the events in *King Lear* or *All's Well That Ends Well* with *The Times*'s probable reporting style. Events can be reported and commented upon, personalities analysed, blame laid, implications discussed through the leader column, the editorial, the letter page, the women's page, the gossip column, the obituary and even the personal columns. The whole programme can be initiated through the editorial conference where, if need be, the teacher can play the part of editor, suggesting possible tasks to the class as sub-editors, for comment and allocation. This approach is only a partial substitute for the formal discursive essay, and students will need pre-examination practice in writing essays and answering textual questions, sometimes under test conditions. But the newspaper scheme of work allows practice in those skills which are required in the successful essay, a knowledge of the play, the ability to marshal and organise facts and the ability to write persuasively, succinctly and to a dead-line.

The CSE Set Text

It is fatally easy to assume that, while teaching the Shakespeare play may require careful thought and preparation, with the CSE text it is sufficient merely to muddle through, or more likely stagger through, beginning at the beginning and reading aloud to the end, too many weeks later. This is a serious mistake, particularly since some CSE classes are likely to have a lower tolerance-level than the academically inclined O or A Level group. The former are more likely to punish the boring lesson with misbehaviour. Partly for this reason, and also in order to net as great a catch of literature as possible, many teachers have decided that short and contemporary is beautiful as far as the CSE text is concerned, hence the popularity of the following nationwide, irrespective of mode or syllabus: *A Kestrel for A Knave; Billy Liar; Late Night on Watling Street; The Loneliness of the Long Distance Runner; The L-Shaped Room; Of Mice and Men; Animal Farm; A Kind of Loving.* The CSE examines literature continuously through the course work folder rather than the end of course examination. It does not require a detailed interpretation of the text in the same way as the O and A Level examinations, thus allowing the teacher a great deal of freedom in the selection and utilisation of texts. There really is no excuse here for a desultory 'doing' of texts. '*A Kestrel for a Knave*' or '*Kes*' is as good a specimen as any for comment; it is a short, contemporary novel which explores topical issues and which is popular with most teachers and pupils (if not all parents).

Introduction. Kes might be introduced as the central text, dominating several weeks' work, or in a more peripheral light as the culmination of a theme, perhaps 'Childhood', 'School' or 'The Family'. In any case it must be introduced in as lively and interesting a way as possible, in order to set the tone and whet the appetite for all that is to come. Irrespective of later subdivision, the initial reading should be a whole-class experience. In almost every case the teacher, rather than a pupil, should read the opening pages, having taken the trouble to prepare the first important reading carefully. It can make a dramatic start to read the first page or so aloud before the students have opened their texts, condensing laboured descriptions if necessary in order to make the maximum impact. This is hardly necessary in *Kes*'s case since the brutal opening is riveting enough. The teacher as he reads can significantly distinguish between characters through their voices, tone, accent and volume, and can accentuate humorous moments. In deciding where to call a halt to this first reading the teacher must take a lead from the class. If they are obviously interested there is much to be gained from revealing as much as possible of characters and plot in this first lesson, and students will only be frustrated by the premature move to writing. There certainly is no need for any sort of written summary of events in these early stages.

Reading. If this early interest is to be bolstered the teacher will need to ensure that the reading proceeds rapidly. He will thus need to know the text intimately, singling out those moments which require careful and public reading and subsequent comment. In *Kes* this will mean focussing on those key scenes which reveal the relationshp between Billy and his kestrel, mother and son, brother and brother, Billy and Mr. Farthing. *Kes*, like many other novels, lends itself to a dramatic reading where two students, or teacher and student, take parts, reading the scene as if from a play, omitting the occasional 'he said' or narrator's interjections. Certain parts will be read silently by the whole class, in class, less crucial ones at home. It is obviously important that the contents of sections set for private reading should be summarised before the class proceeds to the next reading in class. Where the teacher knows that he wishes to omit passages, it is obviously sensible that he should do the reading, having warned the students of these intentions and allowing them the opportunity to read the omissions in their own time. The teacher must maintain a careful balance here; while wishing to encourage the stamina necessary to finish novels, circumspect skipping may be the only way of keeping students' interest to the end, thus convincing them that novels are worth finishing. Throughout, the teacher must be careful not to give the impression that descriptive passages are merely literary padding. While a rapid reading is important this should not be at the cost of under-standing, and oral question-and-answer will highlight facts, ideas and opinions and prepare for later written work. Again there is a balance here, between annoying interested readers by repeated interruptions, and allowing the class to nod off, aware that they will not be called to account for what has been read.

Writing and Discussion. Major writing tasks should either be prepared in class but set for homework or should be postponed until the whole book has been read, otherwise the reading will be unnecessarily protracted and students will be unfairly asked to write with only a fragmentary knowledge of the text. It is tempting to apply O and A Level literature techniques to the modern novel indiscriminately, 'theme-tagging' while the plot is still unfolding. Over-concentration on 'themes' in *Kes* such as 'hobbies', 'bullying' or 'schools' will distort the book, and the relationship between a boy and his kestrel, which is at its heart. It will distract attention away from the contrast between this and a number of singularly unsuccessful human relationsips. The readers' identification with and sympathy for the characters, their understanding of their possible motivation, these are of interest. 'Describe any example of bullying that you have heard about or witnessed' may seem an obvious task but it is also a crude one. Such sensitive issues are best and most safely explored though the relationship between the two brothers, taking students deeper into the book rather than continually back to painful personal experiences or superficial stereotypes. Work should not be set without thought and without good reason. It is far better that students should successfully complete one piece of work associated with the book, after careful preparation and class or group discussion than several routine tasks. If a written task is to be prompted by the book it should be used as a test of understanding of that book, and simultaneously allow scope for discussion and initiative, for example: 'Billy ten years from the end of the novel'. You might as Barry Hines wish to write a final post-script, or write in the 'first person' as Billy's mother, his brother or as Billy himself. Your account might take the form of a lengthy diary entry, a detailed letter or a chapter added to the end of the book. This is perhaps best explored through small group or a pair discussion where students are asked to formulate in rough a description of Billy's situation at the end of the novel and use this as a basis for projection. Students could compile a list of information which would be relevant in deciding Billy's future.

An investigation of the sorts of written work that *Kes* inspires makes rather depressing reading: summary of the main events, a poem entitled 'Birds of Prey', 'My Ideal School', 'Hobbies'. It might be more pertinent to encourage consideration of how the author treats the football game; the account of the paper-round; assembly or careers interview; and then ask students to use the same situation but deliberately alter the tone or form. We might discuss when students felt most sympathy for Billy and then give them the option of writing about the personal experiences which prompted this sympathy. It is true that we need to keep in mind a balance between different types of writing, but this should not mean going to ridiculous lengths to squeeze a poem or a piece of functional prose out of *Kes*. It may well be that such writing tasks are better prompted by more appropriate stimuli.

Notes

1. *English in the 1980s*, Schools Council Working Paper 62 (Evans/Methuen Educational, 1979).
2. Colin Welland, 'Like Angels Trumpet-Tongued', *Times Educational Supplement,* 14 March 1980.
3. *Shakespeare Superscribe*, transcripts from Capital Radio's Set Books Series (Penguin, 1980) makes this point with the help of actors, directors, critics, and teachers.
4. Robert Tanitch, *Shakespeare Tapes* (Ward Lock Educational, 1978).

INDEX